D1615293

Greenhill Books

GERMAN
WAR BIRDS

GERMAN WAR BIRDS

by 'Vigilant'

With a New Introduction
by Norman Franks

Greenhill Books, London
Stackpole Books, Pennsylvania

This edition of *German War Birds*
first published 1994 by Greenhill Books,
Lionel Leventhal Limited, Park House, 1 Russell Gardens
London NW11 9NN
and
Stackpole Books, 5067 Ritter Road, Mechanicsburg, PA 17055, USA

This edition © Lionel Leventhal Limited, 1994

British Library Cataloguing in Publication Data
Sykes, Claud W.
German Warbirds. – New ed
I. Title
940.44943

ISBN 1-85367-164-9

Library of Congress Cataloguing-in-Publication Data available

Publishing History
German War Birds was first published in 1931 (John Hamilton, Limited), and
is now reproduced exactly as the original edition, complete and unabridged,
with the addition of a new Introduction and tables by Norman Franks

Printed and bound in Great Britain by
Biddles Limited, Guildford and King's Lynn

INTRODUCTION

W HEN *German War Birds* was first published in October 1931 it was very much a product of its time. That is to say it gave readers an overall view of what the German airmen did in WWI, although it was limited in its scope by events which were still too close to be fully comprehended. While readers today prefer books with rather more background knowledge, it has to be remembered that in the early 1930s writing about such things was still in its infancy.

The aviation-minded public in the 1930s probably thought they knew a great deal about WWI flying and sadly, the pulp writers of that era did little to add to an enthusiast's knowledge because they knew little more themselves. Not that Claud W. Sykes, who wrote several books under the pseudonym of *Vigilant*, was a pulp writer. He was among the better aviation writers of the period. It is clear too, that many people thought the German Air Service was run on very similar lines to the Royal Flying Corps or the Royal Air Force and therefore wrote appropriately. As we now know, the German Air Service, and especially the WWI fighter pilots, flew a very different war to their Allied counterparts.

The German fighter pilots were far better known to the German public in WWI too. They were fêted as heroes and those that were fortunate enough to win the coveted Ordre Pour le Mérite – the famed Blue Max – became national figures. Their pictures were in every newspaper and magazine, one could purchase portrait postcards of them; when on leave they were treated like royalty or latter-day soccer legends. If they fell in combat they received funerals normally reserved for kings.

German War Birds at least gave the English-speaking peoples of the world an insight into some of the German fighter aces of the Great War, just thirteen years after the end of that conflict. Many, like Richthofen and Boelcke and Immelmann were already well known, Richthofen especially through his own book *The Red Air Fighter*; others were less well known.

Little was known for instance of Rudolph von Eschwege, whose story appears in Chapter VIII, or Hans Schüz in Chapter VII. Indeed, most people only knew about the air fighting on the Western Front, so *German War Birds* was probably the first contact many enthusiasts had with any real knowledge concerning the air battles in the Middle East or Russia. The book was a welcome addition to their libraries for it gave an insight into those far off fronts of Macedonia, Palestine and Galicia.

It also brought some new names to the fore, Rudolph Windisch, Gunther Plüschow and Georg Wilhelm Heydemarck, although the latter would soon become known for his own series of books (*Double Dekker C666, Flying Section 17* and *War Flying in Macedonia*; published in Britain between 1931 and 1935). Another name found in the book is Hermann Göring, in 1931 still some years away from his infamous future.

Of course, the more well-known heroes like Boelcke and Richthofen are well represented in *German War Birds*. Remember, in 1931 books on Boelcke (*Knight of Germany*, 1933) and Immelmann (*Immelmann – Eagle of Lille*, 1935) were also in the future, so *German War Birds*, in 1931, was really breaking new ground in WWI aviation literature.

Also of interest is Chapter VI, concerning balloons. Probably few realised that observation balloons on both sides were attacked so often and so vigorously by fighter pilots in the war, and that they also counted in a pilot's victory score. They were very dangerous things to attack, generally protected by hostile fighting air patrols, not to mention numerous ground gun positions. It is interesting to note that some of the leading German and British aces never touched them, while others made it a regular feature to go after the famed *Drachen*.

Among the leading German aces to score over balloons were Fritz Röth with 20 of his 28 kills being balloons; Heinrich Gontermann with 17 out of 39, Karl Schlegal with 14 out of 22 and Oskar Hennrich with 13 out of 20. Röth is mentioned in this chapter and so is Max Gossner who claimed three among his eight victories. Kissenberth is another mentioned here, but although he scored only once over a balloon, he is famed for being a pilot who wore eye glasses and flew a captured Sopwith Camel – in which he also crashed! Both Röth and Kissenberth won the Blue Max.

The chapter concerning Boelcke's Jasta 2 (Chapter IV) was the first such Jasta history to be so well documented for the British public, but one still feels that the author represented the history as if the unit would have been little different had it been British. That is to say, the English-speaking public with some knowledge of RFC/RAF units would think the Germans ran their units in similar fashion.

This too is borne out by the phrase used on page 56: 'Immelmann had developed a habit of hanging about behind the German lines to lie in wait for any British aeroplanes engaged on photography or reconnaissance work.' It was not a developed habit, but a well defined operational tactic. Unlike the Allied side, where the policy was to take the war to the enemy by flying across the lines and seeking out combat with

enemy aeroplanes, it was German policy to wait for the Allied
flyers to come to them. Those who have read my introduction
to Greenhill's edition of Richthofen's *The Red Air Fighter*,
published in 1990, will understand more fully how the Germans fought their war. Being overall numerically inferior, and
as their Jastas were much smaller in size compared to Allied
squadrons, it was far better to fight them on the German side of
the trenches rather than constantly fly over the lines as the
British did.

In this way they could more readily choose the moment of
contact, strike at the best tactical moment and if in trouble, they
could drop down and land and not be taken prisoner. For their
part, the British units were constantly fighting a westerly
prevailing wind which took them further east *ie* into enemy
territory, had to be on the alert for sudden attacks from above
and or out of the sun, and when it was time to break off and go
home, with fuel and ammunition running low, had often to
fight their way back to safety.

The German Jasta pilots became adept at this type of
fighting, and made the most of their opportunities to engage
Allied two-seater aircraft which were either flying artillery
observation sorties above the lines, or making long or short
range reconnaissances into German air space. There was rarely
any form of fighter escort as would be known in WWII. The
best the two-seater crews could hope for was an escort of their
own type of two-seater, which were either not carrying bombs
if on a bomb raid, or were not tasked with recce or photo work,
thus free to watch the sky for hostile fighters. That in the final
analysis they were as inferior in combat as the aircraft they were
trying to protect seemed to have been ignored by the air
commanders of the day.

The only other hope for the two-seater crews doing their
work was that at least one of the many Offensive Patrols flown

in the general area of their part of the front would ward off any would-be attackers before they could get in amongst them. It was a very hit-and-miss affair, and the losses sustained by the two-seater Corps crews stand testimony to the fact that it often didn't work. For while the British fighters knew what they had to do, once engaged with a German Jasta or two, another could easily sneak in and engage the luckless two-seater, especially as both men had one eye on the task on hand, and only one on the sky.

Most of the successful German fighter pilots came through from being two-seater men. It was recognised that to be a fighter pilot it was better to have experience of flying generally, rather than the Allied idea of sending untried pilots direct to fighter squadrons. In the early days the more aggressive two-seater men would be assigned to the few Fokker monoplanes that units had for protection and hunting patrols. It was these men, of the calibre of Boelcke, Berthold, Loerzer and Jacobs who cut their teeth on Fokkers prior to the formation of the Jastas in late 1916. Initially these Fokker pilots were grouped in KEKs – Kampfeinsitzer Kommandos – at such places as Vaux, Jametz and Bertincourt.

Once the single-seater pilots were grouped together to form the Jastas, the brainchild of Oswald Boelcke, they became veritable hunting packs. Once let loose in the early months of 1917, they took a heavy toll of Allied aircraft, especially during the first major battle of the new year, the Battle of Arras, in April 1917.

It is now history that the fighter pilots of both sides caught the imagination of the public at large, and while *German War Birds* records stories of both single and two-seaters, it is the single-seater fighters that hog the glory.

As well as being among the first books in English to relate any stories of the Great War German aviators, *German War*

Birds was also the fore-runner of numerous books in English [translations] on or about German war pilots. Some have been mentioned above; others were to follow, such as Rudolf Stark's *Wings of War* (1933), Hans Schroder's *An Airman Remembers* (1936), Ernst Udet's *Ace of the Black Cross* (1937). But mention too must be made of two earlier books which predated *War Birds*, the well known *Red Knight of Germany* by Floyd Gibbons (1927 in the USA, 1930 in Britain), and the less well known *The German Air Service in the Great War* by Georg Paul Neuman, in 1920. Neuman's original book, in German (*Die Deutschen Luftstreitkrafte im Weltkreige*), was three times the size of the English version, which was edited by a first war two-seater ace, Captain J. E. Gurdon DFC. Gurdon had to reduce the book's size and left out much which he felt would be of less interest to English readers.

German War Birds is a good overall read and shows just how much of a world war, WWI was, despite the dominance of the fighting in France, on the Western Front. In the air, the German Air Service, as well as the Marine fighter pilots on the Channel coast, were far from defeated, as the German Army and Navy were. In September 1918, just a few weeks from the Armistice, the German fighter pilots inflicted the greatest number of casualties on the combined British, French and American Air Services in any month of the war, and despite overwhelming odds, could have fought on, if petrol had been made available to fly their Fokkers and Pfalz biplanes.

The First War in the Air remains a fascinating period to read about, and research over recent years has led to a re-awakening of this interesting period of aviation history. The re-print of *German War Birds* can only help this interest continuing.

Norman Franks

TOP SCORING GERMAN ACES OF WWI

Rittmeister Baron Manfred von Richthofen	80
Oberleutnant Ernst Vdet	62
Oberleutnant Erich Löwenhardt	54
Leutnant Josef Jacobs	48
Leutnant Werner Voss	48
Leutnant Fritz Rumey	45
Hauptmann Rudolf Berthold	44
Hauptmann Bruno Loerzer	44
Leutnant Paul Bäumer	43
Hauptmann Oswald Boelcke	40
Leutnant Franz Büchner	40
Leutnant Lothar von Richthofen	40
Leutnant Heinrich Gontermann	39
Leutnant Karl Menckhoff	39
Rittmeister Karl Bolle	36
Leutnant Julius Buckler	36
Leutnant Max Ritter von Muller	36
Leutnant Gustav Dörr	35
Hauptmann Eduard Ritter von Schleich	35
Leutnant Emil Thuy	35
Leutnant Josef Veltjens	35
Leutnant Heinrich Bongartz	34
Leutnant Otto Könnecke	34
Leutnant Heinrich Kroll	33

CHRONOLOGICAL LIST OF GERMAN WAR BIRDS WHO RECEIVED THE *BLUE MAX*

Name	Date of Award	Duty	Score	Unit	Remarks	
1916						
Hptm Oswald Boelcke	12 Jan	fighter	40	J2	KIA	28 Oct 1916
Oblt Max Immelmann	12 Jan	fighter	15	FA62	KIA	18 Jun 1916
Hptm Hans-Joachim Buddecke	14 Apr	fighter	15	OFA6	KIA	10 Mar 1918
Ltn Kurt Wintgens	1 Jul	fighter	19	FA6	KIA	25 Sep 1916
Ltn Max Ritter von Mulzer	8 Jul	fighter	10	KekB	KIFA	28 Sep 1916
Ltn Wilhelm Frankl	12 Jul	fighter	20	KekV	KIA	8 Apr 1917
Ltn Walter Höhndorf	20 Jul	fighter	12	KekV	KIFA	5 Sep 1916
Oblt Ernst Fr von Althaus	21 Jul	fighter	9	KekV	Died 1946	
Ltn Otto Parschau	10 Aug	fighter	8	KG1	DOW	21 Jul 1916
Hpt Rudolf Berthold	12 Oct	fighter	44	J4	Killed Mar 1920	
Ltn Gustav Leffers	5 Nov	fighter	9	J1	KIA	27 Dec 1916
Ltn Albert Dossenbach	11 Nov	fighter	15	FA22	KIA	3 Jul 1917
Oblt Hans Berr	4 Dec	fighter	10	J5	KIA	6 Apr 1917
1917						
Ritt Manfred von Richthofen	12 Jan	fighter	80	J2	KIA	21 Apr 1918
Ltn Werner Voss	8 Apr	fighter	48	J2	KIA	23 Sep 1917
Oberst Herman von der Leith-Thomsen	8 Apr	staff	–	HQ	Died	5 Aug 1942
Gen Ernst von Hoeppner	8 Apr	staff	–	HQ	Died	22 Sep 1922
Oblt Otto Bernert	23 Apr	fighter	27	J2	Died	18 Oct 1918
Ltn Karl Emil Schäfer	26 Apr	fighter	30	J11	KIA	5 Jun 1971
Oblt Kurt Wolff	4 May	fighter	33	J11	KIA	15 Sep 1917
Oblt Lothar von Richthofen	14 May	fighter	40	J11	KIFA	4 Jul 1922
Ltn Heinrich Gontermann	14 May	fighter	39	J15	KIFA	30 Oct 1917
Hpt Ernst Brandenburg	14 Jun	bomber	–	KG3	bombed London	
Ltn Karl Allmenroder	14 Jun	fighter	30	J11	KIA	27 Jun 1917
Oblt Paul Fr von Pechmann	31 Jul	recce	–	FA217	observer	
Oblt Eduard von Dostler	6 Aug	fighter	26	J6	KIA	21 Aug 1917
Kapt Peter Srasser	20 Aug	airship	–	Lufts	KIA	5 Aug 1918
Hpt Adolf von Tutschek	3 Sep	fighter	27	J12	DOW	15 Mar 1918
Ltn Max von Muller	3 Sep	fighter	36	J28	KIA	9 Jan 1918
Hpt Rudolf Kleine	4 Oct	bomber	–	KG3	KIA	12 Dec 1917
Ltn Walter von Bulow-Bothkamp	8 Oct	fighter	28	J36	KIA	6 Jan 1918
Ltn Kurt Wüsthoff	22 Nov	fighter	27	J4	POW	17 Jun 1918
Ltn Erwin Böhme	24 Nov	fighter	24	J2	KIA	29 Nov 1917
Oblt Hans Klein	2 Dec	fighter	22	J4	Died	18 Nov 1944

Ltn Julius Buckler	4 Dec	fighter	36	J17	Died	23 May 1960
Hpt Eduard von Schleich	4 Dec	fighter	35	J21	Died	15 Nov 1947
Hpt Alfred Keller	4 Dec	bomber	–	KG1	Died	11 Feb 1974
Oblt Friedrich Christiansen	11 Dec	fighter	13	SF1,1	Died	5 Dec 1972
Ltn Heinrich Bongartz	23 Dec	fighter	33	J36	Died	23 Jan 1946
Oblt Hermann Fricke	23 Dec	recce	–	R2	observer	
Oblt Hans-Jurgen Horn	23 Dec	recce	–	FA221	observer	
1918						
Hpt Bruno Loerzer	12 Feb	fighter	44	J26	Died	23 Aug 1960
Ltn Heinrich Kroll	29 Mar	fighter	33	J24	Died	21 Feb 1930
Kapt Horst Treusch von Buttlar-Brandenfels	9 Apr	airship	–	Lufts		
Oblt Ernst Udet	9 Apr	fighter	62	J15	Died	17 Nov 1941
Hpt Hermann Kohl	21 May	bomber	2	BG7	Died	7 Oct 1938
Oblt Erich Löwenhardt	31 May	fighter	54	J10	KIA	10 Aug 1918
Ltn Fritz Pütter	31 May	fighter	25	J68	DOW	10 Aug 1918
Hpt Hermann Göring	2 Jun	fighter	22	J27	Died	15 Oct 1946
Ltn Friedrich Nielebock	2 Jun	recce	–	FA250	observer	
Ltn Rudolf Windisch	6 Jun	fighter	22	J66	KIA	27 May 1918
Ltn Wilhelm Paul Schreiber	8 Jun	recce	1	FA221	KIA	30 May 1918
Ltn Hans Kirschstein	24 Jun	fighter	27	J6	KIFA	17 Jul 1918
Oblt Otto Kissenberth	30 Jun	fighter	20	J23	Died	2 Aug 1919
Ltn Emil Thuy	30 Jun	fighter	35	J28	KIFA	11 Jun 1930
Ltn Peter Rieper	7 Jul	balloon	–	FfA21	observer	
Ltn Fritz Rumey	10 Jul	fighter	45	J5	KIA	27 Sep 1918
Oblt Josef Jacobs	18 Jul	fighter	48	J7	Died	29 Jul 1978
Oblt Gotthardt Sachsenberg	5 Aug	fighter	31	MFJ1	Died	23 Aug 1961
Hpt Franz Walz	9 Aug	fighter	7	FA304	Died	Dec 1945
Ltn Josef Veltjens	16 Aug	fighter	35	J15	KIA	6 Oct 1943
Ritt Karl Bolle	28 Aug	fighter	35	J2	Died	9 Oct 1955
Ltn Theodor Osterkamp	2 Sep	fighter	32	MFJ2	Died	2 Jan 1975
Oblt Fritz Ritter von Röth	8 Sep	fighter	28	J16	Died	31 Dec 1918
Ltn Otto Könnecke	26 Sep	fighter	35	J5	Died	25 Jan 1956
Ltn Walter Blume	30 Sep	fighter	28	J9	Died	27 May 1964
Ltn Wilhelm Griebsch	30 Sep	recce	–	FA213	KIFA	20 Jul 1920
Hpt Leo Leonhardy	2 Oct	bomber	–	BG6	Died	12 Jul 1928
Oblt Robert Ritter von Greim	8 Oct	fighter	28	JGr9	Died	24 May 1945
Oblt Erich Homburg	13 Oct	recce	–	FA260	observer	
Oblt Albert Muller-Kahle	13 Oct	recce	–	FA6	observer	
Oblt Jurgen von Grone	13 Oct	recce	–	R4	observer	
Oblt Oskar Fr von Boenigk	25 Oct	fighter	26	JGII	Died	30 Jan 1946
Ltn Franz Büchner	25 Oct	fighter	40	J13	Killed	18 Mar 1920
Ltn Arthur Laumann	25 Oct	fighter	28	J10	Died	18 Nov 1918
Ltn Oliver Fr von Beaulieu-Marconnay	26 Oct	fighter	26	J19	DOW	26 Oct 1918
Ltn Karl Thom	1 Nov	fighter	27	J21	Missing WWII	
Ltn Paul Bäumer	2 Nov	fighter	43	J2	KIFA	15 Jul 1927
Ltn Ulrich Neckel	8 Nov	fighter	30	J12	Died	11 May 1928
Ltn Karl Degelow	8 Nov	fighter	30	J40	Died	9 Nov 1970

Kek=Kampfeinsitzer Kommando (single-seat unit); J=Jasta, (fighter squadron); JG=Jagdgeschwader, (permanent group of Jastas); JGr=Jagdgruppe, (non-permanent group of Jastas); KG=Kampfgeschwader, (group of bombing squadrons); BG=Bogohl, (bombing squadron); R=Reihenbildner, (special photographic unit); HQ=Kogenluft; FfA=Feldluftschiffertruppe, (balloon company); Lufts=Luftschiff, (airship unit); FA-Flieger Abteilung, (flying section, generally two-seaters); OFA=Ottoman Flieger Abteilung (Turkish front unit); MFJ=Marinefeld Jasta, (marine fighter squadron); SFl=Seeflugstaffel (naval flying squadron).

CONTENTS

LIST OF ILLUSTRATIONS

Between pages 130 and 131

GERMAN
WAR BIRDS

CHAPTER I

IN the mess of a squadron of the Royal Flying Corps, somewhere in France, an airman was celebrating with his friends the announcement of his D.S.O. That night at dinner he had to return thanks to the friends who had drunk his health. He took the opportunity to pay a tribute to the valour of the enemy they encountered daily and concluded by asking the assembled company to rise and drink to the health of von Richthofen, the famous enemy ace who had taken such toll of them. Every pilot in the room stood up to honour the gallant enemy.

At that time promotion awaited the airman who could conquer von Richthofen and put an end to his activities. Every pilot of the Royal Flying Corps serving on the western front hoped that he might be the lucky man, but none desired his life. They wanted to bring him down uninjured, so that they might have the pleasure of shaking his hand.

When on 21 April, 1918, von Richthofen's Fokker triplane bore him dead to earth behind the British lines, his body lay in state, like that of a deceased monarch. Pilots from far and near came to pay their respects to the last remains of the mighty foeman. Then six officers of the Royal Flying Corps carried his coffin to a grave decked with wreaths sent by every British air squadron in France.

When a British airman fell into German hands alive and unwounded, when a German pilot landed safely behind the British lines, his opposite numbers made all sorts of excuses to prevent his immediate despatch to the base as a prisoner of war. Usually they contrived to carry him off to their mess, where they feasted him royally. Victor and vanquished drank each other's healths and declared that they had thoroughly enjoyed a sporting fight.

In an out-of-the-way corner of the Mesopotamian front Captain Schüz distinguished himself by shooting down many British airmen. His fame spread to the mess of the Royal Flying Corps.

One day a British officer flew high above the German aerodrome by the banks of the Tigris and dropped a packet attached to the usual streamer. Not knowing what it might contain, the finders opened it carefully.

The contents were 200 cigarettes, addressed to " the valiant Captain Schüz, with the compliments of the Royal Flying Corps."

Two British aviators, captured somewhere in the neighbourhood of Kut-el-Amara, were undergoing a weary pilgrimage. Under an escort of Turkish guards they travelled by filthy trains to filthy quarters, and were literally swarming with vermin when chance brought them to the vicinity of a German aviation camp. As soon as the enemy war birds saw their opposite numbers in such sorry plight, they rescued them by force from their Turkish escort and carried them off to their own quarters. There the prisoners indulged in the luxury of the first bath they had taken for months ; they were disinfected and received fresh underclothing. For three days they remained guests of the German airmen's mess, after which they were despatched on their way with sundry gifts to mitigate the discomforts of Turkish captivity.

A British two-seater was shot down over Smyrna and its occupants killed. Their bodies fell into the hands of the Turkish civil authorities, who exhibited them in the market place.

The barbarous spectacle did not last long, for within a few hours a detachment of the German Flying Corps arrived and removed the bodies by force from the Turkish police. They handed them over to the chaplain of the British colony for burial. During the funeral service, which was attended by several German officers, the pilot who had brought them down circled over the cemetery with black streamers attached to his machine.

Such was the relationship that existed between British and German war birds ; the prisoner who fell into their hands was a comrade of the air, whom it was their privilege to assist in every possible way. The dead enemy was a lost friend, and they mourned at his grave.

The following chapters will endeavour to tell something of the lives those opposite numbers led and the exploits they performed.

CHAPTER II

IN the mess of Richthofen's war birds the red wine flowed freely one night, for the renowned ace had received a telegram announcing that the Emperor had conferred on him the third class order of the Red Eagle with Crown. The occasion was, of course, a good excuse for a " binge."

When the time came to drink Richthofen's health, someone enquired how many orders he had already obtained.

" Every one that I can get," was the reply, spoken without boasting. " I should like to have the Oak Leaves for my ' Pour le Mérite'¹ order," he added, " but that is impossible."

" Why ? " asked another pilot, and the ace pointed out that no less a person than General Ludendorff had tried to get the Oak Leaves conferred on him, but the request was refused because they were reserved for the man who had won a battle.

The discussion then turned on the problem as to

¹ The " Ordre pour le Mérite," originally founded by the Elector Frederick in 1667, was remodelled by Frederick II in 1740. Originally a military distinction, it was afterwards enlarged to take in meritorious service in art and science. Unlike some German orders (and some British orders too, I fear) it was always difficult to obtain, and it is worthy of note that it was the only order Thomas Carlyle would ever accept. Roughly, we might say that it corresponds to our Distinguished Service Order, but a very high standard of distinction is required from the recipient.

whether aerial battles actually took place, and Richthofen gave it as his opinion that the fights which took place in the air could not be termed battles in the strategic sense of the word because, no matter how many machines were engaged, the affair always dissolved into a series of individual combats.

I believe that Richthofen was right. Although the number of machines engaged increased as the war progressed until 1918 saw encounters in which 70 or 80 aeroplanes took part, they could not be termed battles. But what of the future ?

Let us hope that there will be no future. Let us hope that the nations of the earth will come to their senses and abolish war.

Yet if mankind still remains foolish, the war birds will fly again—in ever increasing numbers. Some future war might see aerial encounters in which the combatants on either side are numbered by thousands. I wonder, however, whether such a fray would appeal to the airmen who flew out on their happy-go-lucky adventures in those autumn days of 1914.

War was already a horribly complicated affair on the ground. Who does not remember the war-maps of that time, with the double rows of Allied and German flags stretching from the North Sea to the Swiss frontier? An offensive on a grand scale, where brigades and divisions were recklessly hurled into the mêlée, might leave the amateur strategist uncertain whether it was worth while to alter the position of a single flag. Men fought, died and conquered in masses, at a word of command from a general who transmitted his orders over the telephone. It was the age of mass production.

But in the sky men sailed over the clouds to do deeds

of individual daring.   The warrior of the air still had the privilege of playing a lone hand.

Having written these lines, I turn the leaves of a book containing a few illustrations of the machines in which those pioneers of 1914 fought.   What clumsy, cumbrous, complicated affairs they look !   One wonders how they ever managed to get off the ground.

Outside my window I hear a drone in the air.   Some buses from a neighbouring R.A.F. aerodrome are out to-day, and by the sound of them they are very near and low.   That often happens, but to-day there is an unfamiliar sound about them that catches my ear and makes me put my pen down.

I step out into my garden to have a look and discover that the middle of the three buses overhead is an autogiro. This is the first time I have seen one of these inventions which is going to revolutionise the science of flying.

Having stared my fill, back to work !   I take up my pen, and once more my eye falls on the picture of the old 1914 bus. How awkwardly and precariously pilot and observer are seated !

The men who risked their lives in such buses were real heroes.   And so I must begin by paying a tribute to their valour.

Here is an adventure of a German[1] airman whose name I am unable to trace, but it took place in September, 1914.

---

[1] As the title indicates, this book is mainly concerned with the airmen of our late enemies.   To those who would like to read some of the famous deeds of our own pioneer aviators, I would recommend *Flying Fury*, by the late James McCudden, V.C., published by John Hamilton, Ltd. McCudden's first association with aviation took place when he was a mechanic at Aldershot. He embarked for France on 12 August, 1914, and the first part of his book contains a vivid account of war-flying in those early days.

On the morning of that day he was ordered to do a reconnaissance and bring back some photographs of the enemy's positions, which would be taken by an officer from the Photographic Section. Of his passenger (the word " observer " was not yet in use) he had no knowledge, and could only hope that he would prove an adaptable person.

However, all went well. The machine cruised over the enemy at a height of about 2,500 feet, and though it was subjected to intensive fire, it escaped without further damage than a few holes in the wings. After a flight of three hours the pilot came down and was rewarded with much praise by a general of the old-fashioned school, who seemed amazed that he had not broken his neck. What pleased the youthful aviator better was the excellent lunch he received at the general's table.

In the afternoon he enlisted the aid of several chauffeurs in the service of the general's staff to patch the holes and fill his machine with a fresh supply of benzin. Then he wa ted for further orders.

They were not long in coming. A Bavarian major attached to the general's staff had expressed a desire to gather some information concerning the course of the English retreat.

" I hope the major can shoot a bit," thought the pilot, though he said nothing. He knew that enemy aeroplanes had been frequently observed in the neighbourhood, and English airmen were in the habit of flying dangerously close to take pot shots at their opponents. If, however, the major knew how to handle a rifle, he could keep them at a respectful distance.

At about 4 p.m. the gallant officer strolled into sight, carrying a carbine of the type used by Uhlan regiments.

B

"This looks like business," thought our pilot, and decided that the Bavarian major was a stout fellow, whose acquaintance might be worth cultivating.

Flying low, they followed a main road which, according to the major, should bring them on to the line of the English retreat. After a little while the passenger tapped his pilot's shoulder and pointed to a number of small khaki figures of men who seemed too busy making for their new positions to bother about them. No enemy aeroplanes about !

They flew on. Suddenly the major tapped his shoulder again, and shouted something in his ear. At first the roar of the engine drowned all speech, but eventually one word became intelligible through continual repetition.

Paris ! The major wanted to have a look at Paris !

"Paris ?" the pilot shouted. "You want to go to Paris ?" The major nodded and beamed.

The pilot studied his benzin gauge. Yes, there was enough juice to do the trip. So he put his machine's nose southward, and half an hour later the grey mass of a great city expanded before his eyes. Five minutes afterwards he made out the slim framework of the Eiffel Tower and the gleaming white Sacré Cœur church crowning Montmartre hill.

Then the venerable Gothic pile of Nôtre-Dame loomed into sight, and finally the pilot was able to trace the outline of the " Boul Mich," which brought back happy associations of his student days in the Latin Quarter.

"Damn this war which stops me from landing and looking up a few old friends," he thought.

They flew over the town. " Jolly old Paris, damn fine place," mused the pilot, and forgot about the war until peering down he saw the streets filled with what looked like lively masses of ants. Parisians cursing the German Taube [1]—silly asses—after all, the Taube was a jolly fine bird !

From a housetop a feeble flash reached his eye. Some sportsman taking a pot-shot at the bird—or perhaps artillery of sorts on a prepared emplacement. He could not distinguish at that height, and in any case it did not matter, for the marksman could not reach him.

So he continued his tour of the city. Perhaps the major has never seen Paris, he thought, and maybe he won't get another chance. *C'est la guerre*, so we must make the most of this opportunity. A glance at the benzin gauge. High time to be getting home again. But even as he turned his Taube's nose northward, he espied a monoplane heading towards him swiftly from the direction of Juvisy and recognised it as a French machine. He knew that it had the speed of him.

Clouds above him. At 6,000 feet, he judged. If he reached them, he could find shelter from the bird of prey. He glanced round ; the Bavarian major handed him the carbine and began to examine a couple of pistols he had brought with him. Then he pointed to the right, and, following the direction of his outstretched hand, the pilot caught sight of a second monoplane hastening to cut him off. He balanced the carbine and pulled the trigger, at the same moment kicking the rudder. The Taube went into a sharp right-hand turn just in time to avoid a collision with Monoplane No. 1.

The turn brought it broadside on with Monoplane No. 2 and slightly above it. The Major's arm shot out

[1] The German word Taube means pigeon.

and grabbed the carbine, which he fired three times in quick succession.

The pilot saw Monoplane No. 2 shoot up to pass them barely 100 yards away. He had a fleeting vision of a man in it, answering the major with bullet for bullet. Then the French machine reared its nose high in the air ; it rose slightly as the last convulsive movement of its stricken pilot pulled the stick over, and dropped like a stone.

Meanwhile Monoplane No. 1 had circled round to attack the Taube from the rear. With his free hand the passenger emptied chamber after chamber of his revolver into the German machine. One bullet embedded itself in the cockpit ; then the Taube ascended into a thick, opaque bank of clammy mist, in which the roar of the French engine grew ever fainter.

When the German bus emerged into clear sky once more, the pilot realised that he had lost his way, and dropped a thousand feet in search of some landmark that would give him his direction. Suddenly he found himself surrounded by little white clouds, which he recognised as bursting shrapnel.

Shrapnel to the right of him, shrapnel to the left of him. Shrapnel above him, shrapnel below him. The French artillery had got his range with devilish accuracy, and he saw no way of escape save to steer a straight course and outdistance the gunners. But a series of thuds, followed by the splintering of woodwork and ominous metallic clangs, told him that his bus was hit.

Suddenly a white flash blinded him. The Taube's nose went up and the right wing dipped, but with a desperate kick of the rudder the pilot regained an even keel.

A quiver ran through the major's body ; he attempted to rise from his seat, but quickly sank down again. His head dropped forward on his chest, and the pilot saw a thin stream of blood trickling from his passenger's shoulder. The machine began to lose height.

The direct hit that wounded the major had also smashed the propeller, and the left wing was a mass of shreds and tatters, but the pilot kept his head and put his machine into a glide. As he sank earthwards he saw that he was heading for a wood and knew that he was lost if he had to come down in the trees. But luck was with him ; he landed in a field at the very edge of the wood, and though he taxied on until the bus collided with a tree and turned over, he managed to scramble out somehow. Then he fainted.

When he came to, he found himself surrounded by a group of German infantrymen who had seen the Taube come down. An ambulance man was applying first aid to the major's shoulder.

The gallant warrior was carried to hospital ; his trip had cost him dear. The pilot escaped with a badly bruised leg and rejoined his unit that same evening.

A few days later a friend of his was ordered to take a staff officer to reconnoitre the French positions. A heat haze hung over the land, thickening in patches to a dense mist.

Not a pleasant job, thought the pilot, for he knew that he would have to fly low enough to present an easy target to any enterprising marksman, while in all probability the results would hardly be worth the trouble and risk.

But orders are orders. He had the machine brought out and determined to do his best.

They took off, steering by the compass. After about

twenty minutes they ran into clearer air ; the pilot cut off his engine and glided down.

His passenger was able to make out black smears, smudges, strips and dots moving over the green carpet beneath him and, taking them for enemy troops, ordered his pilot to cruise about this territory while he made sketches.

But the men below had observed the big bird sailing over their heads, with the result that it was soon surrounded by the white shrapnel clouds with which the pilot was already familiar. The passenger had also learnt their significance on previous trips, but refused to let them interfere with his work. He became so interested in it that he even told the pilot to drop lower and give him a better view.

But the descent also gave the men on the ground a better mark, and the poilus began to shoot, for in those days there was nothing an infantryman loved better than taking a pot shot at a war bird. Later, of course, when aeroplanes carried machine guns that could sweep a trench, the infantry revised their opinions and developed an unholy respect for the foemen of the air. But as these were early days, the troops in question banged away joyously to their hearts' content.

A number of holes in the Taube's wings testified to the efficiency of their marksmanship. The roar of his engine prevented the pilot from hearing the zips that tore his fabric, but presently his ears caught a fateful clang, and the indicator of his benzin " clock " began to drop. So did the " revs."

Tank punctured, in all probability, or perhaps the feed-pipe. " Try the handpump," he decided, " it may do the trick."

Luckily it did ; the engine kept going. He pulled

the stick and put his Taube into a climbing turn.   Thirty
miles to home and safety—might just do it.   Thank
heavens, we have the wind behind us now !

For the next ten minutes the engine grumbled, but
continued to work.   Then it began to sputter badly.
No juice coming through !   Nothing for it but to land
where we can!

The trouble was that the haze had thickened, so that
he could not tell whether the country over which he
flew was held by friend or foe.   " We'll find that out
when I get down, I suppose," he decided philosophically.

He cut off his engine and glided down through the
haze.   When the ground below him became visible,
he uttered a sigh of relief, for he saw that he was going
to land close to a town of sorts.   Had he gone on another
mile, he would have crashed on the housetops in all
likelihood, but as matters were he could descend in the
surrounding fields, and not so far away he would find
mechanics to patch his damaged Taube and benzin to
replace what he lost from his punctured tank.

Provided, of course, that the town was in German
occupation.   If not, they would be lucky to be marched
off to custody without some preliminary rough handling
by the populace.

He came down on the very outskirts of the town ; a
few minutes later the Taube was the centre of a crowd of
inquisitive spectators. The pilot glanced anxiously about
him in search of some field-grey uniform that would
betoken the presence of German troops.   He found
none.

His hand went to his pocket for the revolver he carried.
If they meant to lynch him, he would not give in
without a fight for life.

" Vive l'Angleterre ! " piped a voice from the crowd.
" Vive l'Angleterre " refrained the chorus. A happy
grin spread over the faces of the pilot and his passenger
as they grasped the situation.

" Does any person here speak English ? " enquired
the passenger in a thick German accent, but—luckily
for him, perhaps—no one did. So with a few words
of broken French and many expressive gestures he
explained that after a fierce encounter with three Boche
aeroplanes *les aviateurs anglaises* had been forced to land
on account of a bullet in the benzin tank. A more
intelligent member of the crowd went off to the nearest
garage to find help for the stranded allies.

He arrived back with a couple of mechanics, a gen-
darme and several red-trousered soldiers who proved most
useful in keeping the crowd back while the hole in the
tank was soldered. Then a supply of the precious liquid
fuel was poured in ; the war birds waved their greetings
to the crowd and sailed aloft to kill some more Boches !

Although the possibilities of damaging an enemy by
dropping bombs from the air were recognised even before
the war, there seem to have been very hazy ideas as to
the most effective way in which this new weapon could
be applied. From an account given by a German
observer of his experiences in October, 1914, the lay
public will learn that the passengers of rival aeroplanes
tried to drop bombs on one another.

In this particular case a German photographer was
ordered to bring his camera to bear on the enemy's
positions. While engaged in this task he was subjected
to heavy shrapnel fire, but as the machine was flying at a
height of nearly 7,000 feet, the missiles failed to reach it,
although the detonations in the air created eddies and

gusts which made it difficult for him to keep his machine on an even keel.

Just as they had finished their work and were about to return, a fast enemy machine appeared, seemingly from nowhere, and tried to climb above them. The two aeroplanes rose in circles, their passengers sniping at one another whenever they saw an opportunity.

The French machine forged ahead, and from a height of some 30 to 50 feet over his enemies' heads its passenger began to drop bombs. The German photographer stood up on his seat and shot at him over his own pilot's head.

After a few attempts the inmates of the French machine came to the conclusion that they were wasting their time and flew away. The Germans returned home none the worse for their experience, but exhausted by their strenuous efforts. It would be interesting to learn whether the enterprising Frenchman ever succeeded in bringing down an opponent in this fashion.[1]

I doubt the possibility, but the passengers in the early machines became efficient enough with their rifles to cause a fair number of casualties on both sides. I have been able to obtain particulars of one curious and tragic case which is worth recounting.

It appears to have occurred somewhat later than the incidents I have already related, because the second seat in the machine was allotted to a regular observer in place

---

[1] In his interesting and entertaining book entitled *One Man's War* (published by John Hamilton, Ltd.), Bert Hall, the American pilot who was a member of the famous Lafayette Squadron, relates how a German airman tried to attack him with hand grenades as late as September, 1915. Hall says that this was the first and only time he encountered an opponent making use of such a weapon, and the affair ended tragically for the thrower, for a grenade fell back into his own cockpit and exploded before he could retrieve it.

of the casual passenger who might be ordered to do some particular sketching or photographic job. But the rifle was still the weapon with which he defended his pilot.

In this case the bus took off just as the sun was rising and gained sufficient height to cross the enemy's lines under cover of some clouds. When about 25 miles in hostile territory, the pilot dropped down to 3,500 feet —the height which his observer had told him would suffice for the job in hand—but was promptly spotted by a hostile battery and shelled.

The enemy had the range too well for his comfort ; the pilot therefore sought again the shelter of the clouds. After a while he emerged, but once more the artillery started, and some infantrymen joined in, but by popping in and out of the clouds he gave his observer sufficient opportunity to photograph their objectives.

The work was completed, apparently without any damage to the machine, and the pilot had just started his homeward journey when his eye fell on the benzin " clock," and he saw that he had only 52 litres left. As he remembered that the indicator had registered 100 only a few minutes previously, he was somewhat worried, and his dismay increased as he saw the hand go rapidly down to 45 and then to 40 litres.

Obviously his tank had been holed. He decided to climb as high as possible and then glide home, reckoning that if he could reach 10,000 feet he would have no difficulty in making the German lines. His altimeter showed 6,000, and he still had the benzin in the emergency tank to fall back on. Things were not looking too bad, he thought.

But both pilot and observer were so busy with their troubles that they failed to notice the arrival of a French machine which had hastened up to chase the enemy home.

When at last they spotted it, it was less than a mile behind them and climbing rapidly.

The pilot took stock of the situation. It was impossible to engage in a climbing match with any hope of success, and equally impossible to go down. He realised that his only chance of safety lay in swift flight, and evened out again in order to cut and run for home while the benzin held out.

But the French machine was the faster. It overhauled the German and cut him off. Then it climbed and turned to swoop.

Nearer came the Frenchman. The pilot saw that his observer was shooting—the enemy too, as he knew from the rips in his fabric and the splintering of his woodwork. But he was too engrossed in his job of getting home to pay much attention to the details of the duel.

He could hardly believe his eyes when he saw the French machine dip by the right and go down in a spin. A lucky bullet from his observer's rifle had killed the enemy pilot. With exultation in his heart he continued his course.

The sputtering of his engine told him that he had no more benzin left, but that did not matter now. He put his machine into a glide and made a perfect landing on his own aerodrome.

He unbuckled the safety belt and sprang from his seat. With outstretched hand he turned to his observer to congratulate him on his valiant and successful fight. But to his horror he saw that his friend lay huddled on his seat—with a bullet through his heart.

Strange as it may seem, at the identical moment when

the German observer loosed the bullet that killed the French pilot and sent his machine crashing, his opposite number must have pulled the trigger to send his own missile on its errand of destruction.

The Austrians are known as happy-go-lucky folk who are inclined to take matters too easily. Consequently their factories failed to deliver the necessary machines for the aviators, with the result that a number of aeroplanes had to be requisitioned from Germany at a time when they were urgently needed on the western front. The Austrians, however, provided some skilful and daring pilots to work them, thanks to the efforts of one man who appears to have been a genius in many directions.

When Emil Uzelac was chosen to organise the Austrian Flying Corps in 1912 he was already famous for the versatility of his accomplishments. He was an officer in the engineer corps with a promising career before him, but he could have served with equal distinction in the cavalry, the Alpine troops, or the navy, for he was a daring rider, a ski-runner who had won many prizes at winter sports gatherings, and he held a master-mariner's certificate. In addition to these accomplishments he was the best fencer in the army and had served as an instructor for a period. Such was his reputation for success in everything to which he put his hand that the Austrian authorities felt convinced that he was the right man to organise their military aviation. Uzelac was 44 years old when he took up his new post, and he knew nothing of flying. He had never even been in the air as a passenger when he was promoted from lieutenant to colonel at one fell swoop and told to get on with his job. " Very well," thought Uzelac, " if I have to create a flying corps, I suppose I'd better learn to fly."

For the next few weeks he practically lived in the hangars of Wiener-Neustadt aerodrome. Every morning early he was up in the air, and although history does not relate the number of machines he wrote off in his experiments, within a month he was the best pilot in Austria.

Uzelac loved nothing so much as playing about with new types of machines until he had mastered all their tricks. " The boss must know all there is to be known about his job," he was wont to remark when he crawled out of the debris of some experimental type of machine he had crashed because he insisted on taking it up without any previous knowledge of its eccentricities, " and I'm not going to let any of our young fellows think they can do things I can't."

He had some miraculous escapes, but in the end there was no type of machine that he could not fly. When he was not in the air, he could generally be found at his desk, grappling with the office routine of the new job or in the hangars, helping his mechanics to repair the damaged machines. Consequently he contrived to make the personal acquaintance of each individual member of his staff and was able to show them that there was no part of their work that he could not do as efficiently as they did it. The riggers and fitters adored the chief who was ready to don overalls and dirty his hands with the best of them.

Uzelac preferred the society of his mechanics to that of his former brother officers. He made it his practice to take each one of them for a flight, and when he landed he made them tell him their impressions of the experience.

" I can always spot if a man has the gift of flying when I've taken him up once," he used to say, and as a matter

of fact many of the best Austrian pilots in the war were
the former chauffeurs, engine-drivers, lorrymen and
mechanics that had learnt to fly under his personal
instruction. Uzelac disliked specialists, and always
insisted on his pupils familiarising themselves with
every type of machine.

He knew that if war broke out his aviators would have
to operate in mountainous country and therefore saw to
it that they had sufficient practice to cope with the
numerous obstacles and difficulties they would be forced
to encounter on active service.   How many pilots of the
western front, I wonder, would have relished the Bocche
di Cattaro as headquarters ?

The town of Cattaro lies on a narrow strip of southernmost Dalmatia, between the mountains of Montenegro
and the bay known as the Bocche di Cattaro.   From the
rocky coast the land slopes steeply upward, terrace upon
terrace of vineyards and olive groves.

Out of one of these foothills Uzelac bade his men
carve a level surface for a miniature aerodrome, and the
pilots that used it had to measure their take-offs and
landings to an inch. Woe betide the blunderer who
missed the landing-ground, for he had no alternative but to
come down on the water of the bay, where his machine
promptly turned over. He was lucky to escape with
his life.

Behind Cattaro were the mountains of the little princi-
pality of Montenegro, gaunt jagged peaks rising out of
deep, precipitous valleys—not an inch of level ground in all
the width and breadth of that Montenegrin land. The man
who escaped with his life after a crash in Montenegro
was certain to fall into the hands of the local banditry, who
dealt with him in their own mediaeval fashion.

Uzelac's pupils learnt to make good landings when they practised at Cattaro.

And when war broke out, they flew forth from Cattaro to attack the Lowçen, that grim Montenegrin fortress that stands on a rock 6,000 feet above the sea.   Then they bombarded the quays of Antivari and the Montenegrin capital, Cettinje ; for three days and three nights they took off and landed in never-ending succession until the Bocche di Cattaro was full of the wreckage of planes that failed to get home.

Bombing was literally a matter of touch and go for them.   They had no percussion detonators on their bombs—only fuses cut to lengths that would cause the charges to ignite just as they touched the ground.   In most of their machines these bombs had to be dropped by the pilots, because the passengers' seats were located over the wings.

One of Uzelac's best pilots was Captain Hegrossky, but when he took part in the attack on the Lowçen fortress he fumbled with a bomb after lighting the fuse (a clumsy job at the best of times), and it rolled under his seat.

One hand he had to keep on the stick ; with the other he could grope blindly for the bomb, and he knew that if he failed to find it and throw it overboard before the quick-match burnt down, it would blow his passenger and himself into fragments.   Under those conditions many a man would have failed to find that bomb through sheer nerves.

But Hegrossky did not know what nerves were.   With his sightless hand he tapped the floor-space under his seat methodically, inch by inch, until he located the bomb.   His fingers crept over its surface until they touched the quick-match ; then he pulled it up and

jerked it over the side.   A hundred feet below him it
burst in mid-air ; if he had found it only three or at
most four seconds later, it would have burst in his machine.
But Hegrossky only laughed.

Another time he was sent to bomb a pontoon bridge
the Serbs had thrown over the Save.   From a height
of 3,000 feet he sent a bomb down which missed its
mark.   " Bad shooting," commented Hegrossky, " I see
I must come a bit nearer."   Down he dropped to 600
feet.

On either side of the river were Serbian batteries that
peppered him hotly.   He did not worry his head about
them, as his chief concern was for his bomb, which had a
fuse calculated to ignite it at the end of a 3,000 feet drop.
So Hegrossky lit it while he was still high up, and came
down with it in his hand.   If he had been compelled to
drop it, he could never have retrieved it in time, but he
held on to it till he judged he was well over his mark.

Then he sent it down, and it fell on the middle of the
bridge.

Hegrossky waited to see that it had done its job before
he climbed up out of reach of the Serbian gunners.

On the Galician front it was equally bad campaigning
for the Austrian war birds, who were ordered to make
long distance reconnaissances to ascertain the positions of
Russian troops marching to the scene of action.   It
was an easy matter for regiments, brigades or even
divisions and army corps to lose themselves from view
in the thick, primeval forests that covered the vast
plains at the foot of the Carpathians.

The Russian generals knew the value of a surprise
attack.   Their armies marched only by night ; in the
daytime they lay hidden in the villages or in the green

depths of the forests. The Austrian aviators received orders to locate the invisible foeman at any cost.

The work fell mainly on two pilots, Lieutenant Mandl, who took Lieutenant Macher as his observer, and Engine-driver Malina, one of Uzelac's finds, who was accompanied by Lieutenant Rosenthal.

If they flew high, they knew they had no chance of spotting the advancing Russians, for, as aforesaid, there was no army too large to be swallowed by those vast forests of Poland and Galicia. The only sure method of discovering the presence of troops was to provoke the concealed enemy to emerge and fire on them.

From village to distant village they skimmed the long, endless cornfields of Galicia. In the open country they flew a few feet above the ground ; when they reached a village or small town, they nearly grazed its housetops. In the Polish forests they scraped the upmost branches of the trees.

For hours perhaps they would fly without setting eyes on a living soul, although every moment brought danger of collision with houses, trees or rising ground. Then at last their labours were rewarded ; some Russian peasant, thrust hurriedly into uniform a few weeks previously and terrified at the sight of the monster that he regarded as an invention of the devil, gave way to his panic fear and, disobeying orders, rushed forth from his hiding place to let off his rifle. Infected by the sound, a dozen of his fellows would spring up from nowhere to join in the fusillade. A minute later a hundred would be firing—five minutes later, perhaps a thousand. Then the pilot would fly up with his wings full of holes, while the observer endeavoured to calculate the strength of the wasp's-nest they had dislodged.

Day after day the two aeroplanes set forth in flights of four or five hours duration, until at last Malina and Rosenthal failed to return. A Russian aeroplane, lying in wait above the clouds, had swooped down on them ; a fight took place in which the two machines collided and crashed to earth.

But their work was done, for as a result of their reconnaissances the Austrian General Staff deduced rightly that the main Russian attack would come from the east and not from the north as they had originally been led to suppose. The blow was heavy enough when it fell, for they lost the fortress of Lemberg and were thrust out of Eastern Galicia, but their armies retreated in time to avoid the encircling movement that threatened complete annihilation.

When the Russians advanced into East Prussia in August, 1914, the German airmen were set the same invidious task of locating the trail of an invisible foeman in vast forests. The Russian armies of the north had more aeroplanes than the forces that were pressing the Austrians in Galicia, so that encounters in the air were fairly frequent, though the pilots on both sides had such long distances to cover in the course of their daily work that they could waste no benzin on hunting one another. They fought when they met by chance—with weapons that were usually ineffective.

When the German armies retreated after the battle of Gumbinnen, a pilot and observer received orders to ascertain the strength of the pursuing Russians. They flew for an hour without incident ; then suddenly they saw a Nieuport monoplane heading towards them. As the enemy machine was some 600 feet below them, as far as they could judge, they decided to ignore it and

carry on with their work. The pilot pulled the stick
to gain yet more height. and as he rose he saw the
Nieuport pass beneath him.

But about five minutes later the observer reported
that the Nieuport had turned round and was pursuing
them. The pilot put his Rumpler into a right hand turn
and circled to meet this pugnacious adversary. When
the two machines had approached to within 200 yards
of one another, the German observer, noting that his
machine was well above the other, snatched up his
carbine and fired. The Russian pilot promptly turned
and made off. The machines of those days could not
climb as high as their successors, but the Rumpler was
a good machine for gaining height, as the occupants of
this one found when a quarter of an hour later they
encountered a large body of Russian troops that promptly
halted and fired at them. Their machine rose comfortably
out of range, and the observer did his work in safety.
A couple of hours later he reported his results at
his headquarters, where he learnt that the pilot and
observer of another aeroplane had been brought down
by rifle fire.

The next day the Rumpler's crew had no luck ; not
a single Russian was to be seen. The observers of the
other machines likewise came back empty-handed.

Had the enemy reinforcements retreated, or had they
been diverted to some other part of the front ? What
additions to their forces were the armies they had encountered at Gumbinnen likely to receive ? That was
the problem for the German staff to solve, and upon the
correctness of the information they received the fate of
East Prussia might depend, for everywhere the Russians
had the numerical superiority, so that an unforeseen

concentration of forces at a weak point could easily
break the resistance.

Day after day the war birds sallied forth to collect the
information so urgently needed. At last one of them,
crossing the frontier and flying nearly 100 miles into
Russian territory, caught sight of a mass of troops, which
he estimated as a division, although he found it extremely
difficult to calculate their numbers because the men were
marching in open order across the fields. There was
no sign of any baggage trains, and he rightly concluded
that the wheeled traffic moved only by night. The
Russians were undoubtedly sending strong reinforcements to East Prussia, but had taken pains to
conceal their numbers from the eyes of prying
airmen.

The next day the pilot of the Rumpler received orders
to make a long distance reconnaissance in the same
direction. Knowing by his comrade's experience that
the Russians avoided the main roads, he decided to scour
the byways in the hope of finding them. But that day
even the fields seemed empty.

His mission seemed doomed to disappointment, but
as he approached an out-of-the-way village, some ten
miles from a main road, he chanced to look down through
the opening in his wing and saw in its long main street
khaki-clad figures, which he recognised as Russian
soldiers. They caught sight of him and began to fire ;
from a neighbouring wood other Russians, hearing the
shots, hastened to join in.

As in Galicia, the Russians were marching by night
and resting in the day time in woods and villages. Thus
they might have deceived the enemy as to their strength
but for the fatal weakness of the soldiers who could never

resist the temptation to emerge from cover and fire at any aeroplane they saw.

When the German airmen knew where and how to look for the enemy, they brought in fairly accurate estimates of the numbers they encountered. Their General Staff received information which enabled them to deduce the strength of the advancing Russians, and thus the war birds of the eastern front must have contributed in no small measure to the success of the operations culminating in the battle of Tannenberg, where the invading hosts were driven into the Masurian swamps and annihilated.

CHAPTER III

WHETHER you consider Gunther Plüschow a lucky or unlucky fellow must depend on the way you look at things. Undoubtedly he was and is a gifted airman, but he never achieved the fame that crowned the achievements of a Richthofen or a Boelcke. As a war bird he enjoyed only a brief flying career, but though it ended with his capture and imprisonment, he was one of the few German officers to escape from Donnington Hall. When he returned to Germany he survived the war . . . and he is still flying.

Plüschow was originally intended for a naval career, but, like so many young officers of his epoch, he was attracted by the adventures that the new sport of aviation offered and put in a request to be transferred to the German Naval Flying Corps. He had an uncle capable of pulling a string or two—a most useful asset—and great was his joy when he learnt that his ultimate destination was to be the German naval station of Tsingtao, in China, where he would have the distinction of being the first airman. In the opening days of fateful 1914 Plüschow thought himself a lucky man.

He had yet to learn to fly. Day by day he hung about the Johannistal aerodrome, but all that January heavy snow fell, and no instructor would take him up. At last February brought better weather, and he received his first lesson.

He learnt quickly ; on the third day he was allowed to take his first solo flight, and within a week he had passed the necessary tests and qualified for his pilot's certificate.

As he was not due to start for the Far East for several weeks, he practised flying in Germany. He made several adventurous cross-country flights and occupied the second seat in the machine of Linnekogel, a well-known German pilot who was trying to break the world's height record.

At their first attempt they were beaten by the cold. When they reached a height of 4,000 metres, their engine froze, so that they had to glide down. But a few days later they tried again.

The world's record, held by a Frenchman, was then 5,300 metres, and when on their second trip they reached 4,900 they thought they were going to beat it. But once more their engine was lamed by the bitter cold, and, try as they would, they could not force their way over the 5,000 mark. When their last drop of benzin was consumed, they came down and consoled themselves with the fact that they had at least flown higher than any other German. But they wanted the world's record, and early in March, when King Winter was beginning to relax his icy grip, they tried their luck again.

They burst through a cloud barrier into a cold blue sky and waved their hands to a Zeppelin that was out on a trial flight. Then they started to climb in grim earnest.

It took them over an hour to reach 4,800 metres, but to their relief the engine worked perfectly. Their hearts and lungs throbbed and panted ; every breath

was a sharp, stabbing pain.   But they did not care, for
their two barographs agreed in recording 5,000 metres,
and they were still climbing.

Plüschow was so fascinated by the spectacle of the
distant earth beneath him that he forgot to keep an eye
on his instruments.   When at last he remembered his
duties, he was surprised to find that the recorded height
remained unchanged, although he knew that the bus
had been steadily mounting.   Conversation being impossible, he held out the five fingers of his right hand to
Linnekogel, and then pointed upwards.

But the pilot only grinned and shook his partner's
hand.   Then he pointed to his own barograph.

Plüschow's instrument had frozen when 5,000 metres
were reached, but Linnekogel's barograph, which received
some slight warmth from the engine, continued to func-
tion and recorded the exact height of 5,500 metres.   So,
with the world's height record to his credit, Plüschow
went gaily off to China via Russia and the trans-Siberian
railway.

Gay days followed—days of idleness and pleasure,
for the youthful aviator's Taube was compelled to take
the longer sea-route and had not even reached the Suez
Canal when he made his entry into Tsingtao.   In Kiauchau
bay lay the *Good Hope*, the flagship of the British cruiser
squadron in the Far East ; the flags of the British and
German Empires fluttered peacefully side by side,
while on the Tsingtao racecourse, which was to be
Plüschow's aerodrome, the football team of H.M.S.
Good Hope played a drawn match with the representatives
of their opposite number, S.M.S. *Scharnhorst*.   On his
flagship Admiral Count von Spee entertained Admiral
Sir Christopher Cradock and his staff.

The visit came to an end. The British cruisers steamed out. " Au Revoir " was the signal that broke out on both flagships.

How could they know that the next meeting was to be at Coronel when Admiral von Spee would send the *Good Hope* and her consort, the *Monmouth*, to the bottom of the ocean, only to lead a precarious existence for another five weeks, a hunted fugitive of the sea until in due course he too found his watery grave !

But the war that caused the death of those two admirals and their gallant seamen was still a part of the unknown future, and meanwhile Tsingtao was at the height of its season. Plüschow found a villa on the side of a hill, which he shared with a congenial comrade ; he bought Chinese works of art to embellish it, he hired ponies and rode, he learnt to play polo. Tsingtao was an earthly paradise and he was due to spend the next three years of his life there. He knew that they would be wonderful, unforgettable years. Golden years of youth !

In July his Taube ended its long journey ; he welcomed it on the quay ; his squad of mechanics unpacked it and bore it off in triumph to the racecourse. For the next couple of days he worked with his men, putting it together, testing, overhauling, taking stock of the spare parts. Then early on the third morning, while the white and yellow denizens of Tsingtao still slept, he went down to the new aerodrome and took off for his first flight.

It was not an ideal aerodrome, measuring as it did barely 600 yards in length and 200 in breadth. Behind it lay the encircling hills, before it the sea. " A children's playground for toy aeroplanes " a brother officer had dubbed it, but despite the dangers and difficulties of

taking off and landing on such a restricted space, with
the certainty of a bad crash if forced to descend anywhere
outside it, Plüschow loved the place. It was all his
own ; in Tsingtao he was king of the air.

His kingdom was a turbulent one to govern ; barely
had he spent a week encircling its boundaries when
treacherous air currents caught him as he hovered some
300 feet above the race course, preparing to land. He
overshot his landing place ; his engine gave out, and
he came down on the edge of a wood that covered the
hillside.

The broken Taube seemed a mass of shreds and tatters,
but the engine was sound. Spare wings and spare
propellers had been sent with the machine, so that in a
few days he hoped to fly again. But when he opened
the huge cases containing these parts, his heart sank,
for the men who had packed them in Germany evidently
had little notion of the toll exacted by the tropics. Wires
were rusted, wood lay rotting, and the disordered masses
were coated with a thick layer of mildew that poisoned
his nostrils.

The offence was rank ; it stank to heaven !

But hope sprang anew in his breast ; wire, wood and
canvas were procurable in Tsingtao, while enough of
the framework remained to give him the exact dimensions
of the wings. His mechanics had already proved their
worth, and he knew his Chinese workmen to be excellent
carpenters and joiners. Nothing was easier than to make
the crippled bird a new pair of wings.

Provided, of course, that the spare propellers remained
intact. But when he opened their cases, the same
foul odour smote his nostrils. His five reserve propellers
were crumbling to dust.

Yet once again his Chinese workmen saved the situation. Day and night they toiled, carving him propeller blades from the stems of seven oak trees—those patient, nerveless sons of the Celestial Kingdom who can stand all day chiselling the delicate tracery of the ivory work that bewitches our European eyes. Inhuman they seem to our European minds, inhuman in their perfection of patient skill . . . but they fashioned Plüschow a new propeller. Day and night he worked with them until the shattered bird was built up anew and ready to take the air again.

Yet why this haste, some readers may enquire. Another, less energetic than Plüschow, would have been content to wait, enjoying the golden hours of idleness until new spare parts could reach him from Germany. But Plüschow and his brother officers had begun to speculate how far distant was the day when Germany could give them no more assistance.

A cloud no larger than a man's hand. An Austrian Archduke has been murdered in Sarajevo, wherever that may be. Somewhere in Bosnia, if we know where Bosnia is. Look it up in the atlas ! An out-of-the-way hole, it seems, peopled by Serbian bandits, so what business has the Austrian Archduke, especially when he is heir to the throne, to go messing about in such wild parts, asking for trouble ?

A ridiculous business it seems to all, especially to those who have passed the greater part of their lives in the East and cannot be bothered to follow the tangle of European politics. But ridiculous or not, it threatens to set Europe by the ears, for in those last weeks of July Austria threatens Serbia, Russia stiffens Serbian resistance, Germany backs Austria, and England and

France are Russia's allies.   What will be the end of
it ?

War !   In Tsingtao's mess Plüschow's brother officers
begin to whisper of war's possibility.   Tsingtao's governor holds anxious conferences with his chief officers of
land and sea.

War is impossible !   July is the gayest month of
Tsingtao's gay season.   The beach is covered with
tents ;   fair maidens of all European nations, clad in
bathing costumes of brilliant hues, disport themselves
in the waves and sun themselves on the strand.   The
" Ostende of the Far East," is the name by which
Tsingtao is known to the white inhabitants of every
European settlement in China.

Every day there are riding and motoring parties.
A tennis tournament is in full swing.   On 1 August, the
English polo club of Shanghai is coming over for its
annual match with the Germans of Tsingtao.   Every
evening there is a dance somewhere, and by far the
greatest number of the foreigners who have come to
Tsingtao to enjoy themselves are English.

War is impossible !

But the war rumours gain ground persistently and at
last develop into solid facts.   Germany has declared war
on Russia to-day ;   to-morrow we shall be at war with
Russia's bosom friend, France.

Will there be war with England ?   That is the vital
question for the German colony of Tsingtao, cut off
from their Fatherland by thousands of watery miles.
So long as the mistress of the seas remains neutral, there
is hope for them.

" War between England and Germany is impossible,"
declares an English girl who has gone out riding with

Plüschow—she danced with him the night before.
Impossible, unthinkable, and all her friends say the
same thing. Utterly impossible for the two leading
white races to fight and slay each other for the benefit
of the grinning little yellow Japs !

But all the same on 4 August England and Germany
are at war.

The gay season of the " Ostende of the Far East "
is over ; the dances are cancelled, the English girls and
their menfolk crowd the departing steamers, while
notices are plastered up forbidding all unauthorised
persons to go near the fortifications. Mars holds Tsingtao in his iron fist.

Then comes the anti-climax. The world is at war,
but Tsingtao remains at peace. Everything is unchanged, save that the foreign visitors have departed.
From Germany come wireless messages, telling of
victory after victory.

Plüschow and his companions seethe with rage. War is
their profession, yet here they are cut off from the conflict and doomed to inactivity.

So they think, until 15 August brings a special edition
of their newspaper, announcing an ultimatum from Japan,
who demands complete surrender by Germany of the
Kiauchau concession. A week is granted for considera-
tion ; if at its expiry Germany does not consent, " the
Imperial Japanese Government will be compelled to
adopt such measures as the situation warrants."

War upon Tsingtao !

During that week's breathing space the railway
communications with neutral China remain intact.
Women, children and all the remaining foreigners are
despatched to Tientsin. The garrison prepares for action.

Plüschow makes a trial flight with his patched-up Taube. In the air all goes well, but when he lands he finds that his propeller is coming to pieces. The Chinese glue is not strong enough to stand the strain of the air ; it is a miracle how the component parts have held together.

Another would have reported the machine definitely out of action, but Gunther Plüschow is made of sterner stuff. The miracle must be repeated daily, he decides, and so the propeller goes back to the Chinese workshop to be glued and pressed again. Henceforth it must be detached after every flight, reglued and reaffixed at the last moment before the next flight. If the gods are favourable the miracle will be repeated, if not . . .

Plüschow has other duties pressed upon him. There are two captive balloons on the books of the garrison, and he has passed through a course of balloon instruction in Berlin. His second in command is a naval petty officer who likewise underwent a course of aeronautics some years ago ; no one else in the garrison knows anything about balloons. So after much labour in the Tsingtao sun Plüschow and his petty officer manage to inflate the monsters ; then they test every rope personally and start to train a crew. Plüschow makes the first ascent alone, but his raw, awkward squad find great difficulty in keeping a tight hold on the unruly " sausage," which nearly succeeds in tearing the ropes from their fumbling fingers and starting a voyage of exploration over the China seas. The car rocks so violently that Plüschow is nearly thrown out.

But after a little practice they do better, and eventually the balloons play their part in the defence of Tsingtao.

On 23 August the Japanese ultimatum expires.

Plüschow makes a flight around the concession, but can see no signs of hostile activity. On the following morning, however, he spies from his balcony some half a dozen black smears on the blue horizon where sea and sky meet, and his binoculars subsequently reveal them as Japanese torpedo-boats. The siege of Tsingtao has begun.

Plüschow soon proves his worth to the garrison, for he makes a flight along the coastline of the Shantung peninsula and is able to report the exact spot where the Japanese have landed, so that the defenders can take measures to hold them up as long as possible. But the Japs are in no hurry ; slow but sure is their motto, and Plüschow does not receive his baptism of fire till several days later, when, flying over the hills at the extreme limit of the concession, he suddenly encounters a troop of Japanese infantrymen. They promptly open fire on him, and he returns to count the holes in his wings, resolving to fly higher in future, now that he has some idea of the range of their weapons.

Slowly but surely the Japanese land forces press forward ; acting on their orders, the German outposts fall back after inflicting the maximum amount of damage. Ammunition supplies are limited ; neither shell nor cartridge must be wasted.

Japanese batteries take up positions on the ground their infantry have won ; Japanese torpedo-boats close in at sea. Farther out Japanese battleships, with an English colleague, the *Triumph*, send their heavy shells into the town and suburbs. Plüschow is forced to take up quarters in the cellar of his villa, but he does not mind that so much ; his chief anxiety is for the hangar that houses his Taube.

Every day he goes out to locate the Japanese batteries so that the German artillery can reply to them, for the big guns have so little ammunition that they must only fire when they can be tolerably sure of hitting a mark.

No easy job for Plüschow.   His propeller is a hundred revolutions too short, and his benzin is strictly rationed. He dare not burden himself with the extra weight of an observer, because he must fly as lightly as possible. He strips the Taube of all unnecessary gear, and often flies without his jacket so as to effect a further economy.

He does not find it so difficult to reconnoitre the enemy's positions as he first anticipated.   With engine throttled and controls in neutral he can keep his height without touching the stick ; both hands are free to manipulate pencil and paper.   He steers by kicking the rudder as he cruises over the Japs, who blaze away with rifles and machine guns.   Plüschow does not worry about them ; his chief complaint is that he gets a stiff neck from bending over the side of the cockpit and staring down the narrow gap at the edge of the wings.

What he thoroughly detests is the start every morning. His Taube, he has discovered, is too heavy a bird for the thin air of these parts, and there are so many treacherous eddies about the foothills. Each separate take-off is a fight for life ; if he starts southward, he is always certain to run into an air pocket which causes a stall. Generally he catches the machine some twenty feet above the surface of the sea, but sometimes he is only a few inches off the waves before he starts to climb again. But the southward stall is infinitely preferable to a northward take-off where he has to scrape the roofs of several villas and invariably risks collision with the church tower. When those obstacles are safely surmounted, he must head for the pass between the Bismark and Iltis peaks, where he is exposed to the buffets of the air currents streaming down the lateral valleys. They always send him slipping over by the right wing, with the prospect of a crash on to the rocks ; yes, decidedly the southern take-off is the least of the two evils.

But north or south the Japs are on the look out for him, and as soon as he rises into view they send a consignment of shrapnel in his direction. Plüschow admits that he does not like shrapnel, which is an unknown element of peril to him, and he considers himself lucky if he can climb out of range in an hour and a half.

His landings have to be made after running the gauntlet of further shrapnel, and though he always passes through unscathed, the disturbances in the air caused by the exploding shells toss his machine about like a row-boat in mid-Atlantic. When he lands and enters the car waiting to carry him to headquarters with his report, the shrapnel follows him along the road. But one morning he hears a familiar sound overhead and runs out of his villa to espy a huge double-decker in the air. He gazes at the enemy machine with envious eyes ; what could he not do if only he had a bird like that instead of his poor little Taube. The Jap airman can fly too, but it is really unkind of him to try to drop bombs on the Taube's hangar. Bird does not eat bird.

In the course of the next few days Plüschow counted no less than eight Japanese aircraft, four of which were seaplanes. The pilots that handled them were expert fliers, but luckily for the Taube they proved poor marksmen with their bombs.

With practice, however, they improved, and soon some of their bombs began to fall uncomfortably near the

hangar.   As they flew over the race-course at a height
well out of range of the German artillery, the only course
open to Plüschow was to circumvent them by guile.

His hangar lay at the northern end of the race-course,
where it was an easy target from the air.   But, working
by night, his Chinese built him a new hangar at the south
end, for which they excavated the site from a bluff of the
hill side.   They covered its roof over with earth and
grass so that it was absolutely invisible from the air,
and then they fashioned out of ropes, spars, odds and
ends of canvas and some old packing cases a dummy
aeroplane which was exhibited on suitable occasions in
front of the abandoned hangar.   Plüschow spent many
a mirthful hour watching the Japanese aviators trying
to bomb it.

Meanwhile Tsingtao's arsenal had contrived to manufacture some bombs for him to drop on the Japs.   These
consisted of old coffee canisters, filled with dynamite,
scrap iron and nails, with primitive fuses fashioned out of
cartridge caps.   Plüschow, however, found them a source
of embarrassment in the machine, and as they generally
failed to explode, they did little damage to the enemy.

He often met Japanese aviators in the air, but, acting
under instructions, avoided combat with them.   One
day, however, when engrossed in his task of reconnoitring
the enemy's positions, he suddenly felt violent disturbances
in the air which he attributed to the eccentricities of a
strong gust from the mountains until he looked up and
saw a hostile aeroplane manœuvring above him.   Its
observer potted him with bombs, none of which fell
anywhere near him, but his brother-officers, who had
seen the enemy machine soar above him, were most
surprised when he returned safe and sound.

A few days later he registered his first and only victory in the air by watching an opportunity to climb above a Japanese machine, at which he fired 30 rounds from a parabellum pistol. After enjoying the satisfaction of seeing his opponent c~ash earthwards, he was sorely tempted to repeat the experience, but his orders to keep himself and his machine intact were too strict to allow him to risk an encounter. The artillery was now so short of shells that it never ventured to fire unless he had definitely located the opposing batteries from the air ; so valuable was therefore his assistance to the gunners that he was warned to keep himself alive at all costs.

But accidents will happen. One day, when he was sketching the positions of the Japanese seaplanes' sheds, he saw a gigantic doubledecker emerge and rise into the air, but went on with his work as he deemed that he had plenty of time before it could reach a height approximate to his. Half-an-hour later he paused to take stock of the situation and was amazed to see the Jap rapidly approaching him.

He decided to climb higher, but soon made the unpleasant discovery that he had reached the top of his ceiling. Meanwhile the Japanese continued to mount.

It dawned on Plüschow that the enemy had laid a trap to cut him off from his base. He promptly turned and fled.

To his delight he found that although inferior in climbing power his Taube was the speedier machine. He reached Tsingtao well ahead of his pursuer and did a deep nose-dive for his aerodrome, plunging through the usual sea of shrapnel.

Meanwhile the ring of the investing forces drew ever closer. The defenders had withdrawn to the positions

on the outskirts of the town which had been chosen for
their last stand, while every day the Anglo-Japanese
squadron bombarded the forts from a distance beyond
the range of the German gunners.   Torpedo-boat S.90
made a dash for the open sea, but, after sinking a Japanese
cruiser, she found her retreat cut off and was compelled
to seek refuge in a Chinese port, where her crew were
interned.   The German gunboat, *Jaguar*, and the
Austrian cruiser *Kaiserin Elizabeth* were sunk in the
harbour when they had fired their last shells, and everyone knew that the end could not be long delayed.

Plüschow still continued his daily work of reconnoitring
the enemy positions, but the pleasure of his first flights
was gone.   The tension of the incessant bombardment told
on his nerves ; his appetite vanished and sleep became
impossible.   All night long he tossed feverishly on his
bed, muttering the instructions he had received for his
early morning reconnaissance, and just when he was
about to fall into a fitful doze, his mechanic would come
to rouse him to the work of a new day.   He had a fight
to subdue his nerves before he could go down to his
aerodrome and watch the mechanics adjust the propeller
after its nightly regluing.

But when he sat in his cockpit and grasped the stick
his steadiness returned.   Doggedly he surmounted the
obstacles he encountered in the course of his take-off
and initial climb, though his heart sank when he began to
sketch the new lines of earthworks that had been thrown
up overnight.   Slowly but surely the Japs pushed their
trenches ever nearer.

How much longer ?   31 October was the anniversary
of the Mikado's birthday ; on that day, their spies
reported, Tsingtao was to fall.   Then captivity in a

German prison-camp would be his fate for the rest of the war.

31 October brought the expected attack. A lucky shot set the petroleum tanks on fire, so that thick black pillars of smoke rose up to heaven. All day long the Japanese heavy artillery pounded the German positions, but when it ceased at sunset the German gunners, emerging from their dugouts, found their weapons undamaged. They caught Japanese columns marching in close order to the final attack and punished them so severely that they were glad to run for shelter. The Mikado had to do without his birthday present.

Tsingtao won a week's respite—if respite it might be called when the thunder of the Japanese guns never ceased. Now the German artillery made no reply at all ; they were keeping their remaining ammunition for the enemy's final rush.

And now they had no airman to locate the enemy positions for them, because the Japanese batteries had pushed forward to within 4,000 yards of the race-course and rendered his aerodrome unusable. He wondered whether it would even be necessary to destroy the Taube ; in all probability the Japs would do it for him.

But on the afternoon of 5 November, he received a summons to the Governor of Tsingtao, who told him that a new Japanese attack might be expected any moment. This time it was bound to succeed.

Plüschow was instructed to leave Tsingtao early the following morning with despatches that he must contrive to deliver to the nearest German Consulate in neutral China.

" If the Japs will let you get off, which I doubt," added the Governor, but Plüschow vowed himself ready to make the attempt. That evening he took leave of all his friends, who gave him letters which he promised to post in China for them. Then, after a last sleepless night, he stole to his hangar before sunrise to make preparations for the final flight.

The aerodrome was in sorry condition, but during the darkness his squad of willing workers had filled in some of the holes made by recent Japanese shells, so that he had a fair run for his take-off. The propeller was adjusted for the last time ; a final handshake with the four German sailors who served as his mechanics—then he climbed into the cockpit.

But scarcely was he a hundred feet up when a violent explosion made his Taube rock from side to side. A shell had burst below him—the farewell greeting of the Japanese artillery.

As he gained height, the sun rose over the sea, and the deep roar of the heavy howitzers hailed Tsingtao's last day under the German flag. Plüschow waved his hand to the little group of mechanics that still gazed skywards, heedless of the shells bursting around them.

He saw the two opposing circles of trenches around the town and the Japanese warships riding at anchor. Flying out to sea, he soared over them, shouting his defiance ; then he made for the coast line and steered a southward course by his compass.

He had planned to come down at Haichow in the province of Kiangsu, about 150 miles from Tsingtao, but when he reached this destination he could find no suitable landing-place. The heavy autumn rains had flooded the whole country for miles. So he flew on, but failed to discover a dry spot.

His scanty ration of benzin was coming to an end,

and he knew that if he pressed onward he might eventually be forced to descend in some out-of-the-way hamlet, the inhabitants of which had never seen a white face. In Haichow there was civilisation of a sort to be found, he therefore turned and flew back. At last, after some reconnoitring, he found a field enclosed by ditches that looked as if it might have been drained into a state of comparative dryness and spiralled down to it.

He landed in a ricefield where the clayish soil was so soft that his wheels promptly sank in up to their axles. The Taube wavered for a second, and then pitched forward gently on to her nose.

Plüschow extricated himself from the mud, discovered that no bones were broken and looked about him. From houses visible in the distance he saw a crowd of Chinese running towards him. Then he began to wonder why everything seemed so silent ; he missed the familiar roar of the Japanese artillery.

But the silence did not last long, for soon he was surrounded by a mob of jabbering, gesticulating Chinese who had never seen an aeroplane before and wondered what sort of a devil had landed in their midst. At first they were too frightened to approach, but when he brought out a handful of copper coins, they decided that he was a mortal like themselves. They hustled and jostled one another in their curiosity to examine the strange bird, meanwhile grinning at the man who drove it and making loud but unintelligible remarks to one another.

But no one seemed inclined to help him, until at length he heard a voice bid him " Good morning," in English.

News travels fast. Mr. Morgan, an American

missionary living in Haichow, had hastened to the
assistance of the unknown white aviator.   This good
Samaritan, who spoke fluent Chinese, was not long in
clearing a way through the crowd for Plüschow.   Then
he despatched a messenger to the local mandarin for a
squad of soldiers to guard the machine and carried his
guest off for a bath and breakfast.

And here we must take leave of Gunther Plüschow as
he sits at Mr. Morgan's hospitable table, telling the
tale of his Tsingtao experiences to the missionary and
his wife, who listen with eyes agog.   Plüschow still
has many adventures before him, but the story of his
escape from the Chinese authorities who wanted to
intern him in Nankin, his voyage to America, whence
he attempted to reach Germany under a forged Swiss
passport, his capture at Gibraltar, his daring escape from
Donnington Hall and his return to Germany *via* Holland
as a stowaway, thrilling as these tales may be, they do
not come within the scope of a book on flying.   Suffice
it to say that Plüschow survived the war and experienced
many more thrilling adventures when he flew over the
mysterious wastes of Tierra del Fuego, the volcanic
lands of southernmost South America.

We can only wish him more power to his wings and
engine, and a " happy landing " wherever he chooses
to fly.

CHAPTER IV

"BOELCKE'S OWN"

IN a very old volume of *Punch* I once saw a cartoon representing a young subaltern in a crack cavalry regiment being put through his paces by an examiner.

" And can you tell what is the use of cavalry in warfare, Mr. X. ? " enquired the examiner.

" To give tone to what would otherwise be merely a vulgar brawl," was the reply.

Now some indiscriminating students of the doughty deeds performed by airmen on both sides in the recent war might come to a similar conclusion. The dashing, daring war bird who fought a valiant enemy in mid-air—man to man, as did the knights of old—certainly did seem to lend tone to what was regarded by many as a vulgar brawl, but that would not have alone justified his existence. The airman's job was (1) to supply accurate information to one set of brawlers about the other's movements ; (2) to prevent the airmen belonging to the other set of brawlers equalising matters by obtaining information concerning his own side's movements.

Resplendent as the knight of the horse and the knight of the air-machine may seem to those who read of their achievements, it is still that vulgar brawler of an infantryman who has to win the war in the end, as he has done for the last few thousand years and will continue to do if the nations are fools enough to indulge in further wars.

The airman, like the cavalry man of old, is an accessory.

A useful accessory, of course, as the Allied forces in France knew well in the early days of 1916. The Germans knew it too, to their cost, for at that period of the war the French and English knights of the air had fairly and squarely beaten their German opponents. General von Hoeppner, who was head of the German Air Service during the war and has written a book embodying his experiences, tells us that the ineffectiveness of the German artillery at that time was due to the excellent co-operation between the Entente gunners and airmen. Whatever arrangements for cover or camouflage were made by any German battery were quickly observed by the sharp eyes of the English and French aviators and shot to pieces with devilish accuracy by their artillery.

The same war birds also made life a super-hell for the German infantry, when, flying low over the trenches and shellholes, they raked their cowering inmates with their machine-guns. Such attacks, spasmodic and planless as they were, did not often do much material damage, but their moral effect was tremendous, for the wretched infantryman felt himself helpless against his assailants ; no movements remained hid from them, no burrowing in the earth offered sure protection from the storms of lead they rained down and no rifle or machine gun seemed effective against them.

The war birds whose machines bore the red, white and blue cockades flew where they liked, and no German airman dared oppose them.

A state of panic spread through the German armies on the western front. German machine gunners and artillerymen got into a habit of firing on their own airmen, some because they believed the false rumour that the Entente aviators ·deliberately painted the black Maltese cross of Germany on their wings so as to approach their objectives unmolested, others because they wanted revenge on the airmen of their own side, whom they considered to have let them down.

Then another rumour gained currency. The Entente aeroplanes, it stated, were built to the designs of a brilliant inventor, who had discovered a light type of armour-plating so resistant that it was not worth while firing on machines protected by it. The crews of the German Archies fled as soon as they heard the dreaded drone of Allied engines in the air.

All of which was very unfair on the German war birds, who were doing their best under adverse circumstances. Whenever they went aloft they had to encounter opponents equipped with machines that could outclimb and outpace them . . . and the odds were too great. For lack of opportunity co-operation between the German aeroplanes and artillery practically ceased.

Few German aviators ever succeeded in bringing back the reports and photographs they were sent to procure, and if by any stroke of luck one of them found himself favourably placed over enemy positions he failed to make use of his chance. Lack of practice had rendered him incompetent to make good records of what he observed.

The ingenuity and daring of the British airmen became notorious. The German infantry and artillery vociferously demanded protection against them, asserting that their own aviators were totally incompetent to cope with the winged enemy.

The German Higher Command knew that something had to be done, and considered ways and means to do it.

They noted, for instance, that although their own
aviators lived short, precarious lives, some few survived
their comrades and began to pile up modest totals of
victories when they gained experience.   There was,
among others, a certain Lieutenant Max Immelmann,
who had become an expert pilot of the Fokker single-
seater early the previous year.

Immelmann had developed a habit of hanging about
behind the German lines to lie in wait for any British
aeroplanes engaged on photography or reconnaissance
work.   On to their tails he would swoop (out of the sun
if possible), and usually the first inkling of his presence
to the victim was the burst from his machine gun with
the new synchronised gear that enabled him to fire through
the propeller.   Down went the enemy in most cases, but
if he was lucky enough to escape the first onslaught,
Immelmann had a trick up his sleeve that enabled him
to initiate a second attack without waste of time.

Pulling the stick well over he made his Fokker's nose
rear up as if he wanted to loop the loop ; then he turned
sideways over the vertical and came out in the opposite
direction.   It was a simple method of gaining height
quickly at the same time as he reversed direction, but
no one had ever thought of it before, and it took the
British airmen by surprise.

Immelmann's heyday was the spring and summer
of 1915, but when his opposite numbers got used to his
methods his successes became rarer.   Many of his
earlier victims flew aeroplanes that were not armed
with machine guns, so that the observer wielding a
revolver or carbine was no match for him, and when
the F.E.2b and De Haviland Scouts made their appearance
on the front they were found to be more than a match

for the Fokkers, as was also the French Nieuport which was brought out about the same time.

But Immelmann was a skilled and daring pilot, and his name will go down to posterity in connection with the famous turn he evolved—which his enemies paid him the compliment of imitating. Unfortunately, however, he was unavailable to help the German authorities over their air crisis which became most acute during the early stages of the Somme offensive, for he fell in June, 1916, shot down by Lieutenant G. R. McCubbin, who fastened on to his tail when he was attacking another F.E. of his squadron.

Immelmann's chief use to his own side was the fact that his name became known to the German public, who had heard so many ominous rumours concerning the inefficiency of their own airmen. But meanwhile the German Higher Command had noted the name of yet another pilot, a young Saxon engineer named Oswald Boelcke, who had taken up flying when he was rejected for active service on account of some weakness in the lungs.

This Boelcke was a friend of Immelmann and, like him, an expert in flying the fast single-seater Fokker. He had shot down a number of French machines in the early days of 1916, but when he was officially credited with his sixteenth victory, thus equalling Immelmann's total, the Higher Command grew anxious on his account. Such luck, they opined, could not last for ever ; sooner or later one of those daring, ingenious British or French aviators would get him.

The gentlemen of the Higher Command were suffering from a bad inferiority complex concerning their own airmen, and so they ordered Boelcke to cease flying.

They told him that the experience he had gained was so valuable that he could not possibly be allowed to risk his life.

They sent him on a tour of the eastern front to instruct Austrians, Turks and Bulgarians in the art of flying, but took care that he never had a chance to fight. Boelcke soon grew bored with life, for he was not a great organiser ; he wearied of the office work his task involved and protested loudly that if he was to instruct the youth of the Central Powers in the art of flying to kill, he could only do so by personal example and inspiration.

Meanwhile on the western front matters went from bad to worse. In the long battle of the Somme, which had just commenced, the Entente artillery and airmen were having things all their own way. In fast single-seaters aces such as Ball, Bishop, Hawker and McCudden ranged high over the battlefields, threatening certain destruction to any German machine sent out on reconnaissance work or any lone fighter detailed to protect it. The situation called for immediate action if the Somme offensive was not to develop into a débâcle for Germany.

We are so apt to think of the Germans as great organisers that it will come as a shock to some readers to learn that the German air force was deplorably managed at that time. But General Hoeppner is not afraid to speak his mind on such matters ; there were not enough single-seater machines to go round, he tells us, and they were never sent to the places where they could be used to best advantage. The whole system needed overhauling.[1]

The Higher Command found a solution of their

[1] *Deutschlands Krieg in der Luft*, by General Hoeppner, pp. 71–75. This book is a revelation in more senses than one.

problem by grouping the pilots of single-seaters into units known as Staffels, a word for which there is no adequate translation. Each Staffel (the literal meaning of the word is a step) consisted of two " swarms " of six machines, which were further divided into " chains " of three machines. These groups were to be known as the Jagd (hunting) Staffels, because it was their task to chase the enemy's fighting machines from the sky. Each Staffel was to be under the leadership of a pilot whose personal achievements would inspire confidence in his subordinates.

Boelcke's name was the first that suggested itself as a possible leader. The Higher Command rescinded the order that prevented him from engaging the enemy and gave him carte blanche to pick from all fronts the pilots whom he considered as the most promising material. At home the aircraft factories were spurred to special efforts, and in August, 1916, they sent to the front a number of aeroplanes equipped with 220 h.p. engines that were superior in climbing ability to anything on the Entente side.

Boelcke had the gift of spotting the type of man he required. Richthofen was one of his first choices, along with Böhme, Max Müller and the younger Immelmann (a cousin of the ace), all of whom afterwards made honourable names for themselves.

' But as yet they had to win their spurs. On 30 August the Staffel assembled at Lagnicourt, where it was officially known as the Royal Prussian Jagdstaffel No. 2. There does not seem to have been an actual No. 1, as far as I can find out, and I presume that, like so many other formations in other armies, it existed only on paper. Boelcke's was the first Staffel for all practical purposes, which was only just, as at that time he was Germany's first airman.

But for a brief space he was also the only active fighting member of the Staffel. Keen as were the youngsters he had gathered together, it would have been sheer murder to expose them to combats with wily, experienced foemen until they had practised on their new machines, all of which had not yet reached the front, and gained some knowledge of the tactics he had evolved for their benefit. For the first fortnight or so the cubs of Boelcke's hunting-pack could only watch their master's feats.

They expected him to " eat an Englishman every day for his early breakfast," and truth to tell, he seldom disappointed them. When he took his place at the head of the mess table and was questioned as to his luck on the early morning patrol, he invariably asked his pupils to look at his face and tell him whether he had a black chin.

" Yes, of course, black as a nigger's," one of the cubs would reply.

" Well then, that's all right," said Boelcke, and the breakfast table knew that he had added one more to his long total of victories. The grime on his chin was caused by the powder from his machine gun ; this meant that he had had occasion to fire it, and when he fired, he generally conquered.

Not that all his victories were easy, for his opponents were wily fighters. On one of those September days, for instance, he encountered a particularly redoubtable adversary in the person of Captain G. L. Cruikshank, who led the Sopwiths of No. 70 Squadron of the Royal Flying Corps. Cruikshank was an old hand who had

flown before the war ; he went to France in the August
of 1914, since which time he had done practically everything that an aviator could be called upon to do in those
early days when a pilot's duties were not so strictly
defined. He had even landed spies behind the enemy's
lines, and when, after a period of home service as an
instructor, he returned to France in August, 1916, it was
his dearest ambition to meet Boelcke in the air.

At 5.45 a.m. on the day when his wish was gratified
he led six other Sopwiths on an early morning patrol.
Crossing the German lines, they encountered a number
of enemy aeroplanes, and in the course of the subsequent
fighting Cruikshank got separated from his patrol.
Over Havrincourt Wood he espied a lone single-seater
and dived on it.

Though he did not know it, his opponent was Boelcke,
who, as usual, had gone out hunting on his own account.
The German ace eluded Cruikshank's swoop, and then
the fight began.

Each of the combatants recognised at once that he
had met a foeman of formidable calibre, and both allowed
discretion to temper their usual valour. They were
too wary to waste useless shots.

For a long time they jockeyed one another to gain a
favourable position, and from the testimony given by the
witnesses of their thrilling duel, both must have given
a brilliant exhibition of flying. At first, one, then the
other, seemed to have an advantage, but at last Boelcke
out-manœuvred Cruikshank and put in a burst that shot
the Sopwith to pieces in mid air. The fragments fell
into Havrincourt Wood.

In reality Boelcke was one of the kindest of men. He
did not want to kill his opponents and often regretted

that by the circumstances of aerial fights his victories so
often involved their deaths. He was better pleased
when he could bring them down alive and entertain them
at his mess.   If they were wounded, he spent much of
his spare time in visiting them in hospital, and he was
most punctilious about dropping notes behind the
British lines to inform the enemy war birds about the
fate of any missing comrade.   Everyone liked him, and
on both sides of the front he was known as a good fellow
and a good sportsman.

On 16 September, Boelcke led his pack out for their
first day's hunting and was delighted to find them profi-
cient in the lessons he had taught them.   The "game-
book" showed the master's name, for Boelcke got his
usual victim that day, but underneath it was inscribed
that of Lieutenant Höhne.   A cub of the Boelcke pack
had tasted his first blood.

On the following day the names of Richthofen, Böhme
and Reimann were inscribed in the book in addition to
Boelcke's.   The "Red Knight" thus began his long
career of victory, his victims being Lieutenant Morris
(pilot), and Lieutenant Rees (observer), the occupants of
a large F.E. two-seater.   They were experienced flyers,
but by demonstration with a model Boelcke had shown
his pupils the F.E.'s blind spot under the fuselage.
Richthofen had sufficient presence of mind to remember
the master's instructions in the heat of the fray, and he
poured a deadly stream of lead into the F.E. from below.
It spiralled down wildly, with pilot and observer mortally
wounded, while Richthofen's delight made him so careless
that he narrowly missed a collision with his victim.

The next day the weather broke, and there was no
flying, but on the 19th Boelcke and his cubs encountered

a squadron of F.E.'s that were undertaking a reconnaissance under the protection of a strong escort of single-seaters. A fight took place over Quéant, in the course of which Boelcke shot Captain Tower's Morane to pieces in the air, while one of the pupils forced an F.E. to land in Delville Wood with a damaged engine and a wounded observer. The reconnaissance had to be broken off, and the Englishmen returned home to report that they had been beaten by " the toughest lot of Huns they had ever met."

Day after day the list of victories mounted up, but naturally the price had to be paid. On 22 September, the pack suffered its first death when Winand Grafe went down in flames ; on the 23rd they encountered six Martinsydes out on a patrol who inflicted further punishment in the course of a sharp fight. Three of the English machines were shot down, Boelcke claiming his usual victim, but a fourth collided with Reimann's machine in the air.

It was piloted by Lieutenant L. F. Forbes, who escaped miraculously with a damaged wing and fought his way home to safety, though he crashed into a tree and was badly injured on landing. But Reimann dropped like a stone to earth, and thus perished untimely the pupil whom Boelcke had considered the most promising of all.

A few days afterwards the English paid Boelcke the compliment of bombing his aerodrome at Lagnicourt. Several hangars were hit but the damage sustained was n t sufficient to interrupt the Staffel's normal activities, for on the following morning we find the master and ᶠour pupils out for their morning patrol.

They ran into six Martinsydes who were looking for

trouble, and in the fight that ensued the famous ace was
the hero of one of the grimmest and most curious episodes
of the whole war.   He picked out an opponent, whom
he sent hurtling earthwards with his first burst ; he
then engaged another in a duel which developed into a
series of tail-chases.   Round and round went the two
machines in ever-narrowing circles, each endeavouring
to get his gun trained on to the vital spot in his opponent's
tail ; at last Boelcke gained this advantage and put in a
murderous burst at short range.

As he came out of the circle, he saw to his surprise that
the Martinsyde was still flying, although he felt certain
that his bullets could not have failed to take effect.   But
his amazement was even greater when he saw the enemy
make no attempt to flee or renew the encounter.   Without any motive the Martinsyde continued to fly in circles,
as if chasing the tail of an invisible opponent.

Boelcke guessed the only possible solution of the
mystery ; his burst, put in at a range where it was
impossible to miss, must have killed the pilot who then
fell in such a way as to hold the controls in the position
in which he had set them the moment before his death.
Impelled by curiosity, but keeping a wary finger on the
trigger-button for emergencies, Boelcke flew back to
the Martinsyde and circled above it for a few seconds.

His surmise was correct.   Leaning over, he contrived
to catch sight of the dead pilot's body sprawling in the
cockpit.   It had fallen against the controls, so that the
machine was bound to continue its aimless course.

Boelcke went back to the fight and engaged another
opponent, who ultimately contrived to escape him after
a long bout of tail chasing, and was lucky to land unhurt
with riddled wings in addition to bullets in his tank,

engine and radiator. The remaining three Martinsydes also got away, though one of them was landed by a badly wounded pilot.

But when Boelcke and his pupils started on their homeward journey, the machine flown by his second victim was still pursuing its rounds, a derelict of the air that was bound to continue the circular course in which it had been set until some circumstance altered the controls or lack of petrol forced it to land. When he flew past, Boelcke dipped his wings in salute to the dead foeman.[1]

On the last day of September two bombing squadrons, protected by six Nieuports and two Moranes, in addition to a number of F.E.'s visited Lagnicourt aerodrome. Boelcke's cubs promptly took the air to fight them, but were defeated by weight of numbers. Three of them were forced to land with machines badly shot about, while Herwarth Philipps went down in flames. Boelcke, however, shot down an F.E., while the damage to the hangars does not appear to have been great.

After that there came a long gap in the roll of honour. Although the efforts of the British armies on the Somme and Ancre to press home their advantage and inflict a decisive defeat on the Germans before the bad weather suspended operations led to fierce fighting by the infantry and consequently also by the aircraft every day that flying was possible, Death took no toll of the Boelcke Staffel, though the list of enemy casualties rose steadily.

Whenever the weather permitted, the English bombers dropped their eggs on the German trains carrying reserves and munitions, while the reconnaissance machines and photographers continued the work that was so vital to

[1] Lieutenant S. Dendrino.

their infantry.   The English single-seaters had their
fair share of successes.

"Every one of our offensive patrols had fights,"
writes H. A. Jones, the official historian, when describing
the aerial events of 10 October, a day on which unwonted
activity followed a long spell of wet weather, " and those
that went in favour of the enemy were all with pilots
of Boelcke's squadron."[1] From German sources it appears
that the Staffel claimed five victims that day.

There followed further bad weather, but on 21, 22, and
23 October, the Staffel was fiercely engaged.   On the
first of those days Boelcke was the hero of another strange
incident when his cubs encountered a squadron of F.E.'s.
The ace singled out an opponent, whose controls he
shot away with his first burst, and the enemy machine
went down in a spin.   The observer was thrown out,
and his body fell behind the German lines, while the aeroplane, with its dead pilot, crashed behind the British lines.

On 25 October, the Staffel claimed three more victims,
one of which, a B.E., gave Richthofen his eighth victory ;
on the morning of the 26th, five De Havilands fought a
magnificent rearguard action against some twenty German
single-seaters and escaped to land with only one wounded
pilot.   But in the afternoon of the same day the Staffel
was able to make four more entries on the " game book,"
which now showed a total of fifty-one victories, twenty of
which were inscribed under the master's name, while the
other thirty-one fell to the pack.   A good beginning.
They had to fight hard for their kills, and they knew that
as yet they were not the equals, man to man, of the
British pilots they encountered in the air.   " Every time
we went up, we had a fight," Richthofen wrote home to

[1] *The War in the Air*, Vol. II, p. 302.

his mother, " and we were quite satisfied when we did
not get a licking."

But if they were not yet feeling their full strength,
they had a leader who was probably at that time the
best ace of any air force. " We always had a wonderful
feeling of security when he was with us," said Richthofen
with justice, for time after time his masterly tactics and
daring interventions pulled one or other of the cubs out
of a tight corner. And so through the month of October
they fought and landed safely and went up to fight again.
It seemed as if one and all bore a charmed life.

But on fatal 28 October, there came an appalling
casuality list. It comprised one name only, but that
name was worth any other six on the Staffel's muster,
for it was that of the master himself.

Boelcke was convinced that he had not yet met the
British or French war bird who could down him. On
principle he always flew as close as possible to the opponent he had picked out and never wasted ammunition
till he had him well sighted. " Then he is bound to go
down," he would explain to his pupils with a smile.

And in a way he was right, for no airman that sported
the red, white and blue cockade could boast of crashing
him when his time came. A collision in mid-air with
one of his pupils sent him to his doom.

It was an ironic accident. Boelcke was engaged on a
round of " tail-chasing," with an Englishman whom he
intended for his forty-first victim, as he probably would
have been if the master had been left to deal with him
single-handed. But a pupil came swooping down from
the sky, with eyes only for the Englishman; whether he
saw only the easy prey and not its pursuer or whether he
thought the beloved master was in danger remains a

mystery. At all events the tip of his left wing touched the tip of Boelcke's right wing.

Only a touch, but it sufficed. The nose of Boelcke's machine dipped heavily, as it swerved from the contact. The Englishman made off and Boelcke's pupil, whose machine had remained uninjured by a miracle, had not the heart to pursue him. He followed his master down, and was horrified to see a wing detach itself from the falling machine.

The Germans gave their distinguished ace a funeral worthy of a crowned head ; from every British aerodrome within reach British warplanes flew over the German lines on peaceful errands. " To the memory of Captain Boelcke, our brave and chivalrous foe," is a typical inscription on one of the wreaths they dropped.

" John Brown's body lies a-mouldering in the grave,
    But his soul goes marching on."

On 30 October, Lieutenant Kirmaier formally took over the leadership of Jagdstaffel No. 2, which by Imperial decree was henceforth to be known as the Boelcke Jagdstaffel, so that all its pilots, old and new, might henceforth be inspired to valiant deeds by the constant memory of the founder who had launched it on its career of fame.

The twenty-five victories won during the month of November showed that Boelcke's spirit still lived in his Staffel. Most of its encounters with English opponents were successful, while the death list remained unaltered. Among the cubs now growing up into full-fledged hounds of the chase a certain Manfred von Richthofen was attracting particular attention. A mighty hunter before the Lord was this young Silesian squire in times

of peace ; many a horned beast of the forest had fallen
to his gun, and it was therefore only fitting that war
should turn him into a hunter of men.

On 20 November Richthofen did the " double event,"
shooting down his ninth and tenth victim, but on 22
November, Kirmaier crashed earthward from a fatal
encounter.   There was silence in the messroom that
night and many headshakings.   Gone was the joy of the
cubs in their kill ; was death always to be the fate of the
man who led them, they asked in awed voice.

And who, they wondered, would be bold enough to
follow the two masters, whose rule had been so brief.

Yet a day later the sadness of Kirmaier's death was
forgotten in the jubilation that greeted a splendid
triumph.   After a duel lasting for a thrilling half-hour
Richthofen shot down Major Hawker.

They knew Hawker's name well enough, for the
English communiqués broadcasted almost daily reports
of his victories.   The "English Boelcke" they called him
in their mess, and, after all, what higher compliment
could they have paid him ?

Nay, he was a greater than Boelcke, for already the
list of his victories had surpassed the half century . . . and
now one of their pack had killed him in fair and equal
fight.   They interred his remains with a funeral that
paid fitting tribute to fallen greatness and rejoiced that
Boelcke and Kirmaier were now avenged.

On 29 November, Captain Walz, an outsider, came
to lead them.   Perhaps this choice was a wise move, for
the superstitious fears that beset all airmen might have prevented one of themselves from doing justice to the office.

The long battle of the Somme drew to its end, and
with December came bad weather that reduced their

activities.   Nevertheless they contrived to enter another
ten victims in their " game-book " that month, bringing
the year's total up to eighty-six.   But 1917 did not begin
too auspiciously, for only three victims were obtained
in its January to set off against the deaths of young
Immelmann and Serjeant Ostrop.

An even greater blow that month was the departure
of their best hunter to fresh fields and pastures new.

The German High Command had now thoroughly
grasped the principle of the Jagdstaffel.   Its selected
bands of efficient lone pilots, men who could shoot as
well as they could fly, were henceforth to be flung on to
any sector of the front where the enemy's machines were
particularly troublesome, and thus gain at least a temporary supremacy of the air that would enable the slower
two-seaters to do their reconnaissance work and photography in peace.   If one Staffel did not suffice, then two
must be sent or even three, until at last the troublesome
foemen were wiped out or forced to keep to the
ground. More Jagdstaffels therefore, decreed the Higher
Command.

" Give us a Boelcke man for our leader," cried each
newly-formed Jagdstaffel.

And so the Higher Command took Richthofen away
from his messmates and put him in charge of Jagdstaffel
No. 11.   Captain Walz wondered whom they would
take next.

But for the next three months the Boelcke pack glutted
itself with many kills.   February—14, March—15,
April—21 . . . such were the numbers of their victories,
against a death-record of 1, 0 and 2.   Not a bad achievement to be carrying on with, they decided, for if
Richthofen was now their rival, were not Bernert and Voss

piling up scores that he would have to bestir himself to
beat.   One day the Staffel wrote down six victories in its
"gamebook," and Bernert claimed five of them.   That
was a record which even Richthofen could not beat ![1]

And Voss, whose fuselage is emblazoned with the
skull and cross-bones, proves himself a veritable pirate
of the air.   A glutton for victories is Voss ; there is
nothing he will not do to increase the Boelcke total.

One day during the German strategic retreat of that
spring Voss was out hunting on his own account, but, as
though warned by some instinct of self-protection, his
prey seemed chary of venturing within striking distance.
Finding his benzin running low, Voss was about to turn
homewards when suddenly he espied through fleeting
clouds a lonely B.E. double-seater that appeared to be
returning from a reconnaissance.

Its observer was frankly puzzled ; he had been looking
for the new German positions but had failed to find them.
No Archies threatened him from below ; no Albatroses
or Halberstadts swept the air above him.

At least so he thought, for he had not seen Pirate
Voss lurking in the clouds.   Down swooped Voss on the
amazed B.E., into which his twin Spandaus poured a
deadly stream of lead.

Down went the B.E. in a steep spin, but its stouthearted
pilot caught his machine in time to make some sort of a
landing in No Man's Land. The bus crashed, but the
pilot and observer extricated themselves from the debris
and made off for the English lines.

It was another victory for Voss and the Boelcke
Staffel, but what proof could he obtain to satisfy the

---

[1] He succeeded in doing so that same month, on 29 April, when his victims
were ; one Spad, one F.E., two B.E.'s and one Nieuport.

exacting officials who alone could authorise him to enter it in the "game book"? No colleague had witnessed the fight from the air, while the German front trenches had been withdrawn so far back that though the troops in the Siegfried Line had probably seen him pounce on the B.E., none of them could have followed its swift descent to earth.

He had no witnesses for his victory, and he knew that the English were advancing. Within the next few hours they were likely to pass the spot where the shattered remains lay, in which case his chance of obtaining the needed evidence would have vanished for ever.

Yet there was one way of procuring proof—a risky way —decidedly risky, but it was the only way. Voss cut his engine and glided down to earth hard by the broken B.E. He climbed out and crawled over the wreckage to the spot where the observer's seat should have been.

Rifle-fire—unpleasantly near too—those English were worming their way forward quicker than he had anticipated. Still there ought to be just time to do the trick —damn that English patrol for poking their noses into a business that does not concern them !

With a last heave Voss wrenched the observer's machine gun free and carried it off in triumph after setting fire to the B.E. to make sure that there should be nothing left for the Royal Flying Corps to salve. As he climbed in, he saw German cavalry galloping up—witnesses—unneeded witnesses now that he had secured the trophy which was the best evidence of all.

Just as he taxied, bullets whizzed about his ears. On came the English patrol ; along the ground sped Voss's machine, still followed by their bullets.

"I hope you will enjoy your scrap, gentlemen." Voss[1] waved his hand to friend and foe as he soared up into the clouds. One more point for the Boelcke Staffel.

Jagdstaffel Boelcke *v.* Jagdstaffel Richthofen. No— Jagdstaffel Boelcke *v.* Manfred, Freiherr von Richthofen alone, for in March the knight with the all-red steed downed ten victims. In April, he claimed twenty-one, as many as the whole Boelcke Staffel between them.

"More power to his Spandaus," thought the hunters of the Boelcke pack in gallant rivalry, "but we'll beat him fairly and squarely in the merry month of May."

May came, but news reached the Boelcke aerodrome at Pronville that Richthofen had gone back to Germany on a long leave. The Higher Command, fearing that his luck could not last for ever, were resolved to preserve him from ill-hap . . . just as they had tried to safeguard Boelcke himself the previous year.

"They won't keep Richthofen out of the fun for long ; he'll see to that," opined one of the Boelcke pack in the mess the night they heard the news. "Meanwhile we can make hay while the sun shines."

But man proposes—the Higher Command disposes. German spies from England reported that pilots were being trained in larger numbers than ever. America having declared war on Germany, a number of lusty young sons of the New World had crossed the Atlantic to be trained to fly at Oxford and elsewhere. Moreover the new Bristol Fighters and S.E.5.'s that the British aircraft factories were about to send to the front would prove

---

[1] Voss left the Boelcke Staffel very soon afterwards to command a Staffel of his own. His death at the hands of Lieutenant Rhys-Davids after a single-handed fight against seven British machines is graphically described in McCudden's *Flying Fury*, pp. 186-7. Like Boelcke and Richthofen he won the " Pour le Mérite " order.

to be quite as good as the Albatros and the Halberstadt, perhaps even better.

" More Jagdstaffels," decreed the Higher Command.

" Boelcke men to lead us to victory," demanded the pilots of the newly-formed Staffels. So orders came, transferring Bernert and Voss to two of them. A few days later Tutschek was appointed to the command of a third.

The Boelcke Staffel fell on evil days.   From the flying schools in Germany came new pilots, raw cubs who had to be taught their business of killing, but the men who could best teach it had been snatched away to lead other Staffels.   The enemy was also showing what good use he could make of the new Bristol Fighters and S.E.5.'s.

Those new machines took some downing ; they were no easy prey like the old F.E.'s and De Haviland Scouts. No wonder that during the merry month of May the Boelcke Staffel had only five victories to record in the " game book," while the roll of honour was increased by three deaths.

In June Captain Walz, war-weary, feeling that he could no longer give of his best, resigned the leadership of the Staffel and went off to Germany to fill an instructor's post.   Bernert returned to take his place, but even he could not stop the rot that had set in.

Bernert was powerless to effect the change of morale that was so badly needed.   Equally impotent was his second-in-command, Richthofen's former friend, the consumptive Zeumer, who had sworn to die in battle before his anguished lungs should compel him to drag on to a lingering end in some sanatorium.   On 17 June, Zeumer met the end he so ardently craved.

In June, July and August only two victories were

written in the "game book," while the losses on the roll of honour steadily mounted.

"No air fights to-day," was a report that figured only too frequently in the Staffel's bulletins. Meanwhile Richthofen had returned to the front and was scoring victory after victory. Pilots of his Staffel, such as Lothar, the Red Knight's younger brother, Wolff, Löwenhardt and Udet were beginning to make names for themselves

The German Higher Command still decreed more and more Jagdstaffels to meet the ever-increasing number of British war birds that took the air.

"We want a Richthofen man to lead us," demanded the newly-formed Jagdstaffels.

But the heads of the German Air Force were sad to see the misfortunes of the oldest Jagdstaffel (that bore such an honourable name) and wondered how they could restore its prestige. Only a complete change of scene, surroundings, leadership and opponents, they decided, could achieve the miracle. The Boelcke Staffel must go to school again and learn its business anew.

They transferred it to Flanders and placed it in charge of Lieutenant Böhme, an old comrade of Boelcke's and one of the earliest cubs in the pack, who had been winning laurels as the commander of another Staffel. Here was the man, they judged, who by evoking memories of the distinguished founder could foster the spirit of emulation while giving his pupils the benefit of the experience he had gained elsewhere. A combination of the old and the new, in fact.

Böhme had no easy task. He found the pilots of the Boelcke Staffel raw, inexperienced youngsters, while the foemen who haunted the air above the blood-drenched battlefields of the Flanders plain were wary, wily veterans.

His first action was to weed out the useless material ; by diplomatic transferences to home service he cut down the number in the Staffel from the usual twelve to seven, so that he could give each of its members the individual instruction they needed.   His success was instantaneous ; in September six victories were inscribed in the " game book," in October eleven, in November eighteen. During those three months only four deaths came on to the roll of honour.

It was vile, bad campaigning that winter, and what a land it was to fight in !   Nothing but shell-holes—how on earth was a pilot to survive a forced landing, they wondered when they first saw the ground they had to cover.

On 5 November, Lieutenant Löffler was shot down and crashed in front of the German lines near Paschendaele. Under constant fire from the infantrymen in the English trenches (the flyer who shot him down would have done him no harm when he crawled out of the debris of his bus, but infantrymen thought otherwise), he made his way from shell hole to shell hole and so returned to fight another day.

And then the weather—rain—rain—rain every day. But, wet or fine, the Staffel went out and on 6 November they returned from a rough buffeting with five victories. On 7 November it streamed in torrents, but they got two more.

And so it went on all that November until on the 29th Lieutenant Böhme was seen fighting over the enemy's lines, but failed to return.   The following day a note dropped by a British pilot told them that he had crashed to his death somewhere in the neighbourhood of Zonnebeke.

They seem to have had some difficulty in finding the right successor, for their records show that Walter von Bülow, a scion of a very famous house, did not take over his command until 13 December. Von Bülow was a good man, with plenty of experience of those Flanders plains with their mud and craters, but he should have waited a day or come a day earlier. The fatal thirteen proved unlucky enough for him, for his rule lasted barely three weeks; on 6 January, 1918, he went down in a dogfight over St. Julien. Lieutenant Max Müller, another personal pupil of Boelcke's, who had rejoined the Staffel in November, took temporary charge, but before his appointment could be officially confirmed he was shot down in flames near Moorslede. Once again the Boelcke squadron was leaderless and suffered accordingly. It contained some good men, such as Löffler, Gallwitz, Pappenmeyer, Plange and Kempf, who were beginning to make names for themselves ; under Böhme and Bülow they had taken the air with confidence, but, try as they might, they were unable to achieve success without a guiding brain to direct their efforts. Lieutenant Höhne, another original Boelcke pupil—the first of them to score a victory—tried his hand at leadership, but resigned after a few days, feeling himself unequal to the task. The number of their victories gradually sank again.

In February Lieutenant Bolle took over the reins. His appointment was a daring experiment, for although he knew his Flanders as thoroughly as the deceased von Bülow, he was not an ace,[1] having only five victories to

---

[1] The German equivalent for " ace," a French expression adopted by the British, is " Kanone." Ten victories entitled an airman to that honourable distinction.

his credit. It was therefore difficult for him to give orders to pilots whose victory totals were far superior to his own, and perhaps equally difficult for them to obey. But Bolle appears to have been a man of forceful character, and before the month was out he succeeded in impressing his personality on the Staffel. Confidence was restored.

The spring of 1918, which brought the long-heralded German offensive, was a difficult and thankless period for the Boelcke Staffel. The rapid advance of their own side caused them to be constantly losing touch with the front and necessitated frequent changes of aerodrome. Naturally they tried to occupy quarters vacated by the retreating enemy, but the English aviators generally took the precaution of rendering their aerodromes unusable before they left, so that much time was wasted in making the necessary arrangements. Their opposite numbers were naturally in as bad a plight, as they were constantly packing up and burning stores and material they could not carry off. Thus the number of flying hours on both sides was seriously curtailed, and victories were few because only few engagements took place.

But when Bolle's men had opportunity, they usually contrived to distinguish themselves, as the following incident will show. One day when Bolle was leading six other Fokker triplanes he fell in with nine De Haviland double-seaters that were returning from a bombing expedition. He singled out the enemy leader, whom he recognised by his streamers, but a dogfight developed, in the course of which he was separated from his comrades and found himself alone in the midst of the enemy squadron, where he was exposed to the concentric fire of eighteen machine guns.

Tack—tack—tack—one in the tank ! Tack—tack
tack—tack—there's one in the engine—tack—tack—
tack—tack—tack—that sounds like an interplane strut
gone. But Bolle did a deep nosedive, and somehow
managed to land with a bus that ought to have gone to
pieces in the air. His mechanics afterwards counted
forty-two hits on it, though he remarked with some
satisfaction that when he said his hurried goodbye to
the company the De Haviland he originally attacked
appeared to have smoke issuing from it.

In due course the other six arrived home, likewise in
battered condition, but reported that they had given as
good as they got. The homeward path of two De
Havilands, they stated, was marked by trails of smoke,
while a third was decidedy out of control. They made
enquiries from the observation posts on the ground, but
were unable to obtain sufficient evidence to put in claims
for victories. One enemy machine was asserted by
eye-witnesses to be in flames, but nobody saw it crash.
No entries could be made in the " game book."

But a few days later one of the Staffel shot down a
De Haviland, the pilot and observer of which were taken
prisoners. In conversation with their enemy guests
round the festive board the Staffel learnt that all the
British machines concerned in the aforesaid fight reached
their aerodrome, but in such a sorry plight that five of
them crashed on landing and had to be written off as
total wrecks.

When the Flanders offensive came to a standstill, the
Staffel was transferred to Laon, where they found themselves matched against French pilots. These foemen
they soon found to be less daring and aggressive than the
British war birds of Flanders, and as soon as the Soissons

offensive started they were faced with the same constant changes of aerodrome that had previously curtailed their flying hours.   Another cause of reduced activity was the restriction of motive power.

Germany had begun to be seriously embarrassed by the iron blockade around her shores.   There was a shortage of food and all sorts of materials, including the benzin needed for their aeroplanes.   The Staffel was strictly rationed, so that a pilot often had to stand by and watch his comrades go up without him because he had already used up his daily allowance.

When the Anglo-French counter-offensive started, the Boelcke Staffel found tasks of an unusual nature to perform, for they were called upon to engage unwonted opponents on the ground in addition to the customary foemen of the air.   One day in August, British aeroplanes and tanks were detailed to carry out a combined attack on Rosières ;   Boelcke's men drove off the enemy war birds and then swooped down to assail the tanks with their machine guns.   They set three of them on fire, and the German artillery finished them off.

In September the Staffel was transferred to the Cambrai sector, where the first three days' fighting brought them eight victories.   Towards the end of the month they had another lucky day when they were able to inscribe eight victims in the " game book."   That September was in fact the best month in the Staffel's history, for they finished it with a total of forty-six victories, the highest they had ever scored in a single month.

Germany was beaten, but despite the constant changes of aerodrome necessitated by the retreat of the infantry, Boelcke's men maintained their usual activities.   In October they shot down eighteen machines, and though

they knew that the end was not far off they stuck grimly
to their work.

On 1 November, their log shows that they encountered
a group of five S.E.'s, three of which they shot down in
flames. On 4 November we find the last entries in the
" game book " ; in the course of two patrols six enemy
machines were shot down, four of which were credited
to Bolle. Then bad weather stopped all further flying.

11 November brought the armistice, with its numerous
safeguards to prevent Germany from starting the ghastly
struggle again. One of these enacted that the German
Air Force should hand over all its machines to the enemy.

It seemed too incredible. There was wild talk in the
war birds' mess that night, but in the end common sense
prevailed and they resigned themselves to submit.

Before they delivered up their beloved planes to the
enemy, they painted in bold letters on the wings and
fuselage of each machine the pilot's name and the number
of his victories.

" Swank," some may say. But British war birds
will understand and forgive the gesture.

CHAPTER V

A GLIMPSE AT THE RED KNIGHT

MORE than a glimpse would be unnecessary, for already so much light has been shed upon his brief but brilliant career. He is the hero of one entire book in this country[1] and probably of several others in his own.

Rittmeister Manfred, Freiherr von Richthofen, was the romantic figure *par excellence* of the war in the air.

He flew an all-red machine,[2] and no other war bird on his own or his enemy's side dared imitate his colour.

He brought down eighty English aeroplanes, and his health was drunk in the messes of the British war birds who strove to kill him.

He was the airman whose feats excited admiration from friend and foe ; his death was perhaps the most startling of them all, for he died in the air but did not

---

[1] *The Red Knight of Germany*, by Floyd Gibbons.

[2] During Richthofen's period of service in the Boelcke Staffel the air forces on both sides painted their aeroplanes in neutral colours in order to camouflage them from the enemy on the ground and in the air. But as all such experiments proved useless, he boldly adopted the opposite course of painting his own machine all red so that it should be easily recognised by friend and foe alike.

His Staffel protested that this amounted to sheer suicide on his part, and at length a compromise was reached. The other pilots gave their machines a red background, but introduced stripes or bars of other colours on wings and fuselages. Thus only Richthofen had an all-red aeroplane, but those flown by his Staffel (and later by his squadron) naturally presented a general red appearance to hostile eyes and ensured the ace some measure of protection.

crash.   His Fokker triplane, bearing his corpse, made
a good landing behind the British lines.

Finally he was engaged to a " mystery " girl, who wrote
to him almost daily.   He promised to marry her after the
war if he survived, but her name was never divulged.
To-day her identity remains a secret which is known
only to his mother and his one surviving brother.

If therefore I did not devote a chapter to him, some
reader would be sure to grumble.   I could understand
and sympathise with such a complaint, because a book
on German war birds that did not give due mention of
Richthofen would resemble a performance of *Hamlet*
from which the character of the Prince of Denmark had
been omitted.   Therefore at the risk of repeating what
other scribes have chronicled I shall endeavour to give
my readers a glimpse of the Red Knight.

My picture shall show him at the height of his fame
in the early days of 1918, when, with a few weeks still
to live, he is the idolised commander of Jagdgeschwader
No. 1.[1] With his war birds he is occupying the captured
quarters of British pilots, for the German " Big Push,"
on which so many hopes were vainly set, is now in full
swing: these are a group of huts, made of the once too
familiar " elephant iron " ; their roofs have been painted
with wavy green and brown stripes to camouflage them
against the attacks of enemy bombers, and the German
pilots complain that they are too small for comfort.

The remains of a hangar which the British aviators
set on fire have smouldered unseen until some chance
breeze has fanned them into flames again.   For the

---

[1] The word can be translated as " Pursuit Squadron."   As aerial warfare
grew, the Staffel of twelve pilots was found insufficient to cope with the demands
made on it, and so the squadron came into being.   A squadron generally
comprised four Staffels, and was known to its British opponents as a " circus."

safety of the German machines not far away the conflagration must be extinguished, and a slim figure, clad in a
ruddy brown leather jacket and breeches, with a silken
muffler tied carelessly round the throat, stands directing
the operations of the fire-extinguishing squad.

He is Manfred von Richthofen. In his hand he
carries a walking stick, cut from one of the propellers
of the British machines shot down, with which he constantly taps the heel of his boot. On his blond head
is perched the cap of the Uhlan regiment to which he
was gazetted when he first joined the army, for Manfred,
descendant of a long line of hard-riding country squires,
received his baptism of fire as a cavalryman.

The cavalry, as he had admitted to the interviewers
fortunate enough to gain access to his presence, has
always been his one and only love as far as fighting is
concerned, and no doubt he envies his armour-clad
ancestors who couched their lances on many a battlefield,
for had he lived in their golden days he could have performed his deeds of valour in the way he preferred.

But now the horse is at a discount. Trench warfare
has banished him to menial service at the base, while
his dismounted rider must perforce take his place in the
line along with the infantry. To find the outlet his
individuality craved, Richthofen was therefore obliged
to school himself to the manipulation of one of those
inventions of modern science which a few years ago he
and his Uhlans affected to despise.

The blaze is extinguished ; the pilots file in to their
midday meal. Richthofen takes his seat at the head of
the long, narrow table in the former messroom of the
English war birds.

Seated on either side of him we may see a galaxy of

knights of the air.   There is Lothar, the ace's younger brother, and himself an ace.   He will survive Manfred, with forty victories to his credit, but is doomed to crash four years after the war when piloting a passenger machine on a cross-country trip; we are lucky to see him here, for a few days hence, on unlucky 13 March, he will be shot down out of control behind his own lines and remain many months in hospital.   Then there is Gussmann, with whom Manfred so often co-operates in the air, and opposite him little Wolff, whose adoring eyes are continually fixed on the Master as he drinks in his every word. Wolff has been in the squadron for nine months, but twice he has been shot down behind his own lines, so that much of his time has been spent in hospital.   So far he has only shot down three opponents, so that he is as yet a long way off the " ace " title, but he boasts that he is Richthofen's rear-guard.   Gladly would he give his life for his hero, but the supreme sacrifice will not be required of him on 21 April, the day that the Red Knight is to meet his doom at the hands of Captain Roy Brown from Toronto ; about a month later, however, it will be exacted in one of the furious battles that are to take place between 11 and 15 May.

Next to Wolff sits another who is doomed to fall about the same time, Weiss, the gifted pilot who often leads Richthofen's own Staffel when administrative business keeps him on the ground.   Yesterday Weiss shot down his fourteenth accredited victim, but in all probability at least a score have fallen to his twin Spandaus, for modesty is his besetting sin. Often he forgets to put in a claim until some comrade insists ; then he argues, disclaims the honour, swearing that in such a dogfight it was impossible to tell who shot down that Bristol

Fighter or who crashed the Camel they ascribe to him. But witnesses come forward to substantiate the claim, and so, very unwillingly, Weiss puts it in. Within the next few days he is destined to increase his total to twenty, and he will have a large share in those battles of May, when on the 11th thirteen English machines will be brought down and on the 15th another eleven. But Weiss will not return from the last of those frays, for he will have gone to join the leader, whose death he has avenged, in the Valhalla that is surely reserved for flying men.

Beyond Weiss you may see one-armed Karjus, who is surely the miracle of the German Flying Corps. As an observer he won the Knightly Cross of the Hohenzollerns, but landed one day with his right arm so badly injured that the surgeons had to amputate it. But when he came out of hospital he determined to fly a single-seater. He had a hazy plan for a re-arrangement of the controls and triggers, but an aircraft designer in Berlin worked it out for him, and instead of his right hand he has a steel hook which he can use most ingeniously. Karjus often leads a Staffel, but to-day he can take no part in the work, for he crashed his machine last week when he returned from a hot fray and must practise in safety behind the lines on the new one of his special make that has just arrived.

Richthofen discovered him when visiting another aerodrome, and was so amazed at his feats that he arranged for him to be transferred to his own squadron, where he has contrived to shoot down quite a number of two-handed opponents.

Further down the table we may see Löwenhardt, who will pile up a score of fifty-three victims before collision with a comrade sends him crashing to his doom, and Reinhard who will lead the squadron after the Red Knight's death, until he goes to Germany to test a new type of machine and crashes it. But Udet will shoot down sixty-three foemen and survive the war to experience many flying adventures in the days of peace. One day he will be forced to land in some African desert, whence he will be rescued by a pilot of Imperial Airways—perhaps one of the men against whom he fought in those stirring days of 1918. If so, they will have much to talk about.

The meal proceeds, to the accompaniment of lively chatter. There is no rule against talking shop in this mess ; in fact Richthofen encourages it, for he knows that an exchange of views may teach his pilots the " whys " and " wherefores " of their daily work. Occasionally he intervenes in a discussion between two other pilots to demonstrate just why one or other is in the wrong.

Richthofen may seem madly reckless in the air, but there is method in his madness. He is not one of those happy-go-lucky fighters, like brother Lothar, who trust to chance for their victories ; every thing he does is done according to plan, and he wants all his pilots to use their heads as well as their hands.

Not that he holds any brief for the man whose discretion is a substitute for valour ; far from it. " I have no use for the pilot who does not go for his man and get him," has he already told several interviewers, and he has likewise no use for the stunting pilot—aerial acrobats, he terms them. He states quite openly that he has never looped a loop and never wants to do so. The airman who finds difficulty in making his left-hand turns may be rejected by other commanders, but Richthofen will take

him if he goes for his man in the air.   That is the secret
of his own success—he picks out his man and goes for
him.   " Never try to shoot holes in a machine," he
constantly tells his pilots, " aim for the man and make sure
you do not miss him.   If you are fighting a two-seater,
get the observer first ;   until you have silenced his gun,
do not bother about the pilot."

The pilot who has too many tricks at his finger-tips
always falls under Richthofen's suspicion.   The Red
Knight watches him carefully when, high above the
battle, he directs the concerted movements of his four
Staffels ;   he sees one of them engage its opponents, but,
deeming that the time has not yet come for his personal
intervention, he keeps his eyes on the stunting pilot.
He notices how he does his tricky half-rolls and side-
loops.   " Yes, he got himself out of a tight corner that
time," he sums up, " and he saved his skin.   But he
saved some Englishman's skin too."

Later he perhaps sees the stunter pull out of the fight.
When he meets him on the aerodrome after the battle,
the fugitive has a good excuse for deserting his comrades,
and Richthofen does not question it.   But a few days
later the man is transferred to another squadron.

The meal comes to an end ;   most of the pilots make
off to their quarters for forty winks before the afternoon
patrol.   After feeding Moritz, the great mongrel mastiff
that he reared from puppydom, Richthofen follows their
example.

In due course a batman wakens the pilots, who make
their way to the aerodrome.   Everyone asks whether
Richthofen is going up this afternoon.   The Red Knight
appears and shakes his head ;   orders have reached him
by telephone that he must go to inspect the new quarters

to which the squadron will be transferred as swiftly as possible, for these, as I have already remarked, are the days of the Great Push. Every day the line is thrust forward, so that the quarters that yesterday were just a convenient distance behind the front will be hopelessly in the rear to-morrow. Richthofen must therefore proceed by car to inspect the latest aerodrome from which the English opponents have been ejected.

So the all-red machine with the streamers is wheeled back into its tent once more, but its owner stays to watch his pilots take off; if he has no use for stunts, he is always most particular about good starts and good landings. Some of the stunting pilots they once sent him from the Johannistal Flying School made terrible landings, he remembers, and shudders as he thinks of them. He could hardly bear to watch them take off, either, but, thank heavens, they have now gone to squadrons where their talents will be better appreciated. " A good bunch we've got now," he thinks.

But they were raw, unlicked cubs when they came to him, and their present excellence is solely due to his training, for the assertion we so constantly hear has not a grain of truth in it. Richthofen is not allowed to pick the best pilots for his own squadron ; like every other commander he has to take the raw material from the flying schools to fill up his gaps, although the survivors of such batches who develop into redoubtable aces are only too often snatched away to command at other aerodromes, because it is the desire of every Staffel in the German Flying Corps to be led by a Richthofen man.

So he watches his war birds take off, and it is amazing how smartly they do it. They just roll a couple of yards along the ground, you would think, and then they seem

to pull themselves up vertically by the left wing. One
and all have this trick.

" Hals und Beinbruch ! " says Richthofen to Wolff.
(May you break your neck and your legs).

German pilots never wish one another anything good.
If anyone unacquainted with their superstitions had
said " Glück auf ! " (Good luck), to one of them as he
was being helped into his cockpit, the pilot would
probably have jumped out again. He might even have
risked a court-martial rather than go up that day, for
he would have been certain that he was going to his death.
But if you expressed the wish that he might break his
neck and his legs, he could feel confident of coming
safely home, with perhaps a brace of victories to report.

Richthofen, the cavalry officer, thinks such superstitions
childish, but he conforms to them because he knows
that their hold over his pilots is too great to be broken.
None of them would have entered their machines unless
they had made sure that they were wearing their special
mascots ; many of them, like their opposite numbers in
the Entente squadrons, wear the top of a silk stocking
under their flying helmets—a fitting lady's favour for a
knight of the air—but for some reason of his own Wolff
always dons an old nightcap that was perhaps the
regular sleeping attire of his great-grandfather.

Richthofen was never superstitious, or at least he said
he was not. He even defied the superstition that
exercised the greatest effect on the German war birds ;
he allowed himself to be photographed shortly before his
last flight. Like Boelcke, another sceptic, he paid the
price.

The Red Knight watches the last machine soar into
the air and then goes to enquire for the car that is to take

him to inspect the new quarters. He sighs as he climbs in ; he would have preferred to have been up aloft in the all-red Fokker triplane, but the powers that be have decreed otherwise.

Why, you will ask, was Richthofen saddled with these duties that might have been performed as efficiently by some disabled pilot ? The answer is that in all probability the Higher Command who were troubled so much on Boelcke's account wanted to prevent him from risking his life too often. About a year previously—when he had celebrated his forty-first victory and overtopped Boelcke's record—some very high personages found it expedient that he should take a long leave ; his successes had caught the imagination of the German civilian population in addition to making him the idol of the flying corps, and it was therefore deemed advisable to preserve him from the fate which, sooner or later, seemed to overtake every ace. To an interviewer he once admitted that the Emperor had forbidden him to fly again when he received him in audience after his fiftieth victory. This prohibition was repeated on another occasion, when he met the monarch at the front, but it does not appear to have had much effect.

In Germany two factions quarrelled over him. One, busy with propaganda, desired that he should cease flying because of the disheartening effect his death might have upon the civilians, whose spirits it was necessary to key up to the utmost, but the other, representing the purely military view, demanded that he should take the air as often as possible so as to inspire his German colleagues to greater efforts. They also imagined that the sight of his all-red machine cast a spell upon the enemy's aviators.

Richthofen was in a position to turn the scale either way . . . and he chose to fly.   If he had expressed the slightest hint that for health or other reasons he needed a long rest or if he had suggested any wish to supervise the instruction imparted to young pilots in the flying schools at home, the propagandist party would have been able to obtain their way.   But he deliberately chose to continue flying.

" I fly from a sense of duty," he once told a friend, adding that he had no material incentive to continue his work in the air because he had obtained every distinction that could be bestowed upon him.   But I imagine that there was another motive ; he was strongly imbued with the spirit of competition.

He was proud of his successes (as we may know from the silver cups that he had a Berlin jeweller make for him each time he was accredited with a new victory) and when his record was established, he made up his mind that no pilot on either side should surpass it.   He was ahead of them, and he meant to maintain his position at the top or die in the attempt.

Not that there was a scrap of meanness in his character. It was a fair fight and no favour; he would not have done anything to prevent a colleague beating his record if he could do it, and those who said that he claimed every victim brought down by the concerted efforts of the Staffel with which he flew in order to swell his own total calumniated him most foully.   His combat-reports are models of fairness, which do full justice to his brother pilots.

Let us peruse, for instance, his official report of the great air-battle of Le Cateau, which embodies his request for the acknowledgement of his sixty-sixth victory.

" At about 10.30 a.m. on 18 March," he writes, " I took off with thirty aircraft of my squadron and led all three Staffels in close order against the enemy, flying at a height 5,300 metres. When we approached the front I saw several English squadrons that had just flown over our lines and were making for Le Cateau. I met the first squadron, which consisted of two-seaters, in the neighbourhood of Le Catelet (15 kilometres north of St. Quentin), at a height of about 5,500 metres. With Lieutenant Gussmann (Jagdstaffel No. 11), I shot at the last of these opponents, a Bristol Fighter. The wings broke away. Lieutenant Gussmann brought him down in the vicinity of Joncourt. Afterwards I reassembled my thirty machines, rose to 5,300 metres and followed two English squadrons that had broken through and reached Le Catelet. When our opponents endeavoured to curve away and return to their lines, I attacked them near Le Cateau. I was the first to come in contact with the enemy, and with Lieutenant Löwenhardt I shot down the machine flying nearest to us, a Bristol Fighter. I saw the English machine go into a vertical dive and break to pieces in the air. Meanwhile my Staffels were engaged in a fierce encounter with the squadrons of enemy single-seaters that suddenly came down from a great height to protect the English two-seaters. At the same time several Staffels of Jagdgruppe No. 2, including Jagdstaffel No. 5, hastened up and joined in the battle. A long circling fight took place. It was impossible for us to retain our squadron formations. Everyone attacked the enemy flying nearest to him. The consequence was a confused mêlée of single combats. It was often quite impossible to distinguish friend from foe. The air was thick with the white streams of

phosphorus ammunition ; through it one saw machines
shot down in flames or going down out of control. I
picked out a Sopwith Camel bearing streamers and
forced it to land in the vicinity of Molain—Vaux—
Aubigny. The occupant was a Canadian who had led
one of the two one-seater squadrons. The enemy's
total loss was fifteen machines, nine of which were shot
down by my Staffels. Our only loss was one machine
from Jagdstaffel No. 10."

This is a brief, soldierly account of the greatest aerial
battle in the war, in which some seventy or eighty machines
came into action. In the opening stages Richthofen,
co-operating with Gussmann, sees an enemy machine go
down, but takes care to specify that his colleague was
the man who ought to have the credit for it ; his own
part in the affair was merely subsidiary.

Some air forces allowed half points for an enemy brought
down by the co-operation of two pilots ; thus McCudden
writes[1] of a Hun being credited between Major Bellew
and himself, but the German air authorities would not
allow this. When it was impossible to judge which of
two or more airmen had finished off a victim, no individual
was allowed to claim him, although the victory was
naturally permitted to increase the Staffel's total.

In the above-quoted fight Richthofen participates in
three encounters. Reporting the first of them, he thinks
that the credit belongs to Gussmann and says so, knowing
that his statement will be reckoned as confirmation of
Gussmann's claim.

In the second affair he and Löwenhardt were concerned.
Richthofen cannot be sure which of them was responsible
for bringing the enemy down and says nothing to pre-

[1] *Flying Fury,* p. 126.

judice matters either way.   If Löwenhardt can make out
a claim that other witnesses are ready to substantiate,
then he can take the credit ; if not, the victory will
simply swell the Staffel's total without increasing any
individual's score.

In the third case he is quite clear about his own
achievement.   He picked out the enemy leader by his
streamers and shot him down.   Affair number three is
confirmed by the victim, Flight-Commander William
G. Ivamy, of Vancouver, who was taken prisoner on
landing and wrote his own version of the fight for
Floyd Gibbons' book.

Richthofen was determined to keep his own place
at the top by fair competition, and so he went on flying.
But the people who wanted to withdraw him from active
service contrived to score a partial sucess.

Unlike so many star performers, Richthofen was an
excellent organiser.   Captain Bodenschatz, who was his
squadron's adjutant, tells us that he went to much trouble
to make sure that the pilots under his command were
equipped with machines as good as those flown by their
opponents ; this involved him in much correspondence
with the aircraft factories.   Moreover, the preparations
for the German spring offensive necessitated a careful
overhauling of all cars and lorries in the service of the
aerodrome, a special accumulation of munitions and
benzin for the pilots, and the fabrication of large tents
to replace the permanent hangars as well as smaller
ones for the sleeping quarters of officers and mechanics.
Emergency landing grounds had to be provided and
sites for wireless stations chosen.

All this labour, which was accomplished during the
winter months when bad weather restricted the flying

hours, was supervised by officers with practical experience.
Richthofen threw himself wholeheartedly into the work
of organising the arrangements for the spring, so that
the gales and storms of winter that brought his pilots
days of leisure and recreation meant hours of desk-work
for their leader.

On 10 November, 1917, Captain Townsend, flying an
S.E.5, was Richthofen's sixty-third victim, but his sixty-
fourth, a Bristol Fighter, was not downed till 12 March,
1918—an interval of four months, during which time
he worked continuously, with the exception of a few
days that he spent hunting in the forest of Bialowitza
after he had attended the peace conference of Brest-
Litowsk, where he was infinitely bored with the wearisome,
protracted negotiations. He hailed with delight his
return to the western front, where he plunged anew into
his office work and spent much time instructing the new
pilots posted to his squadron. Consequently he put
in very few actual flying hours that winter, to the un-
feigned relief of those who wished to see him spared the
fate that had befallen every other German ace.

Richthofen proved himself a capable instructor and
took infinite patience with his pupils, never losing his
temper, but diplomatically weeding out the men whom
he considered unsatisfactory and sparing himself no
pains to develop the capacities of the others.

As a squadron-leader it would be superfluous to call
him a master of tactics, for he evolved the methods of
massed flying that became prevalent in the last year of
the war and compelled his opponents to follow his
example. No longer was man matched against man, but
squadron against squadron, for Richthofen saw clearly
that team-work rather than individual performances

would win the mastery of the air. He therefore did his best to weld his war birds into an efficient team, the members of which could depend on themselves, one another, their machines and their leader.

But this team-work, which is the dominating principle of aerial warfare at the time when we take our glimpse at Richthofen gives him ever less scope for those single combats in which he took such delight at the beginning of his flying career. When he flies—and it is not every day that he can fly now—he must force his all-red Fokker triplane up to some point of vantage from which he can direct the movements of his squadron so as to hurl the weight of numbers on to the weakest point of the enemy's formation. Never again will he have an opportunity like the one he enjoyed on that day some eighteen months ago when, as a new-fledged ace with ten victories to his credit, he met and conquered Major Hawker, whom his comrades knew as the " English Boelcke."

Man against man they fought on that day—a fair fight, without interference from any other machine on either side. He, the younger fighter, had vanquished the older and more experienced ace, and he thrilled with the excitement of the duel to the death. It was the greatest achievement of his career.

Later, truly, he had other thrills, such as the half-hour's fight with Captain Barwell on his Nieuport the previous spring, and the battle with Bird's Sopwith last autumn. But those encounters were only chance exceptions from the universal dogfight where a pilot has no chance to sense his opponent's individuality. It is all team-work now !

So while Manfred von Richthofen is still far away

in his car, one Staffel of the Richthofen team returns from its afternoon match. Down they come, as neatly as they took off, and each new arrival is greeted with a shower of questions.

" Hallo, Wolff, did you get one ? "   No need to ask ; Wolff's beaming face clearly indicates his success. Weiss got one too, it appears, and Sergeant Schultz— that's three to our Staffel. We were five against the enemy's seven, but we licked them all right.

Weiss comes down ; his comrades offer congratulations, but he shakes his head sadly. No, he cannot be sure—no chance of following the enemy down. The Sopwith was out of control, he admits, but it was impossible to see what happened below, for it plunged through a hole in the clouds. He would have liked to have found out, but at the critical moment another Sopwith dived on him and kept him so busy that he forgot all about the first opponent.

"Rot," declares Gussmann, " of course you got him. I saw it all. Out of control indeed ! Why, you shot his wings off, didn't he, Sergeant ? "

Sergeant Schulz is likewise ready to testify to Weiss's victory, so they leave the aerodrome and tumble over one another into the messroom to make out their combat reports. Weiss declines to put in a claim until someone forces a pen into his hand. Then another Staffel troops in.

" We got two," they shout in chorus.

" And we got three," Wolff replies.

After tea they decide to go up again. Wolff starts first, and as soon as he is well up he loops a couple of joyous loops, because Richthofen is not there to see him. Looping the loop is strictly forbidden, but when the cat's away. . . ,

Back they all come in due course. What luck? None at all, not one Tommy's tail to be seen in the sky. Never mind—a good day's work. Off go the various sections of the Richthofen team to clean themselves prior to consuming an enormous meal, while their mechanics, like those attached to any other aerodrome on any front, boast loudly of the merits of their respective buses and the men that take them up.

At dinner the Richthofen team meets its captain, who has returned from his trip, and is eager to hear the news. He listens attentively, asks a question or two and " Yes, you were all good boys," he sums up, " I saw part of the scrap."

When the meal is over Richthofen cuts in for a hand of bridge, but early bedtime is the rule unless a " binge " is scheduled. After the others have retired, the Red Knight extracts a thick bundle of papers from a pigeon-hole of his desk. They form the manuscript of the new book he is writing ; he intended it to be a continuation of "Der Roter Kampfflieger," the chronicle of his early adventures, but, like so many other authors, he has found it taking a different shape to that originally planned. It will be purely and simply a treatise on military aviation, embodying his ideas of the tactics to be adopted by air squadrons—in short a manual of instruction for the Imperial German Flying Corps.

How can he know that a year hence there will be no Imperial German Flying Corps ?

The following morning the early patrol has no luck ; once more not a single foeman to be seen in the air. After breakfast, when the war birds are lounging about the hangars, gossiping and chattering, Richthofen strolls over to the aerodrome, with Moritz at his heels.

All cluster round him.   One of the Staffels secured
its ninety-ninth victim yesterday and is keen on completing
its century to-day.   " All right," says Richthofen,
" suppose I come along and help you get him."

" Yes, yes," they all exclaim, and then, after a pause,
" you'll keep behind us, sir, and at the top of the ceiling,
so that you can put us through it properly."

Team-work again !

He laughs, and with the stick carved from the propeller
of an enemy machine begins to trace diagrams of air-
fights on the moist earth, explaining the advantageous
positions they must aim at securing.   Then he compliments Wolff on yesterday's victory, which he saw from
his car.

" Your fourth, I think, Wolff ? "

" Yes, sir."   Wolff beams all over.   Surely his run
of bad luck is now ended ; only six more and then he
will be into double figures, an ace, worthy to receive the
signed portrait of the commander that goes with the title.

But as the all-red Fokker triplane is being wheeled
out, Manfred von Richthofen looks thoughtful, for he
knows that his team's request for directions from above
means that they wish him to keep out of the fight.

Do they then no longer believe in his invincibility ?
Are they, like the civilians of Germany, so anxious to
preserve him as an adored idol that they no longer trust
him to take care of himself in a dogfight ?   Are they
no better than the gentlemen of the Higher Command
who continually drop hints that it is time for him to take
another spell of long leave ?   Just the time when he
can be spared, they allege—nonsense—this is the moment
of the crisis, when every man is wanted to do his bit if
Germany is to pull off the long-deferred victory !

Richthofen begins to wonder whether he still believes in himself. This time last year he was fully convinced that no man born of mortal woman could conquer him, but now he is not so sure. That crash last July had badly shaken his belief in his invincibility.

That day he realised what his victims must have felt when he sent them down to their doom. If that F.E. had been able to follow him down, its observer could easily have finished him off. Luck—yes, but Luck is ever a fickle jade.

No time to think about that now, for the " Tripe " stands ready, so up we go to help the Staffel get its century !

CHAPTER VI

BALLOONS!

"YOU leave them alone, you young fool! You've only one life to lose, haven't you? You're asking for trouble, my son, in a positively sinful fashion, and by the Lord Harry you'll get it. And if you do bag that ruddy balloon and get away, there'll be another just like it up in the same place to-morrow. You can bet your life on that!"

Such is the typical advice that any experienced old hand of any Flying Corps might have given any green youngster newly arrived from some flying school in his homeland.

The novice pilots could seldom resist the temptations of balloons. Those " blimps," " sausages," or whatever you like to call them, looked such easy tempting marks to the youngsters who did not realise the dangers connected with them. The older pilots usually gave them a wide berth unless in receipt of positive orders to attack them. When a squadron leader was instructed to bring down some particular balloon, he invariably detailed his worst pilot to the job.

The youngsters knew that, but in ninety-nine cases out of a hundred the temptation proved too great. Some of them, however, were lucky enough to survive, and among these fortunate ones was Lieutenant Bormann.

He was only a corporal then, and the powers that be

had just sent him to join the Austro-German forces opposing the Russians in eastern Galicia. For some months he had been flying a double-seater, with an officer as his observer, but he soon grew tired of long-distance reconnaissances and, like all young pilots, he longed to have a single-seater, where he could do both the flying and the fighting.

In fact he yearned to be another Richthofen, and he thought himself on the way to achieve his ambitions when after two months training he was sent to the Galician front and given a Roland biplane with an Argus engine of 180 h.p. and two twin Spandaus machine guns. Corporal Bücker, another youngster with similar aspirations, also had a Roland of like capacity, and Bormann and Bücker congratulated one another because they were the only two single-seater war birds within a radius of several hundreds of miles of Galician plains. So all they had to do was to sail up into the air and crash a few Russians, after which would come promotion and transference to the western front, where their talents would be appreciated.

But this was in June, 1917, a couple of months after the Russian Revolution, and things were not going too well in the former empire of the Tsars. Everything at the front was in a state of disorganisation, and whether the Russian war birds had no machines or whether they had all gone home to celebrate the revolution I cannot tell, but the fact remains that Bormann and Bücker found no foeman to give them an opportunity of the thrilling duels in the bright blue sky that they were longing for.

The Russian army, however, seemed to have a large number of captive balloons, which owed their immunity largely to the fact that hitherto they had been assailed only by slow two-seaters that gave ample warning of their approach. As soon as one of these came anywhere within reach, down went the balloon to safety, and the Germans had to return empty-handed. But Bormann and Bücker, rejoicing in their Rolands that could do over a hundred miles an hour, thought that they would soon make short work of the balloons, whihc would serve for them to practise on until some more worthy foemen turned up.

One day a number of these monsters were reported to be aloft, and the two youngsters laid their heads together. " I'll take the blighter north of the railway line, and you can go for the southmost chap," said Bormann. His companion agreed.

Bormann started gaily off, picturing to himself how he would swoop on that balloon like an eagle after its prey, but he reckoned without the strong head-wind that reduced his speed. The balloon's observer saw him in good time and signalled to his ground squad to haul him down.

Nothing doing. Bormann decided to go and see how friend Bücker was getting on. From the height at which he was flying he was able to note that the southern balloon was still aloft. Every moment he expected to see it go down. What was Bücker doing ? Engine trouble, perhaps, for when they started he had noticed that Bücker's Roland did not seem to be going too well. " In which case his balloon is mine," he reasoned.

With the wind behind him he whirled down on the balloon at top speed and sent a stream of tracer bullets into its envelope before the Russian Archies were aware of his presence. He circled round and observed that the balloon was sinking lower and lower as the ground squad hauled away for dear life. So he put in another burst,

This time a red flame shot out of the envelope ; a few seconds later the whole long " sausage " was one fiery glow. " Any fool can down a balloon," he thought, as he whirled away homewards.

Bücker was not there when he landed, but a minute or two later the mechanics heard his engine in the sky. " I wonder what happened to him," mused Bormann.

" What the blazes did you go butting in on my ' sausage ' for ? " was Bücker's greeting when he clambered out of the cockpit.

" Where were you ? " enquired the amazed Bormann.

" A couple of hundred feet above your head, you silly ass," was the reply.

As no definite proofs were forthcoming, neither got credit for that balloon, but both pilots were dubbed a couple of young fire-eaters by their superiors. Shortly afterwards they parted company, and Bormann found himself on another sector of the long front, in sole charge, with two mechanics for his Roland, another for his machine gun and a batman for his personal needs. He began to think himself a mighty fine fellow, and decided that Richthofen would have to look to his laurels.

A couple of days after his arrival at his new field of action his head mechanic woke him up with the news that there was a balloon in the sky. Bormann went out to sniff the weather and then made up his mind that he would utilise the cover of the low clouds to stalk his prey unobserved.

He made his approach from a height of some 700 feet, and, as he had anticipated, the Russian gunners failed to spot him before he arrived within shooting range.

Bormann chuckled, but his happy mood did not last, for he had completely forgotten the fact that the ground

below him would present a totally different aspect to that
which it assumed when he looked down on it from his usual
flying-height.   In plain words he lost his way and ran
into a low bank of clouds whence he could see neither
the earth, the sky nor the balloon.   He dropped a couple
of hundred feet.

As soon as he emerged from the clouds he became the
object of concentrated machine-gun fire.   The ground
beneath him looked unfamiliar, and the balloon had
vanished ; he could not tell whether it had been hauled
down or was obscured by the clouds.

There was nothing to do but to go home again, and
he was not in the best of tempers when he landed.
His head mechanic made matters worse by tactlessly
remarking that the balloon was still aloft.

" It won't stay there long," snapped Bormann, and
bade the man refill his tank.   He was still such a greenhorn that it never occurred to him to wonder why the
Russians left the balloon standing instead of hauling it
down as they ought to have done when they knew he was
on the prowl.

This time he zoomed up as soon as he had taken off,
though he realised that he must be clearly visible to the
observer in the balloon.   He wondered whether he
could reach the " sausage " before its inmate signalled
to his ground squad to haul him down.

" His funeral anyway," he chuckled, " for here we
come with our little guns—broadside on to the old
sausage—tack—tack—tack—oh, damn, oh blast, there's
a gun jammed ! "

He curved away to remove the jam ; as soon as the
gun was working again, he returned to the attack, but
was far too excited to notice that the balloon remained at

its old height and the ground squad were making no
efforts to haul it down.   It likewise escaped his memory
that in such situations observers are supposed to leap
out and flutter down to earth with the aid of their parachutes instead of sticking in the car and staring at their
assailants, as this one was doing.

" Tack—tack—tack—tack—that's got him fair and
square, but why doesn't the damn thing flare up ?
Let's see—last time just one tiny flame shot out and
then. . . ."   At that moment a lurid sheet of fire burst
forth from the balloon, searing his eyeballs, while a
terrific din seemed to split his eardrums.   A second later
he found himself head downwards, with his Roland
dropping to earth like a stone.

For all his rawness Bormann was a clever pilot, with a
cool head for emergencies.   He cut his engine and
somehow managed to right the machine.

Vastly surprised to find his wings intact and controls
working, he cast a hasty glance at the balloon—or rather
at the mass of black smoke that marked its position.
Then he scurried into the clouds for shelter from the
angry Archies and made off for home.

" Anyhow I got that balloon," he thought, " though
it jolly nearly got me.   I wonder why it bust up in that
sudden fashion."

As aforesaid, he was still young and innocent, but it
seems strange that his superiors did not enlighten him
when he reported his success over the telephone.   Perhaps they did not like to discourage an enthusiastic
young airman who had the reputation of being a regular
fire-eater ; at any rate it was not until some weeks later
that he discovered how a wily enemy sometimes sends up
a balloon filled with explosives, with a dummy observer

in its car—a man of straw, dressed in an old jacket and cap—to lure young fire-eaters to their doom.

Beginner's luck saved Bormann, and he went to bed that night with a resolution to be more careful in future. But the next morning he was roused with the news that the Russians had sent up a whole row of balloons.

" Blasted impudence," he muttered, as he stared at them through his binoculars. As, however, the enemy had obviously lost all sense of shame, it was his duty to instil one. He swore a mighty oath that at least one of those impertinent balloons should rue the day and instructed his mechanics to bring out the Roland. Before he entered his cockpit he took stock of the situation again through his binoculars, and discovered that the balloons were not alone in the air. A whole squadron of aeroplanes was cruising up and down the length of the row, evidently on the look-out for him.

" Bah ! Farmans ! Old lattice-tails ! Don't worry me ! Can't catch me ! " He made a mental note of the Farmans' speed.

" Up and down the line they go—just like sentries on guard outside a palace. I can time my visit so as to reach the northernmost sausage at the moment when they are enquiring after the health of his brother at the southern end. Then I beat it before they can get anywhere near me."

Hopefully he clambered into his cockpit and took off. In less than a minute he had passed the Russian frontline trenches. A glance to southward—the Farmans were out of sight. Excellent !

The Russian Archies gave him their usual welcome, which left him unimpressed. Straight for its objective headed the Roland, and after his first burst Bormann saw the tracer bullets sink home in the long envelope.

Whizzing past the balloon at close range, he caught sight of the observer and wondered what the wretched man would do when the flames broke out. On the occasions of his two previous attacks he had been too excited to worry about the fate of the unfortunate devil in the car ; he had forgotten about his existence, thinking only of the balloon as an animated monster able to do its work without human aid.

He curved away to avoid any damage from a violent explosion like the one that nearly brought him to grief the previous day and circled round, so that he could close in again if his first burst had failed to ignite the envelope.

But this time he had no need to waste further ammunition. From the hull the little red flame had shot out and was growing apace. No explosion troubled his eyes or ears ; this was evidently a well-mannered balloon, ready to die like a gentleman.

Bormann spiralled up to gain sufficient height for a homeward journey above the range of the enemy's Archies. When next he espied the balloon, it was red with the swift greedy flames that devoured it, and a thick column of black smoke shot up to heaven. He wondered what would happen to the observer. Suddenly he saw the car's occupant poise himself on its edge and leap into the air. He was falling—no, his parachute had opened out and was bearing him slowly and gently earthwards.

" Very interesting," thought Bormann.

He knew that observers were provided with parachutes to ensure their safe descent from stricken balloons, but he had never seen the trick done before. Full of curiosity he dropped down to get a better view of the business.

But being, as we have had occasion to remark, somewhat young and inexperienced, he completely forgot about the Farmans until they were almost within range of him.

Although thirsting for the glory of bringing an enemy machine down, he did not feel himself quite equal to tackling half a dozen opponents. Discretion, he decided, was the better part of valour, even if the Farman was the type of bus in which Noah disported himself before the flood, so, tucking his metaphorical tail between his legs, he opened the throttle and bolted for home.

Bormann would be the first to admit that he was a regular greenhorn ; I doubt if he would be offended if you described his conduct on this occasion as that of a " hayseed," or a " sucker." He therefore headed straight for home, and was most unpleasantly surprised to discover that the Farmans had chased him into a barrage put up by the Archies. He had lost so much height when he descended to watch the observer manipulate his parachute that it was dangerous for him to attempt to dodge the enemy's fire by half rolls or side-slips ; his only chance for safety lay in climbing as speedily as possible. His beginner's luck held good, for by a series of hair-raising turns he zoomed up out of reach and got home.

A few days afterwards the Russians sent up a group of four balloons, which Bormann took as a personal affront. He set off to teach them manners, but as it was a cloudy day, he lost sight of them when he got near and only blundered on to them at the last moment, just when he was about to turn back. A strong wind rocked his machine considerably, but he felt that it was impossible to miss such easy targets. He began to compose the speech he would make when he rang up headquarters to report that he had bagged all four.

But he decided that it would be foolish to waste time and ammunition, so he sailed along the line and put in a burst on each of the four. Then he came round in a turn to watch the effect of his marksmanship.

To his surprise and disappointment not a single " sausage " had taken fire, though four observers were gently gliding earthwards. Meanwhile all around him pelted the lead discharged by the angry Archies.

Bormann vowed that whatever happened he would bring down the last balloon of the row. He curved round to attack with the wind behind him, but before he could complete his turn his engine went dead. A glance at his tachometer told him that something must be very much wrong, although the propeller was still revolving.

Meanwhile the Archies had redoubled their efforts. " I'm properly up against it this time," thought Bormann, and began to wonder what life would be like in a prison camp. Probably they would send him to some God-forsaken hole in Siberia.

" Well, at least I can show the Russians how to make a decent forced landing," he thought, picking out a likely meadow. He began to glide down, whereupon the Archies ceased fire and, divining his intention, a number of Russians hastened to his proposed landing-place to prevent him from destroying his machine before he gave himself up.

But evidently Fate thought Bormann was entitled to a further share of beginner's luck, for when he was barely a thousand feet off the ground his engine began to show signs of life. It coughed, sputtered and belched smoke, but its hideous sounds of protest were sweet music in Bormann's ears. He evened out and shot away.

He managed to reach a height of 3,000 feet by the time he reached the Russian trenches ; then, with one convulsive shudder, his engine struck work again. But Bormann did not worry, for he knew that he could get back to safety with a glide, and even if he did not reach his aerodrome, he would come down somewhere within the German lines.

He had difficulty in finding a piece of level ground, for the whole area was pocked and dented with shell holes, but eventually he managed to pancake down and escaped with a bent axle and a couple of broken struts. When however, he examined the interior of his Roland, a different tale was told.

Apparently a bullet from a Russian machine gun had punctured his tank and another had holed the feed-pipe. Deprived of juice, the engine promptly ceased work, but he could not remember switching on to the emergency tank, although he must have done so when starting to glide down, and as he had omitted to cut off his engine it naturally began to work again. The emergency tank was scraped by another bullet which failed to pierce it, and the cause of the engine's final stoppage was a lucky shot which hit the cooler and let all the water out. Several marks on his jacket, boots and helmet told a tale of bullets that had just failed to find their billets.

The whole business gave him rather a shock, for it dawned upon him that : (1) he did not know so much about his machine as he imagined ; (2) that he was not such a difficult target as he had been inclined to presume. He decided that he had had enough of balloons for the moment.

But evidently the Russians had also had enough of him, as for the next few days their balloons made very fleeting appearances and were promptly hauled down the moment he showed his nose in the air. For his part, he was quite glad of an excuse for not attacking them; in fact he was not quite such a fire-eater as when he bagged his first "sausage."

But towards the end of July, 1917, the German Higher Command initiated the offensive that was to drive the Russians out of the corner of Galicia they still held. When operations commenced Captain Wulff and his Jagdstaffel of picked war birds were despatched to the sector in which Bormann was flying, and he knew that his commanding officer would be bound to give a good report of him to the Staffel-leader. He swore that whatever happened and no matter how many balloons the Russians put up he would not show "cold feet."

Early one morning he caught sight of a faint smear through the haze, and when he investigated it with his binoculars he found that it was certainly a balloon. But the visibility was so poor when he went up that he utterly failed to locate his objective and after indulging in a joy-ride to view from the air the unwonted spectacle of a large-scale offensive in progress he returned home. After breakfast he scanned the horizon again with his glasses and, lo and behold—where one balloon had stood, there were now two !

"I've got to get them," he swore, and ordered his Roland to be brought out again. He had been somewhat relieved when he failed to find the balloon on his early morning trip, for his nerves were still badly shaken by his last experience and his original contempt of Archie had developed into an exaggerated respect which was increased still further by several days of enforced inaction. As he subsequently admitted to his friends, he was in a blue funk during the half-hour that he was waiting to start.

Consequently he was overjoyed when he got up and found the haze so thick that once more he was unable to locate his objective, but at the same time he felt ashamed to descend without making a thorough search for it.   Just as he was in two minds what to do, he caught sight of Wulff's Staffel in the air.

That settled it.   He flew across and joined them, happy to be in their company and have all further responsibility taken off his hands.   But before he gained any inkling of their intentions the haze suddenly broke, revealing the naked envelopes of the two balloons.

Cold shivers ran down Bormann's spine.   " If they see the brutes, they'll want to have a go at them," he thought, " and then I shall have to join in."

He set his teeth.   " I'm going for those balloons," he vowed, " and if Wulff's fellows don't see them, I'll show them where they are."   But before he could give the Staffel leader any indication of the whereabouts of his quarry, the haze closed in and swallowed the balloons up once more.

For some time he cruised about aimlessly with Wulff's pilots, wondering whether he would get another sight of the balloons.   Then without any warning the haze broke again, and there they were, quite close at hand. Without a second's pause Bormann turned and headed for them.

He steered for the gap in between two balloons so as to keep the Archies mystified until the last moment. As he approached, he made up his mind that the " sausage " on his right, which, being somewhat higher than its companion, offered the better mark, and bore down on it, opening fire at about 500 yards.

No flame greeted his burst. He pulled his stick hard and jumped over the balloon. Then he circled round to attack it from the other side, but as he came out of his turn he saw the Farmans taking off from the adjacent aerodrome.

There were six of them on the ground, so that he knew he had to be quick about the business if he was to finish off his balloon and get away. He had completely forgotten about Wulff and his Staffel.

Two Farmans were now in the air, and their observers pumped lead at him as fast as their barrels could emit the bullets. Bormann pressed the trigger-buttons of his twin Spandaus.

One Farman had evidently had enough, for it was going down again. Out of control in all probability, but Bormann could spare no time to observe its fate as its companion closed with him just as he was within range of the balloon. So near were the two machines to one another that Bormann had no time to jump or dodge his opponent, but by rolling he contrived to avoid the collision by a matter of a few feet.

When he came out he saw that he was being attacked by four Farmans, but he did not care, for from the balloon's envelope the tiny flame had spurted out that betokened destruction. His ammunition was almost spent, and with an easy conscience he headed for home.

From the haze above a fifth Farman swooped down on him. Bormann gave this unexpected foeman his last burst at long range and pulled the stick. The Farman went into a right turn and tried to dive for his tail, but the Roland was easily the faster machine. High above

the advancing tide of the German offensive Bormann
whirled homewards, leaving Wulff and his merry men to
pick off any stray Farman that came their way.

Later in the day he was credited with his balloon,
which was said to have been responsible for the accurate
fire of a large group of Russian batteries until he brought
it down.

The German offensive was completely successful.
The disorganised Russians were swept out of Galicia,
and Bormann obtained his commission and was sent
off to the Mesopotamian front, where he engaged in
many a tussle with British pilots. No doubt he gave
younger pilots some very sound advice, based on personal
experience, concerning the wisdom of leaving balloons
alone.

But sometimes an experienced pilot caught " balloon-
fever," in which case the attack usually proved fatal,
as in the case of Lieutenant Eschwege, the " Eagle of the
Ægean Sea," whose fate is described in a later chapter.
If the patient somehow survived, he generally became,
like Nimrod, a mighty hunter before the Lord.

Such a one was Lieutenant Fritz von Röth, a good
pilot, but an atrociously bad marksman who had been
concerned in many scraps but never contrived to secure
a victory over an enemy machine.

Röth belonged to a Staffel that flew over a sector in the
neighbourhood of the Mort Homme, where fogs seemed
to be a speciality of the winter climate. For two whole
months the war birds of his mess had found no prey to hunt.

They amused themselves with target practice at
ground marks, betting on the results. This was quite
exciting at first, though it made a big hole in Röth's
pocket, but after a while everyone grew tired of it.

Rōth became careless and made a landing that wrote off his machine. He was fond of that Albatros.

" I'm fed up with life," he announced one day in the mess, and forthwith proclaimed his intention of asking for a transfer back to his old battalion in the trenches. But somehow he refrained from taking this last drastic step and continued his target practice at which he grew steadily worse.

" I don't believe I could hit a balloon," he remarked one day when his marksmanship had been more atrocious than usual.

The following morning the Staffel took the air under the leadership of Lieutenant Kissenberth. They had no particular objective in view, so that all the five pilots were free to hunt any quarry they could find. They searched the air from the bend of the Meuse at Bras to the edge of the Argonne wood and back again, but the only enemies they discovered were a couple of Spads that promptly made off, having no stomach for a fight against odds.

Kissenberth took his Staffel after the Spads until he saw that he had no possible chance of catching them ; then he gave the " wash-out " signal. As the Staffel turned, they saw a group of five or six balloons somewhere far away on the southern fringe of the Forêt de Hesse.

About 2,000 feet high Kissenberth judged them, but he did not bother his head about them. Like so many experienced pilots, he did not like balloons and never attacked them unless some silly old colonel who had taken an antipathy to their species put pressure on him to send a war bird or two after them, in which case duty was duty. On such occasions the pilot entrusted with the job usually got his balloon, because the "sausages" were such easy marks, but in nine cases out of ten he failed to get back past the barrage put up by the Archies or else he fell a victim to some Spad that jumped down on him out of the clouds. "The best thing a fellow can do in such cases," thought Lieutenant Kissenberth, "is to land straight away and hope that the prison camp to which the Frenchies will send him may be somewhere pleasant on the Riviera. And of course there will be another old 'sausage' up the next day in place of the one he shot down." As most of the members of his Staffel cherished similar sentiments concerning balloons, it was not remarkable that they failed to notice Röth's absence until they landed.

"I parted company with you fellows when we passed over Vauquois," Röth afterwards told them, "because I wanted to see whether I really could hit a balloon."

He had an easy task, for no one in the French lines noticed him detach himself from the Staffel. Finding his Archies useless to protect him, the astonished observer in the balloon's car had no alternative but to jump and trust to his parachute for a safe landing. The long, fat envelope proved such an easy mark that even Röth could not miss it, and after he had put in his first burst he had the satisfaction of seeing a long, sharp tongue of flame shoot out. The balloon began to sink, the flames spreading rapidly until within less than a minute the whole envelope was one mass of dancing fire.

"Excellent work," thought Röth, "I'll try another." So, putting his Albatros's nose westward, he steered for a group of three balloons, the observers of which promptly took to their parachutes. A few seconds later two out of the three "sausages" were floating earthwards as burning wrecks.

Röth lost so much height in his attack upon the last of them that he came under a hot fire from the French Archies, but he did not care. He put his Albatros into a sharp turn and whizzed off homewards with the wind at his back to report his success.

Henceforth balloons were his special quarry, and his messmates loved him, for there was no likelihood of any of them being called upon to tackle a " sausage " as long as Röth was on the job. They were only too willing to give him all the help and encouragement he needed.

Röth made a habit of starting out with his Staffel on the usual patrols, just as if he had no interest in hunting anything but Spads. All the time, however, he was looking out for balloons on the horizon.

If he caught sight of one, he did not go for it at once, but made careful observations, noting whether any French machines were cruising about in its vicinity. Then he watched his chance to slip away quietly from the Staffel, and masked his intentions by going off in an opposite direction to that in which his quarry lay.

Generally he found some cover from fog or clouds, but before he emerged from its protection he cut off his engine so that its drone should not betray him to Archie. Then followed a swift, silent glide, and before the ground squad could start to haul the balloon down he was within range and putting in his burst. Out came a stream of phosphorus bullets from the twin Spandaus, and down went the balloon in flames.

Röth seemed to bear a charmed life. His final swoop invariably brought him within the range of the machine guns, and time after time he returned with his wings full of holes, but his body and the vital parts of the Albatros remained unharmed.

In the early spring of 1918 Kissenberth's Staffel was transferred from the Meuse to Aniches in the Arras sector, where they found themselves opposed to some very wily British war birds.

One morning six enemy bombers were reported to be making for Douai aerodrome, and Kissenberth's Staffel took off to intercept them.

They were too late. The bombers laid their eggs, though they did not do much damage. Six Bristol Fighters they were, and Kissenberth's men caught them on the way home and promptly attacked them. Down from the sky dropped an escort of Camels, and the usual dogfight took place.

Lieutenant Gossner, Röth's best friend, was engaged in a tail-chasing affair with a Bristol Fighter, and succeeded at last in fastening himself on to the blind spot where the observer could not reach him with his gun. A well-aimed burst broke the enemy machine to pieces in the air ; first the right wing fell off, then the left, and finally the fuselage shivered into a thousand fragments. "A most unpleasant sight," thought Gossner.

For a vital couple of seconds the spectacle fascinated him so much that he forgot he was not alone in the air. A Camel was just about to fasten on to his tail when Röth, who was some distance below him, charged upwards. The Camel sheered off to avoid a collision, receiving a burst from Röth's Spandaus that sent it hurriedly wobbling back to its own lines.

The Kissenberth squadron returned home in high glee, for they had crashed two Bristol Fighters without sustaining any casualties. All felt certain that Röth had got the Camel as well, but as no one was able to

follow it down, he had no hope of succeeding with a
claim.

Everyone voted it a good fight ; the English, it was
generally agreed, were a far more sporting set of opponents
than the French. But there was a far-away look in
Röth's eyes that evening, for he was wondering whether
there were any balloons to stalk in this sector.

For a couple of weeks he saw none. Then one day
when the Staffel was out on patrol Gossner noticed
Röth steal away in his usual fashion.

He came back to report that he had bagged a " double "
over Marcoing.

Afterwards he saw no more till 1 April, when he
played the fool to some good purpose. On the evening
patrol that day he once again left the Staffel in the air
to pay a call on four balloons that he had espied to the
north of Arras. He sent them all down in flames.

Not long afterwards he was appointed to the leadership
of a Bavarian Staffel operating in the Ypres sector, and
contrived to take his friend, Gossner, with him. For
some little time he appeared to have lost his interest in
balloons.

Often he did not take part in the patrols, but deputed
Gossner to lead the Staffel in his place. On such occasions he went up alone to study the new conditions. In
the mess he was silent and reserved.

" You see," he afterwards told Gossner, " I'd never
been so far north before. Practically all my fighting
has been against the French lower down the line. I'm
up against totally different weather conditions, different
winds and an enemy that employs different fighting
tactics."

But one May morning he judged that he had learnt all

he wanted to know. Under a clear sky, with a north-west wind behind him, he flew the length of the front between Wervicq and Paschendaele. No English machines were about as he set off for the objective that had exercised his brains for several weeks—a large group of balloons that went up daily somewhere between Dixmude and Hazebrouck.

He was greeted with a vigorous salvo from the English Archies, but took no notice. On he went until he was a considerable distance behind the English lines ; then he circled round and with the wind at his back he cut his engine and swooped down on the nearest balloon, which was some 3,000 feet above the ground. He held his fire till he was quite close.

Then he poured in a well-directed burst. The observer jumped for his life, and the balloon went down in flames.

Röth observed another balloon just a bit to southward. Obviously it was intended for his next victim, and down it went. But in order to ensure success he had to drop to a level where the machine guns could join in Archie's efforts to punish him for his impertinence.

All around him the leaden storm raged, but he pushed his stick backwards and forwards and, rising up and down like a switchback, with evasive zigzags at well-chosen intervals, he contrived to spoil the gunners' aim. But suddenly he caught sight of an English aeroplane making for him from the direction of Poperinghe.

" I'm not going to let that fellow spoil my fun," swore Röth.

But obviously something had to be done about this new and unforeseen opponent. Röth went into a long curve that put him on the Englishman's tail, for he was a skilful pilot at out-manœuvering an adversary. The trouble was that he could not shoot well enough to press home his advantage.

He put in a vicious burst at a range that would have sufficed for a better marksman to send his enemy down in flames, but Röth was quite contented to have pricked some holes in the Englishman's wings. At all events his adversary sheered off in a long turn.

" That's given him something to think about for a bit," muttered Röth, " so now for my ' sausage-meat.' " Heedless of the Archies and machine guns around him he winged his way towards the other balloons.

The nearest one to him was nearly 5,000 feet up. " No good," thought Röth wisely, " I'll have to let him go. I can't get sufficient height to deal with him as long as that English machine is knocking around."

But balloon number four was only 3,000 feet up, a height which just suited Röth. Down it went ; out jumped two observers, whom Röth, following the usual custom, allowed to descend unmolested. Then he turned his attention to numbers five and six.

Down they went. Röth might miss enemy planes that were absolute sitters, but those huge " sausages " were simply asking for trouble when he was about. "Any fool can hit those," he chuckled.

Five out of six he had sent to earth, and as each contained a couple of observers, ten men had been forced to jump for their lives. And as he turned he saw that balloon number three, which he had been forced to spare, was gently wobbling earthwards under pressure from her ground squad. Not one of the six was left standing when he went home.

On the way back he spied two more balloons somewhere beyond Hazebrouck and had serious thoughts of
trying to add them to his bag.   But as he approached he
saw a flight of enemy machines heading for the front and,
deeming discretion to be the better part of valour,
decided to call it a day.   Not a bad sort of a day either,
he decided, considering that he had eaten five " sausages."
So back home, to count the holes in the Albatros's
wings.

Röth was lucky, " lousy with luck," as some of the
British war birds who fought against him would have
said, for when he came down he discovered a hole through
the floor of his cockpit, and the bullet that made it
must have missed him by a couple of inches.

Röth's five balloons in one day constituted a record
for the German Flying Corps and gained him the coveted
" Pour le Mérite " order.   Afterwards he seems to
have improved his marksmanship, for he finished the
war with nine enemy machines to his credit as well as
his seventeen balloons.

All of which goes to show that practice can make
perfect.

CHAPTER VII

ODD JOBS

OF the experiences chronicled in the books written by
aviators, the greater portion deal with fights in the air.
We have also some lively accounts of bombing raids, and
occasionally we catch glimpses of the valuable though
less exciting—at least from the reader's point of view—
work of long distance reconnaissance and photography.
But very little has as yet been said about the various
odd jobs that pilots were called upon to perform, especially at the beginning of the war when the best functions
and uses of aeroplanes had not yet been discovered.

One of these irregular jobs was the landing of spies
behind the enemy's lines. On the western front this
practice was much in favour with the French because the
circumstances assisted the spy thus set down ; he landed
in occupied territory, the inhabitants of which could be
trusted to shelter and aid him.

The Germans naturally did not copy the French
example because they would have been forced to land
their spies in a hostile country where every man's hand
would have been against them. But both sides favoured
the practice in the East where agents of Turkish, Arab,
Greek or Armenian nationality could easily mix with the
heterogeneous population in their fields of action.
For obvious reasons, however, few of the pilots who took
part in such work have recorded their experiences.

But communication with besieged towns was found to be a job that naturally fell within the province of the aeroplane. In pre-flying days this dangerous work was done by volunteers who crept past the enemy's lines of investment to worm a secret way into the beleaguered city or fortress, but the invention of aircraft has now rendered it possible for a pilot to sail above the guns of the besieging forces and drop down to safety inside the defences. As however the conditions of modern warfare tend to the abolition of individual sieges (though the group of the Central Powers formed one vast besieged camp during the recent war), the experiences of Adalar Taussig, a Hungarian pilot in the service of the Dual Monarchy, are worth recording.

The siege of Przemysl by the Russians reads like a page of past history. When the Russian autumn offensive of 1914 swept through eastern Galicia and even threatened the safety of the Austro-Hungarian Empire, the garrison holding the fortress of Przemysl repulsed all attacks. The invading Russians had no alternative but to enclose Przemysl within regular siege lines, harassing the defenders until famine and exhaustion forced them to capitulate.

Przemysl held out till April, 1915, and undoubtedly the defenders did much to weaken the force of the Russian forward movement by holding up a large number of troops for many months, so that they perhaps helped to pave the way for the great German summer offensive of 1915, which resulted in the capture of Warsaw and Brest-Litowsk.

During the last week of September, 1914, the Austrian General Staff decided that they must get into communication with the beleaguered garrison as quickly as possible.

1. Oswald Boelcke, father of the German Jastas and victor in 40 combats. Died for the Fatherland, 28 October 1916.

Leutnant Immelmann an seinem Fokker-Flugzeug

2. *(Above)* Max Immelmann. He and Boelcke were the first two airmen to win the coveted Ordre Pour Le Mérite. Died in action 17 June 1916. **3.** *(Left)* Oberleutnant Stefan Kirmaier, commanded Jasta 2 after Boelcke's death and was himself killed in action on 22 November 1916.

4. *(Above left)* The Red Knight, Baron Manfred von Richthofen. Learnt his trade under Boelcke and went on to become the German ace of aces with 80 victories before his own death on 21 April 1918.

5. *(Above right)* Brother Lothar von Richthofen, gained 40 victories during WW1. Died in a plane crash 4 July 1922.

6. *(Left)* Otto Kissenberth was one of a handful of successful German fighter pilots who wore glasses, scoring 20 victories. Died in a climbing accident in the Bavarian Alps, 2 August 1919.

7. *(Right)* Another famous ace who flew with Richthofen was Kurt Wolff. He downed 33 Allied opponents before falling himself on 15 September 1917, to a Naval Triplane pilot. He was flying a Fokker Triplane when he died.

8. *(Below)* Eduard Ritter von Schleich – the Black Knight – (left) with Fritz Ritter von Röth, the successful balloon buster. Röth claimed 20 balloons in his score of 28 victories. Röth committed suicide on New Year's Eve 1918.

9. *(Above left)* Another balloon ace was Heinrich Gontermann. He totalled 18 balloons in his score of 39. Died in a Triplane crash, 30 October 1917.

10. *(Above right)* One more of von Richthofen's students, Karl Schafer, scored 30 victories before falling to the guns of a FE2b near Ypres, on 5 June 1917.

11. *(Left)* Maximilian von Cossel, with his pilot Rudolf Windisch, were a crew with FFA 62 in 1916, on the Russian Front. On 2 October von Cossel was landed behind the enemy lines where he blew up the Kowno-Brody rail line, and was picked up by Windisch the next day. Windisch later became a 22-victory ace but was lost on 27 May 1918 over the French lines.

12. *(Below)* Rudolph von Eschwege was credited with 20 victories on the Macedonian Front, and was known as the Eagle of the Aegean. His 20th victory was in fact a decoy balloon which was exploded when he attacked it on 22 November 1917, killing the 22-year-old ace.

13. *(Top right)* The Black Knight von Schleich survived the war with 35 victories and the Pour le Mérite, serving in the new Luftwaffe in Spain and WW2.

14. *(Middle right)* Hans Adam flew as observer to von Schleich in 1916 when they were a crew with FFA 2b. Later becoming a pilot himself, he gained 21 victories before his death in combat on 15 November 1917.

15. *(Bottom right)* Adolf Ritter von Tutschek, another high-scoring ace – 27 victories but he was to die in combat on 15 March 1918 as commander of JGII.

This page:
16. *(Top left)* Rudolf Berthold – the Iron Knight – had 44 official victories at the war's end, but was murdered by German revolutionaries on 15 March 1920.

17. *(Middle left)* At one time von Riththofen's nearest rival, Werner Voss excelled as a fighter pilot, gaining 48 victories. However, he died fighting a lone duel with seven SE5s of 56 Squadron on 23 September 1917.

18. *(Bottom left)* Ernst Udet, second highest scoring ace of the German Air Service in WW1, with 62 kills. A famous mid-war pilot too, he could not cope with the intrigues of the new Luftwaffe and committed suicide on 17 November 1941.

Opposite page:
19. *(Top)* Herman Göring, a 22-victory ace in WW1, and the last commander of JGI in 1918. Later became the infamous Reichsmarschall under Hitler, and commander of the Luftwaffe. Committed suicide 16 October 1946.

20. *(Left)* Alfred Keller, Pour le Mérite winner for many bombing raids, including some against Paris. Became a Generaloberst in the Luftwaffe in WW2; died in 1974.

21. *(Right)* Kapitanleutnant Horst Treusch von Buttlar-Brandenfels won his Pour le Mérite as an airship commander, flying 19 Zeppelin sorties against England. He survived the war to serve in the new Luftwaffe.

22. *(Above left)* Hermann Kohl, yet another successful bombing pilot who won the Pour le Mérite in WW1. In April 1928 he was part of a three-man crew to fly the Atlantic east to west in 36½ hours, to receive a hero's welcome in New York and Washington.

23. *(Above right)* Peter Rieper was the only balloon observer to receive the Pour le Mérite in WW1. On one occasion he was saved from enemy air attack by non other than Max Immelmann. He was finally wounded on 3 June 1918, then broke a leg when he parachuted to the ground.

24. *(Left)* Leo Leonhardy, bomber pilot with BG6, won the Pour le Mérite in 1918 for his 83 bombing raids. He died in 1928.

Mindful perhaps of Gambetta's achievement in the siege of Paris,[1] they resolved to utilise the progress of science to further their aims. The airman entrusted with the job had no easy task ; aeroplanes were still in an early stage of development, while the weather was abominable and the Russian artillery was reported to be most efficient. Worst of all, there was no proper landing ground within the narrow dimensions of the besieged fortress. So great, in fact, were the risks that no airman could be detailed to undertake the trip, for which pilots were invited to volunteer.

Taussig and another officer named Fessl stepped forward, and as neither would give way to the other, the ultimate choice in Taussig's favour was determined by lot. 1 October was the day fixed for his flight, and he was given to understand that he must start off on that

---

[1] During the siege of Paris in 1870 the defenders endeavoured to maintain contact with their civil and military authorities in unoccupied territory by means of balloons. They could, of course, only do so at irregular intervals as they were dependent on the caprices of the wind, but the total number of balloons that ascended from Paris was no less than sixty-four, the first starting on 23 September, 1870, and the last on 28 January, 1871. The politician, Gambetta, effected his escape from Paris on 7 October in a balloon named the *Armand-Barbès* and arrived safely at Tours, where he took over the joint offices of Minister of War and Minister of the Interior. The energy he threw into his work did much to prolong the French resistance.

Of the sixty-four balloons two were never heard of again ; in all probability they were blown out to sea. All balloons were naturally fired on by the besieging Germans, with little effect ; at any rate none were brought down directly by anti-aircraft guns, although several were forced to descend in territory in German occupation.

Perhaps the most remarkable trip of the series was that undertaken by the *Ville d'Orléans* which descended at Oslo after a fifteen hours' flight, the greater part of which must have taken place over the North Sea.

Those interested in the early feats of aeronautics will find interesting reading matter in a pamphlet entitled *Les Ballons de Siège de Paris*, compiled by the brothers Tissandier, who were well-known aeronauts of the period. This pamphlet contains accounts of all the balloon flights undertaken from Paris during the siege.

day, no matter what weather conditions prevailed.   As
passenger he took a staff officer.

Low clouds veiled the sun when 1 October dawned, while
a strong headwind drove pelting rain into the faces of
pilot and passenger as they were assisted into the machine.

They climbed to 4,000 feet in the hope of rising above
the storm, then to 5,000 but in vain, and finally they were
forced down to 2,500.   They had hoped that the heavy
rainstorms would veil their passage from the enemy,
but over Bubiecko, some twenty-five miles from their
destination they were sighted by a Russian observation
post.   Taussig pulled his stick and hastily climbed to
5,000 again to avoid the attentions of the Archies.

Through the driven rain he made out the outlines of a
large town which he recognised as Przemysl and knew
that he had reached the most perilous part of his trip.
Circling over the fortress, he studied the map with which
he was provided and tried to ascertain where his suggested
landing-ground might be.   He saw several spaces that
might or might not be it, but they all looked very small
and unsuitable.

For some little while he hovered over the town, but
as the visibility was too poor for him to pick his landing-
ground with any certainty, he made up his mind to
drop down to the open space that seemed most promising.
He descended in a steep spiral, under a frantic bombardment from the Russian Archies which had never ceased
their activities from the moment they sighted his machine.

But he made a good landing on a small field intersected
by a military railway and, marvellous to relate, found his
bus undamaged by shot or shell.   Its wings were, however, very sodden and heavy with the weight of the rain
through which he had flown.

The letters and newspapers he brought with him were eagerly devoured by the besieged garrison, while the staff officer hastened off to the commander of the fortress with his despatches.

For five days Taussig rested while his wings dried and the machine underwent some minor repairs. When he prepared to start off again he was overwhelmed by requests from officers and men of the garrison to carry letters to their relations. Eventually his post-bag contained about 1,500 missives, and, even when he was in the cockpit and about to start, men came running up and offered large sums to the Red Cross Fund if he would be their postman.

The Russians guessed that he had no intention of remaining in Przemysl and kept a keen look-out for the commencement of his return journey. As soon as they saw him rise into the air, the Archies opened fire.

Taussig spiralled and circled and described figures of eight to dodge the storm of lead ; it took him a strenuous half-hour to gain a safe height. Before he was out of range, shells burst all around him, but none touched the machine although the town suffered heavily from the falling missiles.

Then the elements took a hand in the game, for the machine ran into a heavy storm. Gusts and eddies continually threatened to upset it ; a thick coating of ice covered his windscreen and the glasses of his " clocks." Sharp icy spikes hurtled down on to the faces of pilot and passenger.

To add to their woes the pressure pipe, which had proved troublesome on the outward journey and been repaired in Przemysl, struck work, so that Taussig was forced to work the handpump with his frozen fingers in order to maintain his supply of " juice." He lost height and descended within range of the Russian Archies again.

All around them whizzed the bullets of the machine guns, and one pierced the cockpit and passed between the legs of his passenger. Another chipped a piece out of his stick, but by a miracle tank and engine remained untouched.

With a windscreen shot to pieces (luckily no fragments penetrated his face), and thus exposed to the fury of the icy blast, Taussig climbed to a secure height again. As if in alliance with the Russians, the wind had changed its direction that very day so that he had it against him on both journeys. But at last, after a struggle of four hours' duration, he reached his aerodrome and descended to count the number of holes in his wings.

Yet, undeterred by his experiences, Taussig was ready to start off again after a few days' rest, and when he had safely done the trip each way a second time he was nominated Przemysl's regular postman. He maintained correspondence between the besieged garrison and the General Staff until lack of food and munitions forced a capitulation in April, 1915.

During the autumn of 1914 and the early days of the following year the German forces in occupation of the Belgian coast had good cause to dread the attentions of the British fleet. At any hour of the day black smudges of smoke on the horizon might reveal the presence of enemy warships ; coast defence batteries were therefore installed, and it seemed quite natural to call upon the winged scouts of the air to co-operate with them. At certain stations groups of seaplanes were kept ready for action at any moment of the day or night.

Then, growing bolder, the war birds went out in search

of the enemy. Regular patrols were instituted to scour the Channel and give timely warning of any impending attack.

One day a certain lieutenant-commander started off to do his usual round. The warm sun, cloudless sky and unrippled surface of the sea led him to deduce a peaceful joy-ride as the bombarding squadrons generally made their raids on cloudy or rainy days when poor visibility rendered them difficult targets for the shore batteries.

" You never know your luck, though," remarked his observer as the two men adjusted themselves in their seats. They took a final glance at their bombs ; the petty officer in charge of their shed gave the signal and the seaplane was just about to glide off when a bluejacket came hurrying up with a message.

A patrol boat had sighted a British squadron out at sea. All seaplanes were to muster to attack it, carrying double loads of bombs.

The observers grinned their delight, but the pilots shook their heads ruefully, wondering how high they could manage to climb with the extra weight. But orders were orders, and as soon as the necessary arrangements were made, the commander led out his little flock of war birds.

As he had foreseen, it was devilish bad climbing, and several minutes elapsed before he had gained sufficient height to espy the smoke of the British warships above the horizon. He had serious thoughts of ordering his observer to throw out a few bombs to lighten their craft.

But he decided to let them remain on board, and eventually he noted with satisfaction that the indicator of his altimeter was approaching 2,500 feet, the minimum height for a swoop on the enemy. At last funnels, superstructures, barbettes and the grey hulls came clearly into view.

The observer tapped his pilot's shoulder and pointed to a bottle he held in his hand. " Like a drink ? " he enquired, though he knew that the roar of the engine must drown his words. Then, recollecting that the other could not take his hands from the controls, he thrust the neck of the bottle towards his mouth.

" Damn you, you blighter ! " swore the pilot, " why the hell did you bring that along when you knew that every extra ounce counts against us ! "

The observer grinned, though he could only guess the meaning of the reply, and took a long pull at the liquid.

The altimeter remained obstinately in the neighbourhood of 2,200 feet ; the extra load seemed to precede all possibility of reaching the required 2,500. " Oh, well, I shall just have to chance it," muttered the pilot.

They were now near enough to count the ships. There were twelve of them, steaming in close formation. Behind them, at some little interval, another. . . .

" The thirteenth !   Unlucky beggar !   He's for it this time," swore the pilot, but even as he pushed the stick down to swoop, he saw that number thirteen was the biggest of the lot.   A battleship of the latest pattern and heavily armoured his naval eye made her out to be.

" No good wasting our eggs on her," he muttered, kicking the rudder-bar savagely.   " Oh, hell ! "

" Oh, hell ! " ejaculated his observer. Two minds with but a single thought. It was sheer midsummer madness to attack a baker's dozen of British warships.

A deep report told the observer that the enemy was ready for him, and, looking down, he saw that the outlines of one of the ships were wreathed in smoke.

Another deafening discharge followed—and yet another. He glanced upward and saw the sky filled with fleecy white cloudlets. The enemy was using shrapnel.

" Miles too high," he reflected, and then the machine began to rock violently.

A gaping rent appeared in the canvas of the right upper wing, and, as far as he could see, its aileron was smashed to bits. Then, somewhat to his surprise, the machine righted herself and proceeded on her way as if untouched.

" Why doesn't that blithering idiot drop his eggs and give me a chance to get away alive," muttered the pilot. The next moment his observer leant over and held up two fingers of his right hand.

" Two only ? Hurry up and get rid of the rest so that we can get home while she's holding together," yelled the pilot as he put his machine into a right turn so as to manoeuvre into position. A deafening roar proclaimed that another shell had burst in front of him.

It came so near that he was quite surprised to find he still had a propeller. But beyond a tempestuous rocking for a couple of agonising seconds nothing happened. He cut off his engine in order to gain the silence needed for a quick interchange of words with his observer.

" How many bombs left ? " he enquired.

" None. Get home, old man."

The pilot could not understand, but he took his observer's word for it. The explanation could follow later. He turned and headed for the coast.

Looking backward, the observer saw that the British warships were steering a westward course. He tapped his pilot's shoulder and showed him the retreating enemy.

The pilot cut off his engine again.

" I dropped them all and got two direct hits," chuckled the observer.

The pilot then realised that he had misinterpreted the signal of the two outstretched fingers.

" Give us a drink," he said.

The observer put the bottle to his mouth for him, but when he removed it and tried to take some refreshment himself, he found it empty.

" Dirty dog ! " he said, tossing the bottle overboard.

" What happened to the other machines ? " asked the pilot, ignoring the reproach.

" Couldn't manage it with double weight. Alone we did the deed."

" I wonder if we'll get home to swank about it," mused the pilot, and somehow or other he did.

Bombing is of course part of the regular work of a flying corps, but although a special type of machine was evolved, with improved arrangements for laying the eggs, the war birds on both sides who were engaged in this occupation could seldom judge accurately the extent of the damage they did. As the proverb says, appearances are deceptive. Man's eye and his camera are both but inaccurate recorders of events taking place at a great distance below them.

These facts once induced a pilot and an observer on the eastern front to perform an odd job that proved most effective in its results.

They had been transferred from the west in the summer of 1916 to serve the hard-pressed armies endeavouring to stay the course of General Brussiloff's offensive, and their aerodrome was situated near Sokal, on the borders of Galicia and Volhynia. On their first long distance reconnaissance they ascertained that the Russian troops opposing their trenches were dependent for munitions and supplies on a single railway line, a hundred miles long, that connected the fortress of Rovno with Brody railhead. German spies reported that the few available roads were in bad condition and that the Russians were short of motor transport, so that the issue of victory or defeat was largely dependent on the maintenance of the railway.

Windisch, the pilot, therefore received orders that he must do his best to destroy this railway line, and, knowing from previous experience the difficulty of achieving success by dropping bombs from the air, he suggested that they should try to land somewhere in enemy territory and blow up the line. Von Cossel, his observer, was delighted with the idea.

They discussed the risks that would have to be taken. In landing on unknown ground they might put the machine out of action by hitting a tree-stump or running into a concealed ditch, in which case they would be stranded in the midst of a hostile population with the prospect of some rough handling before they were marched off to a prison camp, while it was quite likely that they might even be lynched.

But they decided to risk it and broached the idea to their commanding officer, who gave them a free hand. After several reconnaissances they came to the conclusion that the most suitable spot for such a landing was a stubble field about sixty miles behind the Russian lines, which was surrounded by woods on three sides so that they could come down fairly discreetly.

This field was six or seven miles from the railway, which meant that their machine was unlikely to be seen by the patrols guarding the line, although the long tramp to the scene of action involved them in other risks.

Their next procedure was to photograph all the intervening country between the proposed landing-place and the railway ; from their photos they were able to make a serviceable large-scale map. Then they flew over the ground again until they had familiarised themselves with every landmark. But afterwards a difficulty cropped up which had not occurred to them when they first devised their scheme. Neither of them knew anything about mining operations.

A kindly sapper colonel who saw the possibilities of their idea took them under his wing, and for the next week they received daily instruction from him in some woods behind the German lines. When he had put them through their paces sufficiently, they dismantled their Roland of all superfluous gear and loaded it up with the necessary explosives and tools.

It was still dark when their batman woke them. After a hearty breakfast prepared by a long-suffering and good-natured cook they put on their waders and tramped through the mud of a Polish village to the aerodrome where a sergeant and a squad of mechanics awaited them. Their Roland was ready, and after a last look round to see if there was any superfluity they could discard (they were loaded up to the full extent of their carrying capacity) they tested the motor.

Several trial runs were necessary before the Roland took off, and in the air Windisch found considerable difficulty in climbing the necessary height to pass the Russian lines. They were in fact barely 3,000 feet up when they crossed the front trenches and dared not cut their engine, but the darkness hid them well, and their nocturnal flight aroused no protests from Archie.

On they sped through the darkness. The country below them was thickly wooded so that the prospects of surviving a forced landing if the Roland failed to carry her load were not very bright. But the machine behaved nobly, and, as they had anticipated, dawn found them at their destination. The sun was just beginning to pierce the autumn mists as Windisch throttled his engine and glided down to make a perfect landing at the edge of the wood.

They alighted and quickly unloaded their dangerous cargo, which they carried into the wood. Then they put the Roland about; Windisch climbed in and took off. From his cover amid the trees von Cossel watched his departing comrade swerve to avoid a peasant's cart.

The horse bolted, with a terrified moujik tugging frantically at the reins. An unexpected and most unwelcome eyewitness of their arrival, thought von Cossel, and his next hour was rendered uncomfortable by visions of Cossacks patrolling the countryside in search of him. He could only hope that the peasant had not seen the black Maltese crosses on his pilot's wings.

As a matter of fact the *moujik* was too occupied with the primary business of regaining control over his scared steed to bother about the emblems painted on the Roland's wings and fuselage. If he had seen the Maltese crosses he would not have known their significance, for to him all aeroplanes, Russian or German, were inventions of the devil, and the less he had to do with them, the better for his soul's salvation. As he drove on to his destination after he had mastered the frightened animal, he muttered prayers.

Von Cossel found a dry spot in the depths of the marshy wood, extracted some provisions from his rücksack and enjoyed a second breakfast. Hours rolled by, but no one came to disturb him in his sylvan fastness.

About four in the afternoon he prepared to depart. For several days he had devoted much attention to the nature of the clothing he should wear on this expedition, and finally he had hit upon an ingenious compromise, by which he could enter a village, if need be, without attracting attention, while at the same time he was safe from the risk of being treated as a spy if he happened to fall into the hands of the Russian soldiery.

He was in uniform, and yet in civilian garb. The high waders and fur coat he wore were part of his regular equipment, but they did not differ greatly from the boots and coats worn by the Volhynian peasants. The buttons, which were the only distinctive badges of his uniform on the coat he smeared over with dirt to render them less conspicuous, and by pulling the brim of his cap forward he was able to mask to some extent the cockade in the middle of its front that would have proclaimed him a member of the German army.[1] The insignia that proclaimed his military status were thus concealed from all but the closest scrutiny, but no one could assert that he had removed them.

The explosives he placed in his rücksack, which he slung on his back, along with another package containing his electric igniter. Various implements and tools were concealed in his pockets, and a stick, cut from a dead branch, completed his make-up. As he trudged along, bending beneath his heavy load, there was no reason why

---

[1] By the laws of war a soldier may adopt what methods he pleases to gain information or perform a mission behind the enemy's lines, provided that he wears his regular uniform. If he is captured in the enemy's uniform or civilian garb, he is liable to be shot as a spy.

casual passers-by should see in him anything but a Jewish pedlar tramping from village to village on his usual rounds.

When he reached the muddy highroad, a familiar droning in the air made him look up. Two aeroplanes, marked with the German Maltese cross, were sailing overhead, and he smiled, for he knew that they were on their way to create a diversion for him by bombing a station farther up the line and so drawing the attention of all the railway patrols from the spot where he proposed to operate.

He passed children herding the beasts in the fields and peasants gathering in the bean harvest, but no one took any notice of him. Emboldened, he passed through a village to save himself the extra trudge of a detour and attracted no attention except from a couple of peasants who spat as he plodded by them. The Jew, he reflected, was not over-popular in Russia.

Later he met a group of soldiers, who took as little notice of him as the peasants had done.

He was footsore when he reached the railway, and his back ached from the heavy weights he carried, so that he was glad to find a field strewn with haycocks where he could rest in a sheltered refuge. There he waited till darkness fell.

At last he emerged from the warm hay and slunk off to the railway. He peered through the gloom, but there was no sign of any patrol. He extracted his charges and wedged them under the sleepers.

Several times he was interrupted by the passing of the trains laden with munitions and other supplies for the front. As soon as ever he heard the distant rumbling he had to leave his work and seek safety in the long grass at the side of the line, but at last he had fixed all the charges in position. Then he connected them with the ends of his two long coils of cable, which he dragged with him through the long grass. A hundred yards away from the line he halted and dug a hole in the earth large enough for him to sit in comfort and manipulate his electrical igniting apparatus.

A patrol came marching along the side of the line, but found nothing amiss and passed on. Von Cossel ate his supper and whiled away the time by counting the number of trains that used the line in an hour. He regretted that he had to let them pass, but he was working to a timetable which did not allow him to perform the final act before midnight.

Another patrol passed, but it was as unsuspicious as its predecessor. The night grew chilly ; there was a nip of frost in the air that made him want to get up and run about to restore circulation in his limbs. Unable to take the risk, he made shift with a long swig from his flask.

Midnight at last. The next train would run into a whole heap of trouble if things went according to plan, and he thanked heaven that there was no moon.

Every minute seemed a century, but at last a distant rumbling greeted his ears. He crawled out of his hiding-place and peered down the line.

Fiery eyes ... growing ever greater in the darkness ... the headlights of the engine dragging a long train to the railhead at Brody ... munitions for Brussiloff's armies.

Von Cossel fixed his eyes on a telegraph pole that reared its black length above the skyline. The right moment would occur when it was reddened with the engine's glare. With an eager finger on the switch he waited.

The fiery eyes grew larger and larger . . . like the eyes of some primeval monster escaped from a lonely forest in the depths of the Russian wilderness, von Cossel thought, . . . a monster that was raging forth to devour the world.

His heart beat as he saw the telegraph pole gleam red. He pressed the switch : the electric circuit was completed.

A blinding flash seared his eyes, and a mighty roar shook the earth.

Through a red mist he saw the engine rear up on its back wheels like some grotesque steed ; then it plunged sideways, pulling wagon after wagon in its wake.

Von Cossel gave one swift glance at the scene of destruction. Then he started to draw in the two lengths of cable that had carried the deadly current ; he dared not leave them for fear they should betray the line of his flight to the patrols that were bound to search for him.

It seemed an infinity before he had gathered them in, but at last they were wound up. He pushed them into some long grass and slunk away into the darkness.

Down the railway lines came armed men . . . running at top speed . . . while a shrill syren shrieked the alarm signal from the nearest blockhouse. Another, more distant, took it up . . . and yet another echoed it faintly.

Clouds covered the stars ; without warning heavy rain began to fall. Von Cossel swore as his feet sank heavily into the marshy fields. A chill shiver went down his back . . . what if a sudden storm should prevent Windisch from keeping his appointment !

" I'll come if it rains or blows or snows," the pilot had vowed, and von Cossel knew that he would do his utmost to keep his word. But Roland two-seaters were topheavy machines—few pilots liked them—and theirs had shown herself very reluctant to start that morning. What would happen if she broke down *en route* ?

The going was heavy ; von Cossel's feet sank at every step. " Mustn't keep old Windisch waiting if he turns up on time," he decided and made for the high road where he could march at a quicker pace.

To save time he took the short cut through the village he had passed in the morning. It would have been more prudent to take the longer way round through the fields, but this time Fortune favoured the bold. All its inhabitants were abed save a nightwatchman who growled a curse as he passed. Another of those damned Jews, thought the worthy constable, and spat fervently.

Von Cossel had to take to the fields again for the last stage of his journey. Once more the boggy soil gripped his feet at each step, while a stitch in his side made every breath painful. An airman's duties may be strenuous, but they are not the best of training for a long cross-country journey on a rainy night.

But if his wind was deficient, his eyes were sound, for he picked his way unerringly through the dark night to the field where Windisch had landed him that morning. At its verge he hesitated for a second, wondering whether the peasant who turned up so inconveniently that morning might have reported the presence of the aeroplane to the authorities, in which case there would be Russian soldiers waiting for its return. For a moment he fancied he saw a uniformed figure lurking, but when he plucked up heart to approach he saw that it was only a stunted tree.

Then his trained ear caught the welcome music of an engine's drone. He made a last investigation of the trees at the edge of the field to see if the sound in the air had attracted from their hiding-places any concealed Cossacks. No . . . the coast was clear ; von Cossel extracted from his pocket the electric lamp that was to give his pilot the signal that it was safe for him to land.

Windisch throttled his engine and glided down. The Roland taxied to the edge of the wood . . . a perfect landing . . . almost identical to an inch with the one he had made that morning. The two friends clasped hands.

" I brought some grub along, old man, in case you were hungry, and there are your letters and the latest newspaper for you to read on the way home, so what more do you want ? Jump in. Oh, by the way, there's a hell of a mess on the line."

The land of Sinai is known to all readers of the Scriptures as a wilderness, and in Exodus we are told that the children of Israel murmured against Moses for bringing them there. They pointed out in plain unvarnished language that in Egypt there were fleshpots, the contents of which would be very welcome to hungry men.

Moses had evidently forgotten to include an Army Service Corps in his host, so that it eventually required a convenient miracle to put his commissariat on a satisfactory basis and appease the grumblers. But if Moses could have revisited Sinai in the spring of 1917 he would have discovered Brother Aaron's rod to be a back number in the miracle-working line.

Moses would have gaped with amazement at the railway line that the Royal Engineers had built from Kantara on the farther side of the Suez canal to El Arish on the north-east coast of the Sinai peninsula, and he would have stared perhaps even longer at the aqueduct running alongside of it, which obviated any necessity for striking rocks with rods. Truly these English had found a fine way of making the desert flow with milk and honey.

The railway and the aqueduct catered to the needs of the British troops fighting on a front that ran from Gaza to Beersheba. The German-Turkish forces defending Palestine might have agreed with Moses that the engineering feat of their foemen was a miracle of modern science, but they would have had no hesitation in proclaiming it a most inconvenient miracle, because it made possible the employment of much larger forces against them than they had reckoned for. The only way to counteract the trouble, they decided, was by another miracle of modern science, a miracle of a somewhat more explosive nature.

Consequently a certain Lieutenant Falke, a German observer in the Staffel attached to the Turkish forces, received orders to lame the efficiency of his opponents by putting the railway and aqueduct out of action.

By long distance reconnaissances he established the fact that the line was guarded by a series of blockhouses placed at intervals of roughly twelve miles apart. The garrisons of these blockhouses were supposed to patrol the intervening spaces, but Falke came to the conclusion that they were numerically insufficient to keep the whole length of the railway and aqueduct under constant supervision.

There were times, he ascertained, when not a living soul was to be seen along certain stretches, so that it would be quite feasible for the occupants of an aeroplane to land and attack the line and aqueduct with explosives provided that :

(1) A suitable landing place could be found where the aeroplane might take off in any direction.

(2) That the aforesaid landing place was a sufficient distance away from a railway station.

(3) That it lay at a spot where the railway line and aqueduct were in close proximity, so that the wreckers would have no long journeys between the two objectives.

(4) That it was not more than 100 miles behind the British lines, otherwise the aeroplane could not carry sufficient benzin to make detours on the outward or homeward journey if hostile aircraft were encountered.

Further reconnaissances located three such suitable landing places, the merits of which seemed equal. Finally it was resolved to leave the final choice to the last-moment decision of the pilot and observer, who would naturally be influenced by fortuitous circumstances such as the activities of the patrols, the amount of traffic on the line and the movements of any eventual caravan along the regular route, which was generally close to the railway line.

The first attempt was made on 19 April, 1917, a day on which the weather favoured the enterprise because clouds hanging as low as 3,000 feet enabled the two-seater piloted by Lieutenant Felmy to fly over the British lines unnoticed. When they had covered about fifty miles, they found these clouds growing thinner.

At about seven o'clock in the morning their Rumpler glided down to 1,500 feet, from which height its pilot and observer surveyed the possibilities of Landing-ground number two. No British patrols were to be seen, and there was no traffic on the caravan route ; as far as human agencies were concerned, there was nothing to prevent them landing.

Everything depended on the pilot's skill in effecting
a good landing. If the Rumpler sustained any damage
that could not be speedily repaired on the spot, Falke
and Felmy knew that they would never see Gaza aerodrome
again, for it was impossible for them to make their way
back on foot through the sandy wastes. In case of a
break-down the best that could befall them was a
British prison-camp for the rest of the war, but if they
were unlucky enough to fall into the hands of
marauding Bedouins, their future prospects did not bear
contemplation.

But the landing came off beautifully. Its only
spectators were three or four jackals that scurried away
at the sight of the monstrous bird ; when they had
vanished over the rise of a sand dune, everything was as
quiet as they could have wished, except for the faint
rumble of a distant train.

But on their previous reconnaissances they had made
out a rough and ready time-table of the traffic on the line,
and so they knew that this train was due to stop at a
station before it steamed past their landing-ground.
In all probability they could therefore reckon on a
minimum of half an hour in which to do their job. Felmy
put his machine about and prepared for a quick start, while
Falke, carrying his explosives in a rücksack on his back,
trudged off through the sand, using his spade as a walking
stick.

Two hundred paces brought him to the aqueduct,
the pipes of which were carried on the top of a low mud
embankment. About fifty yards beyond it were the
double rows of telephone and telegraph lines that flanked
the railway.

Falke dug a hole under the embankment and laid his

charge. It was an easy job, taking only five minutes by his watch, but he perspired freely over it. When he had finished, he went on to the railway to lay another charge under the sleepers. Having put his machine in order, Felmy came along to help him by placing a third charge under the wires.

They found it harder work, for the British engineers had laid their sleepers truly and well, but with much perspiration they excavated the space for two charges. The next job was to ignite the safety fuses ; each man lit a cigar and puffed at it until its end glowed red.

But the fuses were obstinate ; evidently they did not like the aroma of cigars. The men tried cigarettes, which proved equally useless. But at last rags soaked in petrol did the trick ; the ends of the fuses were ignited, and the wreckers ran for dear life to their Rumpler. Falke looked at his watch, and noted that it had taken them twenty-five minutes to lay the three charges and ignite the fuses.

They had barely reached the Rumpler before two loud explosions set their ears tingling. Mouths, eyes and nostrils were choked with the gritty dust that arose in clouds from the scene of the havoc. A few seconds later a third detonation followed.

As no foeman was in sight, the two men left the machine to survey their work.

They discovered that the charges under the railway line had failed to act ; the fuse had burnt out without firing the charge. But the stumps of what only a few moments ago were long poles showed that both the telegraph and telephone were out of action. Tommy Atkins would be put to some inconvenience, they reflected.

But a bitter disappointment awaited them when they examined the aqueduct. The baked mud in which the pipes were embedded was holed, but the pipes themselves remained intact. They still carried the life-giving fluid to the thirsty troops in Palestine.

The two men held a hurried conversation and decided to try their luck again as they still had an emergency charge left, and no patrols were in sight. They debated whether they should attack the aqueduct or the railway.

Under the broiling sun water is life ; they knew that the Tommies could not fight without water. Besides, the aqueduct was easier to undermine quickly, and the train might be due any moment.

" The aqueduct then," said Falke, and just as he spoke a distant whistle told him that the train was leaving the station. Their time was numbered by minutes.

Quick work with the spades . . . then with eager fumbling hands they placed the charge in position and ignited the fuse. Once more they scurried to their Rumpler.

They were just in time. As the cloud of smoke and dust rose up into the air with a terrific din, something heavy hurtled after them and dropped in the sand a few yards away from the Rumpler. They recognised it as a section of the waterpipe and, with the satisfaction that follows a job well done, they hurled themselves into the machine, which left the ground just as the train pulled up a hundred yards away. An hour later they landed on their aerodrome at Gaza.

But away in the desert, some eighty miles behind the British trenches, the precious water spurted out to form a muddy pool in the sand.

The engineers with the British army of Palestine were, however, prompt in action, and in due course a Turkish Intelligence agent made his way to Gaza and reported that both the telephone and aqueduct were in working order again. Falke and Felmy were instructed to make another attempt to destroy them.

They knew that the difficulties of their task would be more than doubled because the British would tighten up their watch on the lines of communication, but they swore to do their best. This time they chose a landing-place about half a mile distant from the former one, because they found that the railway and aqueduct were closer together there. An engineer officer supplied them with a friction fuse that would ignite their charges more expeditiously.

They had to postpone several starts on account of weather conditions, but on 24 May, they set off at last. It was still dark when they left the aerodrome.

Neither pilot nor observer was particularly optimistic, and they could hardly believe their eyes when on gliding down to the new landing-place they found the desert as solitary and undisturbed as on the first occasion. Once again Falke went off with rücksack and spade on his errand of destruction.

He now knew his job, and his knowledge made for speed.

With Felmy's aid he fixed the charges for the railway, poles and aqueduct within the short space of seven minutes. They were just about to ignite their fuses when they caught sight of two figures on some rising ground about a mile away. A moment later they ascertained them to be a couple of horsemen, who were heading for their machine at full gallop.

There was not a moment to be lost. Felmy manipulated the fuse for the charge under the poles, while Falke attended to the one that was to destroy the sleepers. Then both men raced for the aqueduct.

But even as they bent down to ignite the fuse, shots rang out over their heads. Looking up, Falke saw three men, who had opened fire on them at 200 yards, while at least a dozen others were hastening to join in the fray.

Falke judged the enemy to be close enough to cut him off from the aeroplane. Escape seemed impossible, but he resolved to complete his work of destruction before surrendering. Luckily the fuse ignited almost at once.

" Come on ! " yelled Felmy.

They began to run. They were running for their lives from the explosion that was bound to occur in a few seconds, but they ran in the direction of their aeroplane and, marvellous to relate, they reached it before their foemen, who had halted to shoot in the hope of killing them before they put the final touches to their work.

Consequently Falke and Felmy won the race to the Rumpler, which they reached through a shower of bullets. Lead whistled over their heads as they climbed into their seats, but while Felmy taxied Falke swung his machine-gun on to the snipers, who promptly took cover.

By a miracle both pilot and observer were unhurt, by another no bullet found a vital spot in the Rumpler. Just as their wheels left the ground a series of detonations occurred.

All three fuses did their duty, and when Falke looked back he saw a great hole in the railroad, while a heavy jet of water spurted out on to the sands of the desert. Although he was out of range, he could not resist the temptation of saying good-bye to Tommy with a final burst from his machine gun.

Anyone who has read a book on flying by some well-known instructor will note the oft-repeated command to the novice to learn everything there is to be learnt about his engine and the various parts of his bus. At the aerodrome the beginner will hear the same precept by word of mouth.

If he takes it to heart, the knowledge he acquires will stand him in good stead one day, for, however perfect may be his touch on the controls, the man who leaves the care of his machine entirely to his mechanics is more than likely to find himself in an awkward plight sooner or later. Not that I mean to cast any aspersions on the mechanic fraternity, most of whom are stout enough fellows, but some day or other the pilot has to make a forced landing that involves minor damages. If he knows what to do, he is all right ; if not, he can only wait and swear till help arrives. In fact, knowledge is power.

The truth of this proverb came home to a Staffel of German pilots that were sent to help the Turkish forces in Mesopotamia. Their long journey began in the comfortable trains of Central Europe ; then, after leaving Constantinople, they changed into the less comfortable rolling-stock of Asia, which took them, if I remember rightly, as far as the railhead of Aleppo. There they were hoisted with their belongings into ox-wagons which jolted them for several days along roads knee-deep in mud until they reached the highest navigable point of the Euphrates.

There they embarked on rafts which conveyed them to Baghdad, and with every day of the journey the little band of pilots grew more and more conscious of the imperative need to make the most of the resources they had brought with them, for if they had to depend upon spare parts from Germany the war would probably be over before they got them.

They were supplied with a liberal equipment for the four Parasol monoplanes that were to bomb the English forces advancing on Baghdad and the Fokker that was to shoot down the enemy's single-seaters, but when they reached their headquarters they found themselves in sorry plight, for one Parasol was lost in a storm on the Euphrates, while the other three were severely damaged.

The pilots assisted their squad of mechanics, and with heroic efforts they got the Parasols ready for action just in time to take part in the siege of Kut-el-Amara. Day after day they bombed General Townshend's beleaguered forces, while the Fokker, piloted by Captain Schüz, shot down several British aeroplanes that were attempting to drop down the supplies of which the garrison stood so sorely in need.

General Townshend capitulated, but the war in Mesopotamia still went on. Despite careful handling, wear and tear began to tell on the Parasols and the Fokker.

Captain von Aulock, the leader of the Staffel, worked day and night in Baghdad. With his mechanics he organised a park for spare parts where the machines could be repaired ; he arranged a system of transport, set up his own smithy and saddlery and commandeered a building in which he superintended the manufacture of bombs by a staff of local workmen.

Then his supplies of benzin began to run short.

He sent a detachment across miles of open country to take possession of a derelict English petroleum distillery at a little village close to the Persian frontier and manufacture the precious fuel.

His labour troubles were heart-breaking. Neither the Turks nor the Arabs showed any capacity or inclination for the work he required of them, so that he had to spend many weary hours rounding up Armenian and Persian craftsmen. He also found timely aid from some German Balts who had served in the Russian armies on the Caucasian front until they found an opportunity to desert, while among the Indian prisoners captured at Kut there were some who showed aptitude for special tasks. But everyone had to do two men's work.

Despite these heroic efforts the condition of the machines degenerated daily. On any other front they would have been scrapped long ago, but in Mesopotamia there was nothing to replace them. Captain von Aulock knew that it would take months for new aeroplanes to reach him, even if the people at home kept their promises to send them, which was extremely doubtful.

At the front the machines flew daily when no expert would have deemed them capable of getting off the ground. Somehow or other they held together in the air, when by every law of mechanics they should have gone to pieces, and the men in them did their work. But at last the day arrived when they could do no more ; the three Parasols were consigned to their last resting-place on the scrap heap, and it was only a question of days before the Fokker would have to follow them.

" If we can't get new machines from home," thought Captain von Aulock, " we shall have to make one here." So he summoned his pilots to a conference in Baghdad.

At first they were amazed and incredulous, but when they began to discuss ways and means prospects began to look a little brighter. The main essential was there— a reserve 120 h.p. Mercedes engine that they had brought with them from Germany ; moreover it was in good condition.

After some debate they resolved to model the new aeroplane on the B.E. type. The pilots had observed the habits of B.E.'s flown by their British opponents, and spoke highly of their qualities. The B.E., one and all declared, was the best possible machine for work in hot climates, though one or two modifications might be introduced that would even make for an improvement on the original model.

For struts, spars and ribs there was ample timber to be had at Baghdad wharf, and Captain von Aulock found a native carpenter who could be trusted to work under supervision of one or other of the pilots. A Turkish officer who had done a course at a European technical school volunteered to be responsible for turning out the propeller.

Their greatest difficulty lay in finding the fabric for the wings as they had used up all the material they brought with them. After several experiments they found some bales of a coarse native cotton which answered their purpose. Then they remembered that they had no varnish with which to stretch and coat the new bird's wings. Further experiments followed, and eventually they discovered a mixture of white of eggs and raki (date spirit) which served their purpose excellently.

When the machine was finished, the fuselage was somewhat shorter and the wings somewhat narrower than those of the B.E.'s from which they drew their inspiration ; these variations from the original model were purposely introduced because they thought they would make for greater speed. Every pilot in the Staffel did something to contribute to the construction of the new machine, and the knowledge that they had acquired about machines when they learnt to fly now stood them in good stead.

The cooler was taken from an English seaplane that Captain Schüz had shot down on one of the last days that he was able to fly his Fokker ; clocks and instruments came from the same source. A Russian machine gun, captured by the Turks in the Caucasus, that had found its way to Baghdad—Heaven alone knows how or why—constituted the armament. The wheels were taken from a motor-car belonging to the Turkish Military Automobile Corps.

News travels swiftly in eastern cities, and though the designers tried to keep the date of their trial flight a secret, all Baghdad turned out to see it.

I do not know whether the man who first took off in the home-made B.E. got any decoration, but I imagine he deserved one for risking his life in such a contrivance. In all probability he was as surprised as the spectators when he found himself climbing serenely up into the sky. But the new machine, which was christened the " Baghdad Baby," flew perfectly, and only a few minor alterations were necessary before it was reported fit to be despatched to the front.

Captain Schüz wondered what the English war birds thought when they saw this new and strange B.E. flying over their lines for the first time. A few days later they enlightened him in typically British fashion.

An airman flew high over the German aerodrome and

dropped a sack containing a few rusty old spare parts. Attached to it was a label, on which was written " With the compliments of the Royal Flying Corps."

Inside the sack they also found a letter which congratulated them on the flying capacity of their B.E. It also informed them that if any more spare parts were needed, the Royal Flying Corps was able to book orders. Cash on delivery.

We have related in this chapter how at various times airmen on different fronts carried out successfully the jobs of postman, miner and aircraft designer ; it therefore seems child's play for a Staffel of them to undertake the tasks that in times of peace are carried out by the vans of the butcher, the baker, the grocer, etc. In the German offensive of March, 1918, we find the airman as assistant to the commissariat department.

When the offensive had died down after pushing the enemy back for some considerable distance, a German division on the Ancre found itself in a parlous plight, being compelled to entrench hastily in exposed positions that were continually under enemy fire. No communication trenches could be dug, so that intercourse with the base was possible only by night. Under these circumstances it proved impossible to supply the division with food and munitions until a Staffel of infantry flyers was called upon to lend assistance.

Left a free hand as to how they should carry out their work, the airmen secured a number of sandbags, each of which could be packed with sixty rounds of ammunition two large loaves, two tins of preserved meat, twelve light-signals and ten packets of first aid dressings.

As each aeroplane was able to take ten such sandbags, the Staffel could count on delivering 6,000 rounds of ammunition, 200 loaves and 200 tins of meat per journey. The delivery was carried out in a way that impressed the front line man with the efficiency of the Flying Corps far more than any thrilling duels of aces in the sky, according to the admission of a pilot who took part in the work.

CHAPTER VIII

A MAN of medium height and slender build, with finely chiselled features and keen blue eyes. Face and hands as grimy as those of any mechanic, a uniform greasy with oil smears.

This is the portrait we have of Lieutenant v Eschwege, whom the Bulgarians named " The Eagle of the Ægean Sea."

He was an ugly duckling when he first began to stretch his wings, and no one thought that he would ever make a first-class flyer.

From the military academy Eschwege was gazetted to a mounted Jaeger regiment in August, 1914, just in time to take part in the war, but after six months of the trenches he decided that he wanted to be an aviator and put in a request for transference to the Flying Corps.

Like Richthofen, Eschwege felt that the massed effects of modern warfare gave him no scope to express his individuality, and we see another point of resemblance with the Red Knight in the fact that the instructors of the flying school he attended were within an inch of sending him back to his regiment as incompetent because he crashed so many machines. But his keenness induced them to persevere with him for five months, at the end of which period they passed him as competent to fly a two-seater. Perhaps one or other of them realised that

ugly ducklings sometimes grow up into noble swans—
and eagles.

For ten months Eschwege flew a two-seater employed
on long distance reconnaissance work on the western
front ; then, feeling his powers growing, he yearned for
the responsibility that falls to the lone fighter and applied
for permission to return to the flying school and undergo
the necessary instruction. His request was granted,
and in due course he was sent to the Balkan front to
join a little group of German war birds that had their
headquarters at Drama, in Greece.

It was a remote corner of the war, which the newpapers
of both parties liked to forget, for what did their readers
care about the events in far-off Macedonia when the daily
deeds of war birds in Flanders, Artois and the Champagne
gave them so much more fruitful material ? On the
western front the daring Immelmann and the gallant
Boelcke rose to fame and fell to death, while Richthofen,
the Red Knight, fascinated friend and foe alike by his
dazzling victories. Who, then, wanted to hear about a
lonely eagle by the coasts of the Ægean Sea ?

The German hero-worshippers who took their reading-
matter from the newspapers and idolised Immelmann,
Boelcke and Richthofen have probably never heard of
Eschwege, but when I look up the Balkan situation in
General Hoeppner's *Deutschlands Krieg in der Luft*,[1] an
impartial survey of aerial warfare, written with official
precision and very sparing of names (in its index I find
only three references to Richthofen and no mention of
Immelmann's name), Eschwege receives his due meed
of praise. " It was essentially owing to Lieutenant

[1] " Germany's War in the Air."

v Eschwege and the Jagdstaffel he created that we were able to hold the enemy more or less in check."

That one sentence in such a work speaks volumes.

Drama is a town of Macedonia, some seventy or eighty miles to the north-east of Salonica, and during the latter years of the war it was the headquarters of a German Staffel detailed for service on the Struma sector of the Salonica front, where Turks and Bulgarians, with some German and Austrian assistance, opposed a mixed host of English, French, Italians, Serbs and Venizelist Greeks.   In the air as on land the weight of numbers was on the side of the Entente, and for a long time five or six German aeroplanes had to contend against some forty or fifty machines of the Royal Flying Corps.

Moreover, the Balkan railways afforded such bad communications and transport that at one time Captain Heydemarck, the commander of the Drama aerodrome, received orders that his aviators must be careful to avoid accidents of any sort because it is impossible to supply them with spare parts.   It was well for the war birds of Drama that the Eagle of the Ægean Sea was an inmate of their nest.

At first the Eagle's merits escaped official recognition, for through an unhappy combination of circumstances his victories lacked the confirmation he was required to furnish before he could have them credited to him.

One English opponent he forced to land behind the Allied lines with a motor shot to pieces, but there were no witnesses to testify to his success.   Another foeman from the British aerodrome on the island of Thasos he forced down on to the sea, and as the fight was witnessed by a Bulgarian observation post at the mouth of the Mesta river, he felt sure of his first official victory because he had only to send in a report embodying the evidence of the men who witnessed his triumph to secure credit for it.

But when he sought out the members of the observation post, he learnt with dismay that the Bulgarian regiment from which they were drawn had been transferred a couple of days previously to the Monastir sector. In the hustle and bustle of war he was unable to track down his witnesses.

Then Fate, realising the injustice done to him, sent two easy victims across his path. The first was a British two-seater that flew over Drama to take a shot at a Bulgarian company drilling on the parade-ground. Returning from a flight, Eschwege came upon the enemy machine unawares, and though his machine gun jammed time after time, he persevered until a lucky shot penetrated the motor and forced the foeman to descend. The two occupants of the English machine were made prisoners.

His second victory was yet easier, for two Serbian Flight-sergeants, ordered to pilot a Farman from Florina to Salonica, lost their way and prepared to land on Drama aerodrome.

Great was their surprise when they were greeted with a vociferous outburst from the Archies ; realising their mistake, they started to climb again, but before they could escape, Eschwege took off and rose above them. A well-directed burst from his machine-gun gave an unmistakable hint that their wisest course was to go down again. They made an excellent landing and were marched off as prisoners, while Eschwege amused himself with a trial flight in their machine.

With these two gifts from Fate to encourage him, the

Eagle started off on his victorious career. It was not long before he came into conflict with Captain G. W. M. Green, whose name bore an ominous reputation in Drama aerodrome.

Green had shot down several of the Staffel's best men, and it soon dawned on him that there was a new Fokker pilot in the enemy's ranks who might prove an opponent worthy of his notice. In company with a certain Lieutenant Owen, he started out one February morning in quest of this redoubtable foe.

Some 6,000 feet up in the sky the British war birds found their quarry and dived on him. Unfortunately for Green, his machine gun jammed at the critical moment, so that he had to pull out of the fight to attend to it. Owen put up a plucky resistance and fought the Fokker down to 1,800 feet, but he was inexperienced and allowed Eschwege to close with him. From an advantageous position the Eagle got a burst in on his tank ; he was forced to land, but contrived to set fire to his machine before he was captured.

Lieutenants Sydney Beare and D. E. Hyde, who were Eschwege's next victims, likewise managed to burn their Nieuport before they gave themselves up, but Lieutenants Ingham and Maxwell of the Royal Naval Air Service were not so lucky, for their Sopwith two-seater was smashed to atoms against a sheer cliff of the Macedonian mountains. Their bodies were never recovered, but lay rotting in some deep, inaccessible gorge, a fitting resting-place for the victims of an Eagle.

Eschwege's reputation spread to the British aerodromes at Thasos, Stavros, Monuhi, Badinal and Orlyak. His Fokker was now known to the opposing aviators,

who generally gave him a wide berth. He had to go
a-hunting for his quarry, and as his hunting-ground was
a sector about 120 miles in length, there were naturally
many days when he returned empty-handed.

But one day he was heading homeward after using up
nearly all his benzin in a fruitless chase up and down
the line when suddenly he caught sight of white, fleecy
shrapnel cloudlets over Angista. Their message was
plain enough ; British airmen were bombing the railway
station. Eschwege put his Fokker's nose in the direction
of Angista, while his keen eye searched the air to ascertain
the number of his opponents.

There were only two—B.E.s with 140 h.p. engines,
but one of them looked to be handled by a skilled pilot.
Eschwege's heart thrilled with joy at the prospect of a
tough fight, and he zoomed up into the blue to gain
sufficient height for his swoop.

He judged the distance nicely and soon had the nearest
of the two foemen well sighted, but the Englishman
avoided his burst by a sharp curve ; meanwhile his companion, executing a neat climbing turn, put himself on
to the Fokker's tail. All around Eschwege the bullets
whistled ; a sharp metallic clang told him that his motor
was hit, and a second later he felt two burning stabs in
his right arm. There followed a round of tail-chasing,
but the Englishman hung on grimly to his advantage.

Eschwege saw that defeat was inevitable unless he
could manage to somehow shake off this persistent
opponent. Quickly his brain grasped the best way of
escape ; pulling the stick hard, he sent his Fokker
rearing up so steeply that the Englishman barely avoided
a collision by going over on to his right wing in a
side-loop.

Down went Eschwege's Fokker, wing over wing, but a few hundred feet off the ground he evened out and looked about him for signs of the enemy.

At last he sighted the two machines far away over Lake Takhino ; imagining him out of control and bound to crash, they were on their way back to their aerodrome at Monuhi to report that the German single-seater that had given so much trouble during the past weeks was now eliminated.

" Not so fast, my friends," muttered Eschwege, and started off in pursuit.

But when he tried to rise again, he saw that his rev-counter was dropping rapidly and his engine had begun to cough.   Obviously no benzin was reaching it from the tank ; the automatic pump had ceased to work. He tried his handpump, but the coughing continued, whereupon he knew that his main tank must have been holed.

But his emergency tank, with at least half an hour's benzin in it, remained intact.   There was plenty of time to have a go at the Englishmen and get home, he decided.

He switched on to the emergency tank ; the engine ceased coughing and the revcounter's indicator crept up again.   Eschwege started off in pursuit, and soon found himself rapidly gaining on the B.E.s.   Before he got within range he sent out a burst from his machine gun as a challenge to them to turn and fight.

They heard him and circled round.   A minute later the three machines were at it, hammer and tongs ; a Bulgarian observation post that watched the fray from the seashore was unable to join in as the gunners could not distinguish friend from foe.   But at last the

Bulgarians saw one of the B.E.s glide off in the direction of Monuhi.

Fastening on to the more inexperienced of the two pilots, Eschwege shot his motor to pieces and thought he was going to finish him off before he could get home. But the other machine, which Eschwege rightly deduced to be flown by Green, came to the rescue in such masterly fashion that the Eagle was forced to relinquish his victim and fight for his own life again. For some time the two pilots chased one another's tails, seeking a chance to put in a burst on the blind spot, but, as so often happens when skilled foemen meet in the air, a deadlock ensued. Neither gave the other an opening, and at last, as if by mutual consent, they separated and made off for their respective aerodromes. Eschwege had used literally the last drop in his emergency tank when he landed.

The doctor's examination diagnosed only two flesh-wounds in his arm, and after they had been dressed, he was able to take his place at lunch in the mess, where he was loud in his praise of Captain Green.

Green had every reason to be proud of his share in the day's work, because his companion was a novice, newly arrived from England and therefore quite unskilled in the ways of Ægean eagles. By his masterly counter-attacks he twice saved him to fight another day.

Green saved his companion's life, but not his machine, for the officer in charge of the Bulgarian Archies on the shore of Lake Takhino telephoned late that evening to report that only one B.E. had reached Monuhi. The other had been forced to land on a marsh that covered part of the lake and lay some five hundred yards away from Ahinos village. From Monhui a motor boat had

put out to rescue the pilot, carrying a squad of mechanics
who made an examination of the machine, which they
probably hoped to salve.

" Not if I know it," swore Eschwege.

Early the following morning he went up in a two-
seater with an observer and a load of bombs.   Swiftly
they skimmed the lake, darting hither and thither like
a monstrous dragon-fly in quest of its prey.

At last they caught sight of the B.E. with its nose
deeply buried in the swamp and its tail sticking up in
the air.   Eschwege glanced towards Monuhi, but could
see no signs of life ; the war birds of the Royal Flying
Corps and their mechanics were still sleeping the sleep
of the just.

The early bird gets the early worm, and this worm was
a morsel that no eagle need disdain. Circling round the
lake to get into position, Eschwege pushed the stick
down, and as they passed over the bogged B.E. his
observer loosed four bombs.   Four columns of mud
rose into the air.

Once more the Germans circled round the lake, and
once again they swooped on the B.E. which both pilot
and observer pounded with their machine-guns.   Then
Eschwege gave a yell of derisive triumph and set his
course for Drama and breakfast.

Later they listened with unconcealed glee to the
telephonic report of their Bulgarian allies.   Again an
English working-party had inspected the shattered
machine, but their investigation lasted hardly a minute.
Then they put off and went back to Monuhi.

For several weeks the tail of the B.E. remained visible,
but at last the mud of the swamp swallowed it up.

One morning the commander of Drama aerodrome

was aroused with the news that British warships were bombarding Cavalla. Ten aeroplanes were said to be assisting them ; what could Herr Lieutenant Eschwege do about it ?

Eschwege replied that he would start at once, and ordered his mechanics to bring out the Albatros he was now flying. He took off, but instead of making for Cavalla, he winged his way south by east to the mountains. At last he turned to take stock of the situation.

From afar he beheld the houses of Cavalla, with their white walls dyed crimson in the rising sun. Then he surveyed the harbour, where the masses of grey water thrown up by the bursting shells were clearly visible. Far away on the horizon he espied dark smears which he knew to be British warships, but as yet he could see no sign of the ten aeroplanes.

He flew out to sea, going into a sharp right-hand turn which put the sun behind him when he approached the bombarding ships, and at last he caught sight of the winged allies that circled in the air above them.

There were only eight of them—not ten, as originally stated, but even so they were too many for the fiercest eagle to engage. However, Eschwege had sworn that he would do something, and he meant to keep his word.

He began to study the formation of the enemy's 'planes and noted that the lowest of all was a Farman two-seater ; the others were fast S.E.s and flew at least a thousand feet above their companion.

The Farman, it was clear to him, contained an observer who watched the effect produced by the bursting shells and wirelessed the range to the gunners below. It was in fact the brain and eyes of the fleet, while the seven scouts above were there to protect it—in case any eagle should conceive some wild notion of interfering with the business on hand.

"I'll settle that Farman," vowed Eschwege, and zoomed up to gain height for a dive. He climbed until he reckoned he was a good 4,000 feet above his intended victim.

Then he cast a hasty glance down. There lay the English leviathans, belching fire and smoke from their iron mouths, while far away in Cavalla their shells, directed by the Farman's observer, were now bursting with deadly effect on the harbour where the German mine-layers rode at anchor. A German submarine was likewise there, if rumour's tongue spoke truth.

Out of the sun shot the Eagle of the Ægean Sea, and before the seven sentinel birds were aware of his presence, he had streaked through their midst. His wires sang in the air as he bore down on the Farman.

Now he had it well sighted, but he held his fire, for, come what might, he dared not miss with his first burst. The seven sentinels, hastening belatedly to the rescue, would see to it that he had no time for a second.

On sped Eschwege's Albatros. Neither the observer nor the pilot of the Farman seemed aware of his coming, so engrossed were they in their work—and so fully confident in the vigilance of their protectors overhead.

Five—four—three hundred yards away ! Now is the right moment ! Tack—tack—tack—tack—tack ! —Damn that left gun ; it's jammed. No it hasn't— —tack—tack—tack—tack—yes, it has. Never mind ... the right one's going ... tack—tack—tack ! Got him !

His Albatros was barely fifty yards away when he saw the Farman's nose dip, and down she went, her descent clearly traced by a thin line of smoke. Eschwege swept round in a sharp right-hand turn and fled for dear life from the vengeance of the seven sentinels.

But when he glanced over his shoulder he saw the Farman fall to pieces in the air. The heavy fuselage shot seawards to dive into the depths, while the broken wings fluttered slowly after.

With delight Eschwege saw that the distance between his Albatros and the S.E.'s was increasing. Finally the pursuers gave him up as a bad job.

A telephonic report of his success had reached Drama Aerodrome before he landed. When he alighted, his comrades told him that the bombardment had ceased. " I expect you can do with some breakfast now," one of them said as they hustled him into a waiting car.

" Tell them to stop at my quarters first," replied Eschwege, and smiled as he loosed a button of his leather jacket. When the S.O.S. call came, he was in too great a hurry to dress ; he simply put his flying-kit on over his pyjamas.

About six weeks later a Bulgarian observation post found the bodies of the Farman's pilot and observer, which were washed on shore. Eschwege was relieved to learn that their deaths must have been instantaneous ; one had a bullet through the heart, the other through the brain.

The Germans buried them with full military honours. The British aviators of Monuhi and Thasos were naturally loath to let Eschwege and his comrades enjoy their leisure hours in peace and quiet ; by night and day the flyers of Drama were on the alert for the visitation of bombers seeking to destroy their nest. Many of them paid for their daring, for nothing pleased Eschwege so much as to rise into the air before the raiders were aware of his presence and overhaul one of them before he could get home. He gave one B.E. such a mauling that it was forced to land close to the Takhino marsh ; the machine was worth no more than its price as scrap-iron, but its pilot, bleeding from four wounds, managed to crawl out and reached Monuhi. A couple of days later Green resolved to avenge the loss.

He found Eschwege alone in the air and spoiling for a fight. The two champions met over Lake Takhino, but after a few short exchanges Green found himself in an unfavourable situation from which he could only extricate himself by a daring nose-dive. He seemed bound to go down into the water, but at the last moment he caught his engine and made a good landing at Monuhi. Eschwege was full of admiration for the skilful manœuvre which saved his opponent in the nick of time, and later he learnt from a prisoner that Green's machine-gun had jammed at the crucial moment.

Lake Takhino seems to have been a favourite battle-ground, for that same week Eschwege encountered a Nieuport over its waters and forced it to land in so damaged a condition that it was not worth salving. The pilot was wounded in the lungs, but survived.

As spring gave way to summer, the bombers' visits became more frequent. Their opportunities seemed too good to be lost because even if they failed to secure a direct hit on a hangar there was always a likelihood of their incendiary missiles setting fire to the dried up grass around it and so causing a blaze that might entail serious consequences.

Eschwege ascertained that the period between eleven and three was the time of day most favoured by the bombers and resolved to lie in wait for them. One day he therefore transported himself and his machine to the advanced landing ground at Iralti, where he hoped to cut them off on their way back to Thasos.

Higher and higher rose the sun towards its zenith ; the baked soil beneath him seemed to burn his feet. Hour after hour passed by, yet no sound came from the direction of Thasos, the peaks of which were faintly discernible through the heat haze.

At last his ears caught a faint drone in the air. He raised his binoculars to search the sky, but the haze was too thick. No signs of the enemy.

The humming in the air grew ever louder, and after minutes that seemed like hours Eschwege fancied he could discern three black specks in the sky.

The Eagle's fiery impulse bade him stretch his wings forthwith, but he restrained its promptings, for he knew that a premature move would spoil everything. The bombers must be allowed to reach their objective and drop their eggs, after which he could catch them on the way home. Once more he possessed his soul in patience.

Now they were near enough for him to distinguish their types. There were two great Farman bombers, with a single-seater Sopwith water-plane to protect them against attacks from eagles ; Eschwege swore loudly, as he realised that they were bound to see his machine on the ground, in which case it would be all up with the surprise attack he had planned.

Did they see him ? They were flying so low that he could espy the observer in one of the Farmans leaning over to take a look at him. Then four little dots detached themselves from his machine.

" That's coming damnably near me ! Thank Heaven, a dud ! " A cloud of dust rose into the air, choking his parched throat and veiling the enemy from his sight as they passed on towards Drama.

" Crash! crash ! crash ! No duds that time, but damned bad shots ! Missed me by a mile or two, I should think. So, now then, up and at them ! Damn and damn again ! What the hell's up ? No sparks ! Why won't the blasted engine fire ? "

He tried again, but the engine remained dead, so he climbed out and swung the propeller frantically. Then back into the machine, and switch on. All in vain— the propeller remained motionless. Switch off again !

Terrible is the rage of an eagle with lamed wings when he sees his prey escape him.

" Where's that damned can ? I'll give the cylinder a dose. . . . . Now try the prop. again ! Engine ought to be all right now ! Back into the machine . . . . Lord, it's firing at last. Question is—can I catch them ? I'll have a shot at it, anyway."

Their task accomplished, the two Farmans and their guardian Sopwith were winging their way back to the island nest. As they approached, the Sopwith pilot, recollecting some engagement perhaps and scenting no danger for his charges at the journey's end, hastened ahead. Neither he nor the occupants of the Farmans heard the whirring of the eagle's wings behind them, while the haze hid from their careless eyes all sight of the avenger that drew ever nearer.

Tack—tack—tack—tack—and devil take the hindmost !

The observer of the hindmost Farman turned roun and swung his machine gun in the direction of the pursue

" Too late," muttered Eschwege, " you can't dodge me this time. I've got you fairly sighted, and now you're for it ! Oh, damn that gun ! " But in his eagerness to remove the jam, he forgot the difference in the relative speeds of his Albatros and the Farman until he was close upon his prey. Then he had to pull his stick frantically to avoid a collision by rising above the Englishman.

" Thank Heaven . . . gun working again . . . I'll get you yet . . . Lord . . . there's the Sopwith ! "

The truant escort, seeing the danger to his charges, had turned to attack the Albatros. But Eschwege put in a couple of bursts that made this adversary sheer off in a wide right-hand turn. Then he looked round for the Farman.

" Where the hell is he ? That's funny ! Did I crash him after all ? No . . . he's down there . . . nearly home, but I'll get him yet. All the Sopwiths in the world shan't stop me. . . . Nose down and dive for him ! "

The coasts of Thasos loomed larger and larger as the eagle swooped on his prey. Once more the Farman's observer prepared to defend himself.

" That's right . . . shoot away, old fellow . . . shoot as much as you like ; I've got you all the same . . . tack—tack—tack—tack—tack—tack—hurrah ! "

From the Farman's motor steam rose up as the machine sank lower and lower towards the water.

No need to finish him off. The Eagle became a man who saw that two other brave men would be forced down to the sea in a machine that was not provided with floats and would therefore be bound to capsize the moment it touched the surface. With relief he noted that both the Farman's inmates were alive and apparently active enough to swim for safety.

The wheels touched the waves, and, as he had foreseen,

the battered Farman turned turtle.   But the pilot and
observer disentangled themselves from the wreckage
and started to swim for the shore.

" Only about five hundred yards to the island,"
calculated Eschwege, " and they're sure to send a boat
for them."   He waved his hand in friendly greeting to
his late adversaries and saw them wave back.   Then he
put his Albatros about and returned to Drama.

About a fortnight later Eschwege shot down another
English machine, and this time the pilot and observer
were made prisoners.   When he met them in the airmen's mess at Drama, he immediately enquired after
the fate of the Farman's occupants.

The observer was picked up in a boat, his captives
told him, but the pilot was too badly hit to keep afloat
till help came.   Eschwege's face wore a gloomy look
for the rest of the day.

But, undeterred by their losses, the war birds of Thasos
came again and again to bomb Drama Aerodrome.   As
usual, Eschwege lay in wait for them, and on one occasion he
had a fight with four Sopwiths, one of which he brought
down although he had a narrow escape for his own life.

He had heard them coming over at about half-past
eleven one morning and went up in pursuit at once,
because he found himself unable to bear the strain of
waiting till they had laid their eggs.   But as soon as he
joined battle, he realised that he had to deal with four
resolute opponents who were determined to give him no
chance.   They got rid of their bombs at once and made
off for Thasos in close formation.

Eschwege bore down upon the hindermost of them,
but before he had him sighted the other three turned and
attacked him.   He avoided their bursts with a sharp

turn and tried to fasten on to the tail of one of the assailants. But the Sopwiths manœuvred cleverly, and, with tracer bullets ripping past his ears, Eschwege was forced to curve away again. Five times he returned to the attack, but in vain ; the team-work of the British war birds forced him to withdraw each time. As he started to climb into position for a sixth onslaught he saw that he was over the sea.

Great was the Eagle's rage when he beheld the near outlines of Thasos. Casting discretion to the winds, he swooped on the lowest Sopwith.

Once again the other three attacked him, but he did not care. One victim he meant to have, even if he paid the penalty with his own life.

The pilot of the lowest Sopwith pulled his stick, but before he could rise the Eagle of the Ægean Sea was on to him. " Tack—tack—tack—tack—no jam this time. Good old gun ! Got him ! "

From the fuselage of the stricken Sopwith a flame shot out. A fearful explosion followed as the machine burst into a thousand fragments.

Eschwege pulled the stick hard against his chest, but before he could rise a cloud of black smoke enveloped him. Gusts, and swirls, mightier than any he had experienced in the worst storm, tossed his Albatros hither and thither like an autumn leaf.

After a few hectic seconds he found his machine under control and rose to fill his choking lungs with pure air. Then he looked round for the other three Sopwiths. They were not too far away and he thought that with luck he might catch another of them. But as he started off in pursuit his engine began to sputter. The rev-counter fell to 800 and then to 600.

Eschwege looked at his altimeter and ascertained that he was barely 1,500 feet above the sea.

He had lost height in the swoop on the Sopwith, and now he could do nothing but put his machine about and make a desperate dash for the mainland, with the certain knowledge that he was doomed to drown if his engine failed him.   From a height of 1,500 feet it was impossible to cover in a glide the four miles of water that separated him from the shore.

He had not covered one tenth of the distance when his engine stopped dead and the revcounter went back to zero.   Mechanically he put his machine into a glide, knowing that by the laws of mathematics he had no possible chance of making the shore.   He was bound to come down in the waves, and if he extricated himself from the Albatros before it sank, he would only prolong the agony.   Even if the English in Thasos or the Bulgarians on the mainland saw his plight, neither could send a boat to reach him in time.

Then his quick brain seized upon the one desperate chance.   A steep vertical dive might set his dead propeller going again.   Then the engine might catch ;   if not . . .

" No need to think of the ' if not.'   Stick forward and nose down before we drop too low to do the trick ! "

He saw the sea rush up to meet him. 1,200 . . . 1,000 . . . 800 . . . 700 feet, said the altimeter, but the propeller still remained dead.   500 . . . 400 . . . 300 no signs of life. 200 . . . 100 . . . 90 . . . .

Even as Eschwege fumbled desperately at his belt, the mighty pressure of the air did its work, and the propeller began to revolve.   Then the engine started to work again.

Eschwege evened out and set off at full speed for

Drama. When he landed he soon discovered that the engine had suffered no damage in the fight with the four Sopwiths. It was simply fouled with the gases generated by the explosion that occurred when he sent one of their number to destruction.

But the English bombers remained undeterred, and one night they had the audacity to drop their eggs when the war birds of Drama were celebrating with wine and wassail the last evening of their Commander, Captain Heydemarck, who had received promotion. Eschwege had just proposed his health when the commander of a Bulgarian observation post telegraphed that the English bombing squadron had left Thasos.

Great was the wrath of the assembled company, all of whom were looking forward to one of those festive evenings in which airmen of all nations were wont to indulge whenever they had time and opportunity. But as someone wisely remarked that it was not yet certain that the Tommies were making for Drama, they continued their carouse. A little while afterwards a second message announced that the Englishmen were undoubtedly heading for the Staffel's advanced landing-place at Xanthi. " In which case we are unlikely to be disturbed, gentlemen," remarked the master of the ceremonies. " So fill up your glasses." But Eschwege fidgeted and looked glum.

Ten minutes later the worst of tidings came through. Eschwege's new Halberstadt, which was housed at Xanthi, had been badly damaged.

His wrath knew no bounds. That Halberstadt had been obtained with blood and tears, for the powers who directed these affairs in Germany seemed to know nothing and care less about the little nest of war birds in Drama.

Anything was good enough for them—any old ante-diluvian machine would do for such a remote front, and they could tie it together with bits of string till it fell to pieces and then indent for more string if they still wanted to fly.   Before his eyes rose up visions of pilots on the western front who could write off a machine before break-fast and take up a new one after lunch.   And now his Halberstadt, that had cost him so much trouble to get, was washed out !

Eschwege rose to his feet and swore that he would bomb Thasos in revenge that very night.   Heydemarck wanted to go with him, but the others protested, and as the commander was still shaky from a bad bout of malaria, he allowed another aviator, a certain König, to take the observer's seat.   While they donned their flying kit, Heydemarck telephoned to the aerodrome to have a Rumpler brought out for them.

At midnight they departed beneath the light of a full moon.   The company came to see them off and then returned to the dining-room of the mess.

Half an hour later someone strolled on to the terrace, and, glancing south-eastward, saw a red glow in the sky. All trooped out to look at it.   Then the telephone bell recalled them to the messroom.

A Bulgarian officer rang up to tell them that Thasos Aerodrome was on fire.   They filled their glasses to drink to the healths of Eschwege and König, after which the carouse went on merrily until once again the tele-phone interrupted it.   Two English aeroplanes were making for Drama, reported the Bulgarian at the other end.

So the English had conceived the daring idea of firing the Drama hangars just as Eschwege and König would be returning.   A cunning counterstroke, the company decided, but surely their own men were too wily to fall into such a trap. But they felt unable to settle down to further potations until they had more definite news, so once more they piled themselves into their cars and whirled off to the aerodrome.

There was no need to light any flares ; they would only show the enemy his target. Eschwege could get home blindfold, if need be, and he was quite used to landing in the dark. The main thing was that he should arrive back before the counter-raiders dropped their eggs.

Sharp ears caught the distant drone of an engine in the air. " It's the Rumpler ! " someone cried.

Out of the darkness the Rumpler glided down and made a perfect landing. Eschwege and König alighted.

Their tale was soon told. Less than half an hour's flight took them to Thasos, where a well-placed bomb speedily disposed of the search-light. The Archies threw up a series of star-shells, but the shooting was wild and the lights in the air only served to show up the target to the bombers. Four eggs hurtled through the air to fall in close proximity to a hangar. These König followed up with two incendiary bombs, after which Eschwege curved away sharply.

A red glow illumined his wings, and when he was able to look back, he saw that a hangar housing six machines blazed fiercely. Around it little tongues of flame ran along the dried grass.

Eschwege put the Rumpler about and sailed over the scene of destruction again. Below him he saw minute figures—a squad of busy ants, they looked like.

" No you don't, brother Tommy," he muttered. " That shed has got to burn."

He pushed his stick forward and sent the Rumpler down in a steep dive. Then König brought his Spandau into play, scattering the fire-fighters in all directions. Heedless of the Archies, the Rumpler cruised over the aerodrome until its occupants saw that the conflagration was too strong to be quenched by human devices. They then set off home.

"But what about the English aeroplane that was 'phoned to be coming over?" enquired one of their listeners.

Eschwege laughed. "Those Bulgarians heard the echo of our engine in the mountains and mistook it for another machine. That's all there is to it."

The company returned to their wine and made a merry night of it, and the following morning Eschwege learnt over the 'phone that the first report from Xanthi had greatly exaggerated the extent of the damage. The few minor injuries his new Halberstadt had sustained were already repaired.

On 3 October, 1917, Eschwege shot down his sixteenth victim, and to friend and foe it seemed as if he bore a charmed life. At Drama, Thasos and Monuhi war birds came and went, but the Eagle of the Ægean Sea still ranged the mountains triumphantly. He was a terror to his enemies and a strong comfort to his friends.

But one day a comrade reported to him that Balloon Section No. 17 of the British Salonica Force had sent up a blimp in the neighbourhood of Orlyak.

"Well, good luck to it," said Eschwege. "It won't worry me, and I shan't worry it." Which was really a very sensible remark for him to make.

Some newspaper correspondents used to try to persuade their readers that captive balloons were easy things to deal with. From the tone they took the layman in such matters might almost have been led to assume that they were put up to provide the enemy's pilots with a little innocent fun.

Youthful aviators, fresh from the flying schools, sometimes used to think so too.   The sky is full of perplexities for the greenhorn ; until he has acquired his " air-eyes," he has great difficulty in sighting the foeman he goes out so joyously to encounter.   The wily enemy ace who stalks him he never sees at all—until perhaps just the moment before he is sent crashing earthward, out of control or in flames.

But the captive balloon, the blimp or sausage, is such a nice, easy mark, the youngster thinks.   It can't hide itself in the sun ; it just waits there for you to try your new gun on it.   " Leave it alone, you young fool," counsels the old hand, " you don't know what a mess of things you'll make.   You may get it, but ten to one the Archies will get you.   And if you do send it down, what's the good ?   There'll only be another one up in its place to-morrow."

Such words of wisdom Eschwege would probably have imparted to any new arrival from the flying school. But instead of following their sound advice, he secretly filled his ammunition belt with incendiary bullets.

Like all experienced war birds, he favoured surprise tactics ; he therefore winged his way to the mountains so that he could attack from out of the sun.   When he judged himself within striking distance, he throttled down his engine so that its sound could not betray him and glided down the sausage.   Neither the Archies nor the balloon's observer (whose glasses were riveted on the Bulgarian trenches) saw him.

Tack—tack—tack—"got him all right.   Why doesn't

he blaze up ? " Eschwege's Halberstadt was within twenty yards of the monster, whose observer, finding the situation somewhat too unhealthy, climbed up on to the edge of his car and gazed down dubiously at the ground far beneath him. But, choosing the least of two evils, he took the plunge, and his parachute opened and bore him safely to earth.

Leaving him to descend unmolested, Eschwege curved away and circled round for a fresh attack. Once more he saw his bullets rip the envelope, but when he glanced back to ascertain their effect, the balloon remained intact.

Yet again he attacked, and this time a flame shot out of the hole made by his bullet. " Hurrah, that's got him ! "

Sped on his way by a shower of shells from the Archies that were forced to remain silent while he attacked for fear of injuring their own balloon, Eschwege flew back to Drama in triumph.

There was no new balloon up at Orlyak the next day ; there was in fact no sign of a balloon for the next fortnight, by which time Eschwege ought to have recovered from his attack of " balloon-fever." But when on 9 November, another sausage was reported to be up, he swore that nothing on earth should prevent him from sending it down again.

Like its predecessor, this second balloon seemed blessed with a cat's nine lives. Twice Eschwege watched his bullets go home in the silver-grey envelope, with no apparent result except the tragic fate of the observer, whose parachute failed to open. With ever-increasing speed the unfortunate man hurtled down to his doom.

When Eschwege attacked the first balloon, the English Archies had failed to distinguish themselves, but now they were getting the range better. He felt the bullets from the machine-guns strike his wings, but despite their uncomfortable attentions he stuck to his task until both his Spandaus jammed and refused to be righted. There was nothing left for him but to fly home again and own himself beaten.

All that day he brooded.

On the following morning his friend König went off to bomb the new English aerodrome at Lahana, and when he returned he advised Eschwege to leave the balloon severely alone in future as the number of Archies defending it had been considerably increased. But Eschwege merely shook his head sadly.

On 15 November, he rang up to enquire whether the balloon was still there. The answer was in the affirmative ; moreover, in addition to the extra Archies, three aeroplanes were detailed to guard it.

Eschwege hung up the receiver and went straight off to the aerodrome, where he instructed the sergeant in charge to give him a belt of incendiary bullets.

15 November was decidedly his lucky day. Heavy rain-clouds hung low in the sky, and under their cover he was able to creep up invisibly to within striking distance. Then he pushed the stick down and swooped on his quarry in a daring nose-dive. He knew that he must finish the business at the first attempt, for the British war birds up aloft would see to it that he had no second chance.

But everything went off " according to plan." The clouds covered him so well that the watchers in the sky were unaware of his presence until he had his objective

sighted.   His first burst ripped the hull, from which a
crimson flame promptly shot out.   He turned away to
flee from the storm of shrapnel, and when he looked
round he saw the blazing mass sink slowly earthward.
Archies to the right of him, Archies to the left of him,
volleyed and thundered, but miraculously he reached
Drama aerodrome untouched.

The next day the threatened storm broke ; for a whole
week the fury of the elements was such that not even an
eagle could venture forth.   On 19 November, the sky
cleared and the sun shone forth once more.   Eschwege
went to the telephone.

" There's another balloon up at Orlyak," was the
reply to his question.

From his face König read the import of the message
Eschwege had received.   " Don't be a darn fool," he
said, but the other, growing wise in the art of deceit,
responded that he had no intention of tempting Provi-
dence.   He promised not to attack the sausage that day,
but surely he might be allowed one peep at it.   Besides,
the three English machines would be there to guard it, and
surely they at least were his lawful quarry.

His coming was looked for, and, with their usual
daring, his British opponents of the air did not wait too
long for him.   Hardly was he aloft when he saw two
black specks in the sky, which on nearer inspection
turned out to be a B.E. two-seater and a Sopwith Pup.
Over Kalendra he met them.

He felt himself so invincible that day that he threw
tactics to the winds and headed straight for the B.E.
without a thought for the Sopwith sitting on his tail.
One burst from his machine-gun sent his heavier opponent down in flames, and when he turned to engage the

Sopwith, lo and behold, its pilot was diving for his own lines.

When Eschwege returned to Drama his commander took him aside and warned him to be cautious. Lance-Sergeant van Ahlen, the only other single-seater pilot in the little Staffel, had been shot down over Porna and forced to land with a leg wound that would keep him out of action for many weeks. If anything happened to Eschwege before a substitute could be obtained from Germany, the consequences might be very serious. Eschwege dutifully promised to take no unnecessary risks.

But he had the " balloon-fever " too badly to be able to keep his word, and that same afternoon he once more set off in the direction of Orlyak. The balloon was up, but as soon as he came into sight, its attendants hauled it down hastily and the Archies began to bark defiance. Four enemy machines were in the air ; these he attacked, but they instantly sheered off to shelter behind their Archies. Eschwege returned home empty-handed to brood again.

On the morning of the 21st his mechanics watched him fill his belts with incendiary bullets. One of them ventured to remonstrate with him, but Eschwege clapped the man jovially on the shoulder and told him not to worry.

Luck was on his side, he vowed, and the man who did not play high when his luck was in deserved to lose.

Under a grey sky the Eagle of the Ægean Sea set forth on his last flight.

As he approached Orlyak, he saw the balloon swaying gently in the morning breeze. In its car he espied the observer.

" I trust for his sake the parachute is going to behave itself," he muttered grimly.

As on several former occasions the clouds seemed to conceal him from hostile eyes, for the Archies that had barked so noisily at his last approach remained silent. Their gunners, he imagined, would consider him unwilling to face them after the warm welcome they had accorded him the last time. So he calculated his distance and swooped down on the balloon.

" If they haven't spotted me," he thought, " I can get right up to the brute and make sure of it with my first burst." He therefore held his fire till only a few yards separated him from his quarry.

Then he sent forth his stream of incendiary bullets. He saw a flame shoot out of the envelope, and as he curved away he looked back to feast his eyes on the scene of destruction. But at that moment a terrific din smote his ears, while his Halberstadt, enveloped in smoke, began to toss hither and thither as on the day when he smote down the Sopwith over the sea. A pillar of flame broke out from the balloon, and the members of the Bulgarian observation post who witnessed its end cheered wildly.

They naturally did not see the flames lick up the dummy observer, the man of straw in the cast-off cap and coat who had been placed there to lure Eschwege to his doom. They only saw the Halberstadt emerge from the smoke-cloud in a right-hand turn. So they continued to cheer.

Then all at once silence fell upon them, for they saw the Halberstadt's left wing dip as it went down out of control in a long side-slipping dive.

When they telephoned to Drama what they had seen,

their news seemed too incredible for belief. Eschwege was invincible—a veritable monarch of the air—and the Bulgarians must have been mistaken. For hours a little group waited about the empty hangar, hoping against hope.

When they finally realised that he would never return, they still refused to believe the worst. Somehow he would have regained control of his machine and made a landing of sorts. Probably he was now enjoying the hospitality of the British war birds' mess and swapping yarns with the pilots there. Eschwege had always got on so well with the captive English airmen they entertained at Drama.

But late that afternoon a British machine flew over their aerodrome at a great height and dropped a streamer. When it was picked up, they found a note informing them that Eschwege was dead.

The explosives with which the death-trap was filled had done their work, for, as the pilots of Drama afterwards learnt from a prisoner, they were of sufficient strength and quantity to wreck any machine within a hundred yards radius. The charge was fired from below by electrical contact.

And so at last the Eagle of the Ægean Sea fell to earth with broken wings.

Three days later another streamer was dropped by the enemy. Attached to it was a packet containing Eschwege's few personal belongings and a couple of photographs, the first of which showed his coffin being carried to its last resting place on the shoulders of six pilots of the Royal Flying Corps, while the second was a picture of his grave, covered with the wreaths that were a last tribute from his opponents of the air.

The Bulgarians put up a monument in Drama to commemorate his fame, and although less than a year later they were compelled by the fortunes of war to retreat to their own land, every pilot of every flying corps that took part in the war will hope that the Greeks have suffered it to remain intact.

CHAPTER IX

SOME OTHER WAR BIRDS OF DRAMA

" NO weary legs hamper him ; he does not have to
crawl over the dead or stand up to his knees in
the mire. He is the pampered aristocrat of the war,
the golden youth of adventure.

" He leaves a comfortable bed, with bath, a good
breakfast, the comradeship of a pleasant mess, the care
of servants, to mount his steed. When he returns, he
has only to slip out of his seat. Mechanics look after
his plane, and refreshment and shade in summer and
warmth in winter await alike the spoiled child of the
favoured adventurous corps who has not quite the gift
and never quite dares the great hazards as well as the
one who dares them to his certain end."

Thus wrote a certain journalist who visited the British
forces on the Somme when he wanted to contrast the
comfortable life of the flying man with the hardships
suffered by his sorely tried brother-officer of the front
line. Yet perhaps it was only just that the aviator should
enjoy such compensations, for from his corps Death
reaped the largest proportionate harvest. " A short
life and a gay one," was his motto, and whether he dared
all or not quite all, the chances of his survival were
remote. The brevity of his life gave him a right to its
gaiety.

But what of those war birds that had to look forward

to the brevity without the gaiety—brevity with all sorts of discomforts ?

The little group of German war birds in Drama and their British opposite numbers in Thasos and Monuhi had to put up with :

(1) Malaria. However fine the meshes of the nets under which they slept, the crafty mosquitoes found the way to their blood. Of the forty odd British aviators in Thasos, at one time over twenty were put out of action by malaria. All the Balkan lands are hotbeds of this scourge, and the Struma marshes, which formed a long sector of the front, were the worst fever-lands in the whole Balkans.

(2) An educated Greek once remarked to the writer that even the cleanest houses in the best quarter of Athens were never free from bugs. Bedclothes, etc, must be well shaken every day. But Athens was probably cleanliness itself compared with Drama, Monuhi and Thasos. " Kill that you may not be killed," Captain Heydemarck states to have been the theory that the German aviators were compelled to put into practice every night during the hours that they should have been resting. Their opposite numbers were in the same plight.

(3) Heat. In the summer they could only fly in the very early morning or in very late evening, and even then in their shirt-sleeves. Aerial photography was impossible because in the middle of the day, the natural time for such work on account of the shortness of shadow, the heat of the sun melted the gelatine from the plates. Fixing and toning baths in the dark room had to be kept on ice.

Oil became as thin as water and leaked all over their machines ; engines went on strike. Lieutenant Rottka and Sergeant von der Weppen were once compelled to abandon a reconnaissance flight immediately after leaving the aerodrome because the hot oil affected the engine to such an extent that the propeller suddenly dropped 200 revolutions. Only the pilot's skill saved the machine from the consequences of a bad stall.

(4) Cold. In winter the thermometer was likely to fall to depths as startling as the heights to which it could rise in summer.

(5) Thin mountain air, with unaccountable gusts, eddies and currents. Even if no foemen were encountered in the air, flying was often a matter of life and death. A pilot about to land might suddenly encounter an airhole at the last moment that would send him down in a side-slip.

Macedonia is a treeless land, deforested by centuries of war and Turkish misrule. The soil is therefore unable to form reservoirs to take the rain, which runs off the ground in sheets to find its way to the nearest stream. Thus the land grows ever nakeder, and the barren rocks of the mountains absorb large quantities of heat from the sun, which they give off again by night or on cloudy days. Then vertical air-currents are formed which combine with the fierce horizontal winds to create dangerous eddies. Many an aeroplane was caught by these eddies and smashed against sharp crags or sheer cliffs before the pilot could regain control.

Whenever a Drama pilot complained about discomforts he had experienced on the western front, the others would reply : " At least there was decent air there."

(6) No—the list of woes must cease, otherwise it might completely fill this chapter. Let it suffice to say that the conditions on the Macedonian front were all

in favour of a short life for the Drama war birds and all against a gay one.

But their cheerful readiness to adapt themselves to every emergency prevailed over the adverse circumstances, and I believe that they contrived to exact a fair amount of fun out of life. They were a friendly set of war birds who lived on the best of terms with their Turkish and Bulgarian allies, the neutral Greeks in whose land they were fighting and their English enemies. They kept up the traditions of hospitality despite constant food shortages, and every British pilot who fell uninjured into their hands was feasted before being despatched to a Bulgarian prison camp.

The food problem was often a real trial to them, for they lived in a barren land, the tillers of which could only earn a scanty living by the sweat of their brow, while the deficient railway system made the arrival of comforts from home a matter of uncertainty. Even the good things of life that are supposed to come from the east were often conspicuous by their absence.

When Lieutenant Leslie-Moore, one of Eschwege's victims, was dining with them the evening after his capture, they had to apologise because they were unable to provide him with a cup of coffee to round off the meal.

" That's all right," replied their guest. " I'll get you some." And in the letter which he wrote to his commander announcing his safety he inserted a request that one of his brother pilots would drop a supply of coffee for his hosts' mess. His message was dropped over the English lines the following day.

Subsequently a British machine appeared over Drama and dropped a packet attached to a streamer. But unfortunately a strong wind was blowing that day, which carried the streamer away to some distant gorge of the mountains, where it was impossible to retrieve it. So the German mess at Drama still went short of coffee.

But with or without their coffee they fought hard and put up an amazingly good show against odds. Owing to the shortage of machines and spare parts the loss of a single bus meant a severe handicap, so that they often resorted to desperate measures when hard pressed. But perhaps their most amazing feat was Lance-Corporal Wethekam's landing on a mountain.

He had gone out one morning in a two-seater Albatros with Lieutenant Eckhardt, who was instructed to take some photographs of the enemy's positions. When they were engaged in this task, they saw a B.E. approaching, but Eckhardt judged that he had plenty of time to finish his job. After taking his last photo, he gave the signal to return ; Wethekam put the Albatros into a right-hand turn and started for home.

The B.E., which had the advantage of height, overhauled them rapidly. At about 300 yards distance the British pilot dived and found the blind spot on the Albatros's tail. Eckhardt felt a violent blow on the head, and the next moment his face was blinded with streaming blood.

Wethekam grasped the situation. His observer was out of action, and his machine, an antiquated model, had no forward machine-gun. There was nothing for it but to cut and run. But whither ? They had passed the trenches of the Struma front and were heading for mountains where there was no possible landing place. The pursuing B.E. pilot saw his opponent's dilemma and redoubled his efforts.

Wethekam zigzagged to avoid the B.E.'s fire, but

bullets sped all about him. He heard them strike
various parts of the machine ; then, all of a sudden, the
rudder refused to answer to his kicks. His lateral
controls were shot away. Before him was a mountain
ridge which he could not avoid, although it looked to
taper up into a knife-like edge, and behind him was the
B.E. His observer had fallen from his seat and lay
helpless in the cockpit.

Just at that moment the revcounter began to drop,
and after a few spasmodic efforts the propeller ceased
to turn. " Engine touched," deduced Wethekam, " and
that just puts the lid on it."

Evidently the B.E. pilot thought so too. As far as
he could see, his victim was going down out of control
to crash on the rocks, so that the poor devils inside the
Albatros would be lucky if they escaped with their
lives. Should they sustain serious injuries that prevented
them from crawling down to an inhabited valley, they
might bleed or starve to death before anyone found them
in that remote, inaccessible spot.

No call for him to add to their troubles, he decided,
and, turning, he made off for his own aerodrome. If
his late opponents could save their lives, well then,
good luck to them !

Wethekam glided down to the ridge and was thankful
to find it not quite so knifelike as it appeared in the
distance. He imagined that he might have been able
to make quite a decent landing if only he had been able
to turn and come down along its length.

But any sort of a turn was out of the question, for
all his lateral controls were shot away. The only thing
he could do was to pick out the best possible spot for
a descent on the course he was taking.

Wethekam tried to keep his machine's nose up and prolong the glide until he had carried on past the sharp barren rocks of the upper heights, in which case he might be able to drop to safety in some Alpine pasture. But as soon as he pulled the stick the Albatros began to stall and threatened to go into a side-slip.

There was therefore no alternative to coming down on the ridge. He determined to try a pancake, which would, of course, smash the undercarriage, but there was just the chance that Eckhardt (provided he was still alive) and himself might survive the crash.

When, however, his wheels were only a matter of yards above the ridge, he saw that the idea was impossible. It was too narrow a landing-place for even a pancake, and the Albatros would go hurtling over a precipice on the further side. He pulled the stick frantically.

The wheels touched the rocks, and Wethekam went up again with a bump. Once more he nearly side-slipped. Then, seeing that it was no use trying to delay the inevitable, he put the Albatros's nose down again.

To his joy he saw that what he had taken for a sheer precipice was only a steep dip, beyond which lay a fairly gentle slope, strewn with boulders, of course, but he could chance them. So down he pancaked, and shut his eyes as the Albatros crashed. A second later he opened them again and crawled wearily out of the wreckage. A violent pain shot through his right ankle, but he was not worrying about it, for at least there were no bones broken. He could use his legs.

Then came the gruesome task of extricating Eckhardt, whose face was covered with blood. Unable to diagnose the wound, he adjusted the emergency dressing that the observer had tried to put on when he was hit, and after making him as comfortable as possible, started to hobble off in search of help.

He was in luck. In a matter of two hours he reached the hamlet of Dovishta, where he found a Turkish detachment commanded by a German officer. Better still, there was an Austrian doctor with them, who gave him the attention he needed and then set off with a guide and stretcher-bearers to rescue his observer.

The doctor found that Eckhardt had received a bullet through the cheek which must have touched the optic nerves. Skilful treatment subsequently saved the sight of his left eye.

Wethekam escaped with a sprained ankle and a number of bruises, while the mechanics who were sent up the following day to see if any part of the Albatros was worth salving, reported it a total wreck. Their examination showed that an English airman must have flown over the mountains in the course of the afternoon and dropped a few bombs to make sure of its destruction.

A few days later another photographic party had a narrow escape. On this occasion an Albatros piloted by Sergeant Stattaus, with Lieutenant Lenz as observer, was sent to Thasos to take photographs and bomb the harbour and hangars. Lenz carried out the first part of his job satisfactorily.

When he arrived he had noted six English single-seaters on the aerodrome, and before he started the bombing he looked down again and saw that there were only four. Two had evidently gone up in search of him, but as his altimeter showed over ten thousand feet he deemed that he had sufficient time to lay his eggs before running for home. He instructed Stattaus accordingly.

But as soon as the pilot curved to manœuvre his bus over the targets the Archies below started to make things uncomfortable for him. Disregarding them, Stattaus came round in a right-hand turn, and four times Lenz pulled the lever that released his eggs. Then the Archies got his range.

"Whew ! That was most unpleasantly near," he thought, " and that was still nearer ! " All around him the air was full of the little fleecy shrapnel clouds, while the machine began to rock like a rowing boat caught in Atlantic rollers.

Suddenly a sharp metallic sound rang out, and the indicator of his revcounter dropped. Slowly and yet more slowly the propeller went round until it finally stopped dead.

" Engine pipped of course,".thought Sergeant Stattaus, and glanced at his altimeter. " But I've height enough to glide to the mainland if they'll let me."

If—But if those two Sopwith single-seaters chose to attack him he would lose height when he dodged their bursts and risk being forced down on to the sea where his Albatros would turn turtle the moment she touched the water. Pilot and observer would have to swim for it or drown.

The Archies were now firing busily, and Stattaus saw that their shells were bursting overhead instead of below him. That meant that he had already lost considerable height.

Glancing down, Lenz espied the two Sopwiths about 1,000 feet below him and spat out a couple of desperate bursts from his machine gun which sent them curving away for dear life. But as the Albatros was losing height with every second of her glide the English machines were above him when next he looked round for them.

The nearest Sopwith dived, but Lenz, an old hand with the machine gun, gave him such a warm welcome that he was glad to sheer off again. With a sigh of relief the observer saw that his pilot had contrived to keep a straight course so that they suffered no unnecessary loss of height.

About a minute later the second Sopwith came down to attack, but once again a well-directed burst repelled him. Then the miracle of miracles occurred, for, glancing back, Lenz could hardly believe his eyes when he saw both his opponents heading for Thasos.

What had induced this unexpected retreat he never ascertained. The English war birds of Thasos were daring flyers and courageous fighters who often paid with their lives for ill-timed audacity. Lenz could only gasp with amazement as their outlines grew fainter and fainter.

Now they were only distant black specks, while the coast of Macedonia loomed large before them. Stattaus steered for Iralti, praying that he might have enough height to take him over the marshes that lay between the sea and the aerodrome there. The Albatros cleared the marshes, but could not quite reach the aerodrome, and Stattaus brought her down on rough ground where a dip was masked by shadows thrown by the setting sun. Consequently he crashed and washed out his undercarriage but as the damage suffered by the engine was easily reparable, they felt satisfied with their day's work.

Although their environment did not give the Drama war birds many chances of indulging in the usual diversions that beguiled the lighter hours of flying men on the western front, they nevertheless found opportunities for an occasional good laugh. There was little incitement to paint Drama red, and leaves were few and far between, but they contrived to extract a lot of fun out of life, as their keen brains contrived to manufacture humour from the most trivial incident.

One night they were talking shop in the mess, and, as often was the case, a long discussion took place on the respective merits of one- and two-seater machines. Eschwege, their ace, was naturally all in favour of the lone hand, but found himself in violent opposition to a certain gentleman, to whom we shall refer as X.

"I'd sooner go back to the trenches than fly a single-seater," declared X, but when he had gone off to bed, some bright spirit remembered that they were only a couple of days off 1 April. "Let's work it on old X," he suggested, and everyone, including their commander, Captain Heydemarck, agreed.

So the very next day X received a telegram to the effect that he was transferred to the western front, where he was to report for duty at Richthofen's aerodrome at Douai and join the famous ace's squadron.

X received the news when they were seated at lunch, and from his crestfallen face his comrades saw that he did not doubt the authenticity of the missive, even though he was instructed to leave Drama on 1 April. So in order to cheer him up, they arranged to give him a farewell dinner that evening and let him drown his sorrows in the flowing bowl.

All the world loves an April fool, and so the secret was kept in spite of the number of persons who had to share it. The Bulgarian commander of Drama pressed X's hand warmly when he came in to say good-bye and paid a fitting tribute to his doughty deeds ; his mechanics brushed away their tears with honest but grimy hands when he took leave of them and his machine. Genuine grief, however, was displayed by the Greek family on whom he was billeted, for they alone of all the inhabitants of Drama were not let into the secret. X had often romped with their children and flirted with the young ladies of the house, who were inconsolable in spite of assurances by his brother-pilots that he would soon return. So, armed with a large bouquet from his sorrowing hosts, X took his seat in the car that was to convey him to the station.

A place in the train had been reserved for him, and, leaning out of the window, he shook hands with all the messmates who had come to see him off. The signal was given ; slowly the train rolled out of the station.

But the stationmaster was in the plot too, for after steaming a couple of hundred yards the train came to a stop, and backed into Drama. A porter tore madly down the platform, waving a telegram and shouting at the top of his voice for X.

The amazed X fumbled with the wire, but when he opened it, the perplexity on his face increased every moment. On the platform a mixed assembly of Germans, Bulgarians, Greeks and Turks stood watching him with countenances wreathed in ever-widening grins.

The telegram informed X that his appointment to Richthofen's Jagdstaffel was cancelled and that he was nominated, as from the first of April, to the supreme command of the Flying Corps recently raised by the brigands of Albania.

X's pained look relaxed into a smile. " That's all right, boys," he remarked to the German war birds who had crowded into his compartment, " I don't care a damn as long as I can stay here and fly my old machine. So what about a drink ? "

The German pilots sometimes found their Bulgarian allies a sore trial, for the latter were always putting in requests to be taken up in an aeroplane. They naturally gave sound reasons to mask these desires for joy-rides, but Captain Heydemarck's good nature had its limits, and finally he put his foot down. One day, however, the Bulgarian liason officer attached to their Staffel begged the privilege of a flight for a certain colonel of the artillery and backed up his request with a letter from a general on the Bulgarian staff.

Heydemarck was powerless to resist such pressure, and detailed Sergeant Stattaus to take the colonel up the following morning. Lance-Sergeant van Ahlen, the second single-seater pilot in their Staffel, was ordered to escort the passenger, while Heydemarck carefully instructed both pilots that they were not to get into any mischief while their distinguished guest was in their charge.

The Albatros two-seater flew over the artillery positions that Colonel Trifonoff wished to reconnoitre and swung round to return to Drama, van Ahlen following in his Roland. Suddenly he caught sight of two other aeroplanes rapidly approaching him and recognised them as B.E.s.

The English planes attacked the Albatros, having failed to notice van Ahlen who was some 3,000 feet above them. He promptly dived on the tail of one of the B.E.s, whose pilot was completely taken by surprise and curved away to avoid his burst. The other English machine abandoned its attack on the Albatros and tried to fasten on to the Roland's tail.

Van Ahlen saw that Stattaus and his Bulgarian passenger stood every chance of getting home safely if he could keep the two English machines occupied for sufficient time. A neat turn brought him on to the tail of the B.E. that attacked him first and after a couple of bursts his opponent made off. He was obviously in trouble, but before van Ahlen could finish him off the second machine came to his rescue.

A lively bout of tail-chasing followed which ended to the Englishman's advantage, for a hard metallic clang told van Ahlen that his engine was hit. A few seconds later he saw the indicator of his pressure gauge drop and realised that a bullet from the same burst had holed his tank.

Van Ahlen switched on to the emergency tank, and his languid propeller showed signs of returning vigour. " Now then, I'm ready for you, Mr. Englishman," he thought.

But unfortunately for van Ahlen the Englishman had anticipated matters while he was busy with the switch, and he had the Roland nicely sighted. Once again van Ahlen heard the bullets rattle against his engine, and once more he saw the indicator drop.

A strong smell of benzin invaded his nostrils ; benzin squirted over his face and ran down his glasses. " Damn the blighter," he muttered, " he's the devil's own luck—pipped my emergency tank, I suppose, and now I'm for it ! "

He tore off his glasses and looked up to discover the feed pipe punctured ; he therefore turned off the cock, cut his engine and prepared to come down. He saw that he was over the plain, but otherwise he had no inkling of his whereabouts and surmised that in all likelihood he would have to land behind the enemy's lines.

"At all events," decided the practical van Ahlen, "I must keep out of his burst till I'm down." He put the Roland into a vertical dive and saw the ground rush up to meet him, while all thoughts of the enemy were driven from his head by the need of concentrating on the task of the moment.

In the nick of time he pulled out of his dive, made a good landing, taxied and came to rest in some long grass. He unbuckled his belt and crawled away ; in a dip of the ground he found a convenient ambush and looked up to see what the Englishman was doing.

The latter had followed him down and was now circling at a low height over the Roland, which he evidently intended to destroy. After however emptying a couple of drums on it, he rose again and flew off in the direction of Monuhi. Van Ahlen emerged from his hiding-place and went to investigate the damage.

It was not so bad as he had anticipated. The B.E. observer was a good enough marksman in the air, but he had obviously been a bit careless with the easy ground target, for examination showed that the Roland had sustained no further damage. Van Ahlen saw that there was enough juice to take him home if only he could manage to patch up the emergency tank's feedpipe.

But how to repair it ? He knew that an isolation band would be the very thing but unfortunately he had forgotten to bring one with him. He pulled out his cigarette case and smoked gloomily, wondering whether the English or the Bulgarians would be the first to find him.

Suddenly an idea struck him—the leucoplast strip

covering the old wound in his left arm would serve the purpose excellently, at least it would hold long enough to get the machine home.

It was not a pleasant job, and afterwards the doctor at Drama cursed him for a fool. But he did not care, for the trick worked, and he escaped from a spot which he afterwards discovered to have been behind the English lines.

Van Ahlen was often detailed to escort photographic expeditions, but invariably found such tasks tedious unless he looked for trouble. In this respect, however, his sight was excellent.

On one occasion, shortly after he had obtained his new Halberstadt, he was ordered to protect Captain Heydemarck, who wanted to photograph the Struma trenches in the neighbourhood of Lake Takhino. The Rumpler, piloted by Lance-Corporal Wethekam duly arrived over the positions between the lake and the sea, but Heydemarck found his work difficult as a strong side wind was causing the machine to drift very pronouncedly. Wethekam lost so much time in manœuvring his observer into position that the English Archies found his range and proceeded to make matters uncomfortable for him.

The gunner officers guessed that Heydemarck wanted vertical photographs and put up a barrage to cut him off from his objective. Soon the Rumpler was enveloped in a sea of the little white shrapnel clouds that looked so innocent.

"We'll carry on," explained Heydemarck to Wethekam in their language of signs, and then he saw black clouds mingling with the white. Looking round for the cause of this new trouble, he espied a monitor, barely a mile out at sea, the gunners of which were evidently itching for some target practice. Heydemarck saw that he was likely to make a bad job of the photography, but resolved nevertheless to go through with it. He remembered a trick that had pulled him out of a similar tight corner in France and instructed Wethekam to drop 3,000 feet. The pilot flew off in a long curve and returned to the objective at the lower level.

As Heydemarck hoped, the ruse deceived the gunners, who continued to blaze away at the old range, with the result that he got all the photographs he wanted. When the work was finished and Wethekam had put the Rumpler's nose in the direction of Drama, Heydemarck looked up to see where van Ahlen was.

But the Halberstadt was nowhere to be seen. Heydemarck wondered whether a lucky shot from the Archies had brought it down, but a moment's reflection told him that that was impossible as it had been flying a good thousand feet above their topmost range. A duel in the air was likewise ruled out, because the bright blue sky held no hostile planes. Heydemarck leaned over and swept the ground with his glasses.

The earth disclosed no sign of any tragedy, and as the mystery seemed insoluble, there was nothing for them to do but go home without their escort. They reached their aerodrome unmolested and, on landing, enquired whether anything had been seen or heard of van Ahlen.

But no one had any information ; no report had come through from the Bulgarian observation posts.

" Maybe he got into a fight that carried him out of your view," someone suggested.

" Not one Tommy in the air to-day ; I'll take my oath on it," Heydemarck replied.

Which shows how deceptive the air can be, for from his vantage point above the Rumpler van Ahlen had seen a Sopwith two-seater take off from Monuhi aerodrome. Its observer had marked the photographer down as an easy prey.

But the Sopwith's crew did not see the Halberstadt above them, and were decidedly surprised when it dived. However, they dodged the first burst and turned off in a long curve, with van Ahlen after them.

He ended a fierce bout of tail-chasing by pumping a stream of lead into the Sopwith's engine, eventually forcing it to land at Radulevo where the British occupants were taken prisoners by Bulgarian infantry. Consequently Lieutenant Brady, the pilot, who was badly wounded, spent some time in hospital at Drama, while his observer, Lieutenant Moore, dined at the German pilots' mess that night and went on to the prison camp at Philippopolis the following morning.

All of which shows how deceptive the air can be, except to the man who is on the look-out for trouble.

Lieutenant Lenz was another warrior who always seemed to be seeking more than his fair share of trouble, but he invariably returned home unscathed. His hair-breadth escapes from ticklish situations were so numerous and so often was his mach ne untouched when by all the laws of aerial warfare it should have been shot down in flames that some wit in the mess christened him " The Virgin," because it was evidently beyond the power of man to harm him.

The following is a typical example of one of Lenz's escapes. He was ordered to do a long distance reconnaissance in a Rumpler piloted by Sergeant von der Weppen and photograph the harbour and camp at Salonica, but

when the machine had flown some ten or twelve miles both
its inmates began to be disturbed by the unwonted calm
of the bright blue sky.   It did not seem natural to them
that they should have travelled so far without meeting
any hostile planes or receiving attention from the Archies
that were generally alert enough.

It was a positive relief to them when at last they heard
the familiar sounds and saw the white shrapnel cloudlets
about their airy path.   Von der Weppen put the Rumpler
into a sharp left-hand turn to get out of trouble's
way.

Crash ! crash ! crash ! Suddenly the Rumpler rocked
violently, and an ominous metallic clang smote their ears.
The engine began to sputter, while the revcounter
dropped.   It was not long before they were able to hear
themselves speak, for after a while the motor struck work
altogether.

" Can we get home in a glide ? " Lenz enquired.

Von der Weppen looked at the altimeter, which showed
close upon 13,000 feet and ventured the opinion that
they might manage to make the aerodrome of the German
Staffel at Hudova on the Vardar front, as the wind would
help them that way, but there was no possible chance of
getting back to Drama.

" Hudova then let it be," said Lenz.

But they were evidently out of luck, for as soon as they
started the wind changed suddenly.   It was dead against
them now and reduced their speed considerably.   At
last, after a flight that seemed to last for hours, they
made out the water of Lake Doiran.   The altimeter
showed that they were barely 2,000 feet above the ground.

" We might perhaps reach the Bulgarian trenches,"
said von der Weppen, " or again, we mightn't."

But they were dropping fast, and before they could pass the English trenches, there was the barrier of the Archies to surmount. Neither of them minded Archies when flying with a sound engine, but to the wounded bird, deprived of motive power, the anti-aircraft gunner is a formidable foe, for the curve that carries the machine away from his shrapnel means a loss of height at the critical moment,

But even more to be dreaded is the hostile single-seater that lurks at the top of its ceiling, waiting for just such a chance. His dive involves the gliding cripple in turn after turn, with the inevitable certainty of a landing behind the enemy's lines.

Better risk being smashed up by a hundred Archies than meet one Sopwith, thought Lieutenant Lenz, but the luck of the Virgin held good, for a survey of the sky showed not one English plane.

But now the Archies began to manifest signs of life and—to make matters worse—some sportsmen in the trenches joined in with machine-guns and rifles.

" Only 1,500 feet," remarked von der Weppen.

" I'm not going down without a fight," swore Lenz, depressing his gun so as to spray a shower of lead into the trenches. " That will spoil their fun," he chuckled, when he saw the Tommies scuttling for cover.

He gave them another drum to damp their ardour, and then saw to his delight that he was past the front line. But the Bulgarian trenches were some considerable distance away.

" Can we do it ? " asked Lenz.

" We've only 600 feet of altitude," ·replied von der Weppen.

Lenz glanced at his map and made a lightning calcula-
tion. There was nothing for it, his deductions told
him, but a landing in No Man's Land.

" Needs must when the devil drives," he muttered.

" 300—200—100 feet—now for it—and the Lord
only knows what we're going to bump into—never
mind—ground looks all right so far ! "

The wheels touched the surface, but before the machine
had finished its run the English batteries started again.
Luckily their shells pitched wide, and Lenz showed his
contempt for the bad marksmanship by making a cursory
examination of their Rumpler's injuries. He found that
a splinter had penetrated the crank-case, but otherwise
the machine seemed intact save for a couple of broken
ribs.

Von der Weppen dismounted the machine gun, which
he hoisted on his shoulder ; Lenz retrieved his photographic apparatus. Then they sprinted for the Bulgarian
trenches, which they reached unscathed.

They decided to wait there till nightfall on the chance
that something else might be salved from the Rumpler
if the English gunners did not shoot any better than
they were doing when it came down.

Lenz's luck held good ; in the darkness they led a
Bulgarian patrol to the spot where the Rumpler lay and
found themselves able to retrieve the engine and the
forward fixed machine gun in spite of the fact that the
artillery must have fired at least 200 rounds in its direction
while several aeroplanes had cruised over the spot and
dropped their eggs.

Archie was a sore trial to the Drama war birds, for
not only were they exposed to the attentions of the
British anti-aircraft artillery on every outward journey,

but the homecoming was likely to end with a vicious peppering from Turkish or Bulgarian gunners. The Turks, for instance, never learnt to distinguish between the black Maltese cross painted on the German buses and the tricolour cockade that distinguished the allied machines.

Reproaches and remonstrations simply met with a polite apology and a promise not to repeat the offence—which was broken the very next time that a German machine flew anywhere near a Turkish battery. One day Captain Heydemarck endeavoured to ascertain from a Turkish officer their mess was entertaining the reason of this pernicious habit.

The Turkish soldier loved his German ally, was the answer, and was deeply grateful to him for the noble work he did in the air. But whenever a machine distinguished with black crosses flew over a Turkish Archie, the gunners promptly conceived the notion that it might be an enemy cunningly disguised with the German emblem so as to deceive the simple-minded followers of the Prophet.

" But no such case has ever been known to occur," pointed out one of the Germans.

The Turk shrugged his shoulders. " That is true," he replied with a smile, " but our people are convinced that one day the English are sure to practise some such trick. We endeavour to show them how impossible it would be, but they prefer to take no risks. It is obviously the will of Allah that they should cherish such absurd notions."

When Allah is invoked, further argument is useless with a Turk, and the German war birds therefore took care to fly at the top of their ceilings whenever duty took them anywhere in the vicinity of a Turkish anti-aircraft battery.

The Bulgarian gunners showed a splendid impartiality. Not only did they subject every British, German, French, Serbian or Turkish aeroplane to as hot a fire as they could contrive, but they shot with equal zest on their own aviators. Filled with the joy of life, they looked upon every machine in the sky as their lawful prey, irrespective of its nationality.

Remonstrances were as useless with them as with the Turks. They promised to amend their ways and continued to shoot at every aeroplane they saw.

One day Captain Heydemarck received a telephone message from the Bulgarian G.H.Q., requesting his presence for a conference. He could land at Belisa aerodrome, said the Bulgarian officer who rang him up, and every preparation would be made to receive him.

"No doubt," thought Heydemarck, smiling ruefully, and reminded the speaker at the other end as tactfully as he could that there was no need for the Bulgarian Archies to take any part in his reception.

"Of course not," replied the Bulgarian, "it would be utterly impossible for them to make such a silly mistake as you suggest."

"H—m ; I sincerely trust so, but if they have any lingering doubts about our nationality, tell them that I shall fire a white light as a signal."

"Very good ; our anti-aircraft batteries will all receive instructions to that effect."

Heydemarck started off in a two-seater Albatros piloted by Lieutenant Siebold. First he had to do a short reconnaissance, but this caused him no trouble as neither the English war birds nor their Archies seemed

aware of his presence over their lines.   When the work
was done and the machine's nose set for Belisa, he gave a
sigh of relief.

As he had left the Drama aerodrome in charge of a
capable subordinate he was inclined to look upon the
trip as somewhat in the nature of a holiday.   Moreover
Major Popkristeff, the commander of the Bulgarian
pilots at Belisa, was noted for his lavish hospitality.
In fact everything in the garden seemed lovely.

" Crack—crack—crack ! "   Siebold   went   into   a
sharp right-hand turn to avoid a shell that burst perilously
near.   " So the Tommies have woken up to our presence
at last," he thought, " and I suppose we have asked for
trouble, seeing that we're barely 4,000 feet up."

Crack—crack—crack !   The next shell burst even
nearer than its predecessor, and Siebold put the Albatros into a series of frantic zigzags while Heydemarck
looked back to ascertain the whereabouts of the obnoxious
gunner.

" Those Tommies must have a very long range to-day,"
he thought.   Then he saw a third shell burst below
and in front of him.

A glance at his map told him that he must be flying
over the Bulgarian anti-aircraft batteries of Demi-Hissar.
He made a hasty grab for his pistol and fired off a white
light, which broke and fell to earth in a shower of stars.

To make assurance doubly sure he repeated the pre-
arranged signal, but the only reply was yet another
shell which burst uncomfortably near the Albatros's
right wing.   Siebold exerted himself to screw the utmost
speed out of his machine.

Heydemarck fired signal after signal, all of which
were answered with further shrapnels.   With dismay

he noted that his pilot's curves to avoid instant destruction had lost so much height that every moment they became an easier target.

Suddenly the bombardment ceased. " Have the idiots found out who we are ? " wondered the sorely tried Heydemarck, " or are we merely out of range ? Oh, Lord, there they go again ! " Then a sharp clang told him that the engine was hit.

The revs. dropped from 1,600 to 800, and, looking down, Siebold discovered that he was flying over the valley leading up to the Rupel Pass. It was hardly the place that he would have chosen for a forced landing.

They were steadily losing height, but apparently the engine was not completely disabled because the rev-counter mounted again to 1,200. " Probably a cylinder gone west," thought Siebold, " in which case we might just do it."

But the distance was too far to cover in a glide, and they were in the midst of mountainous country where the mildest result of a forced landing would be a total write-off of the machine. There was therefore no alternative but to crawl along as far as possible with a sputtering engine and trust to luck. At last the outlines of Belisa hove in sight, but at that moment the revcounter went back to 800 and stayed there.

" A block of three cylinders conked out," diagnosed Siebold and glanced at his altimeter. 900 feet ! He throttled down to half to ease the strain on the engine.

Down dropped the wounded Albatros ; Heydemarck saw the aerodrome squad laying out the big T that marked the correct landing-place. With his engine coughing badly, Siebold passed safely over the sheer drop on its south side, but at the very moment when his wheels touched the ground, the propeller stopped dead. He was only just in time.

But when the Germans showed their Bulgarian allies the battered Albatros and swore horrible vengeance against the gunners of Demi-Hissar, Major Popkristeff only grinned and bade one of his men fetch the log-book.

In it was written under the previous day's date :

" I was unable to carry out my long distance reconnaissance as per instructions because I was heavily shelled by our own anti-aircraft batteries at Demi-Hissar."

" They serve them all alike at Demi-Hissar," grinned the gallant major.

Captain Fuad Bey, commanding the Turkish militia company in the Drama Garrison, was a hospitable man who was always ready to oblige any of the German aviators with the loan of a horse if they fancied equestrian locomotion in their spare time. But as such requests were generally conveyed to him by an interpreter, he had no opportunity to make the acquaintance of these German brothers-in-arms. One night he determined to repair the omission and invited their whole mess to dine with him.

They were ushered into a room where they sat on low divans, but as none of them could speak Turkish and their host's French [1] was practically nil, the conversation was somewhat restricted. However, Fuad Bey seemed to set no store on the Koran's prohibition of alcohol for all true believers, and so for a while host and guests passed the time quite pleasantly by drinking one another's healths.

---

[1] Very few Turks knew German, and so by a strange irony of circumstance all communications between Turks and Germans generally took place in the language of their French enemies.

The fare set before the Germans seemed rather strange to their European palates. There were no hot dishes, but most of the edibles had a very sharp taste, in addition to being smothered in sauces that prevented them from guessing the nature of the ingredients. But, out of politeness to their host, they sampled all the dishes, and most of them made a fairly decent meal.

In the courtyard a military band struck up a lively quick-step march which Captain Heydemarck recognized as the Turkish National anthem. At his whispered instructions all the German war birds stood up and saluted.

They sat down again, but immediately the band started a fantastic tune which they took for a waltz. It sounded familiar, but no one could recall having danced to it.

Suddenly their host nudged Heydemarck and stood up. When he saluted, it dawned on the amazed Germans that the band was playing " Deutschland über alles" in their honour.

Then a door was thrown open, and Fuad Bey led them into a room where a table was laid in European fashion.

Revelation number two. This was the real dinner. What had been placed before them in the ante-room (some of them had partaken quite liberally thereof), was merely a series of *hors d'œuvres* that were intended to whet their appetites. " Save me from my friends," murmured one of the war birds, tenderly rubbing a full stomach.

CHAPTER X

THE strangest episode of the war in the air is perhaps
that which I have related in Chapter IV concerning
a Martinsyde pilot killed by Boelcke, who lay lifeless
in the cockpit while his machine continued its flight.
Later in the war I believe another similar incident
occurred, but I doubt whether the tale I am about to
relate has any parallel.

Somewhere in Belgium a German two-seater started
out on a reconnaissance, and when the task was fulfilled
the officer [1] (observer) instructed his pilot to fly home.
But on the way back they came under heavy fire from
anti-aircraft batteries. Shells burst all around them.

The pilot pulled his stick in a desperate endeavour
to climb out of the danger-zone, but before he could reach
the safety of the heights he felt a terrific explosion over
his head, which was followed by a violent blow that
seemed to cleave his skull in twain. Flames danced
before his eyes.

Then he found himself flying into a thick black cloud.
He felt relieved to be still alive and looked round to see
how his observer was faring.

He could not see an inch before him. In a dazed
manner he wondered how he had come into such a dense

---

[1] In most of the German two-seaters the observers were officers and the pilots
N.C.O.'s.

cloud ; he remembered that before the explosion the air around him was obscured by gaseous vapours, but he had had previous experience of anti-aircraft fire and it seemed to him unusual that the smoke should condense to form so thick a cloud.

He called out to the observer, but received no answer. He looked again, but it was impossible to see anything. Mechanically he steered in what he supposed to be the direction of his own lines.

The black cloud seemed endless. Below him he heard or sensed the enemy's shells bursting, and they gave him the direction. When he judged that he had travelled far enough, he cut off his engine and glided down in the hope of getting out of the thick darkness.

" Put up your nose, man ! " he suddenly heard the observer say, and obediently he pulled the stick.

" What's up with you ? You nearly ran into that church tower ! " the observer's voice continued a few seconds later in querulous, feeble tones.

Then the pilot realised the truth. " You'll have to guide me, sir," he replied, " for I can't see."

" I'll do my best," gasped the observer.

" How are you, sir ? " asked the pilot.

" I believe I'm done for, but keep her nose up."

From a field a group of spectators watched the eccentric behaviour of an aeroplane that seemed to have some difficulty in making up its mind where to land. First the pilot descended until it looked as if he was bound to crash his machine against the roof of a high building ; then he thought better of it and rose into the air again. He turned and appeared to be making for the enemy's lines once more, but his observer staggered to his feet, and, clutching his shoulder, shouted directions to him.

The machine's nose went down and it was about to hit the ground, but at the critical moment the pilot evened out and glided down towards the field. The machine shot past the heads of the astonished spectators and came to earth in a pancake that smashed the undercarriage.

When the bystanders ran to assist its inmates, they found the observer dead. The pilot's face was covered with blood, but he appeared to be breathing.

Ambulance men brought a stretcher and carried him to the hospital, where a doctor made the sad diagnosis that his sight was irretrievably gone. A splinter of shell had passed through his head and severed the optic nerves.

Mortally wounded, the observer had managed to guide his blind pilot to earth. Only an iron will kept him alive during those last few moments—until his task was done.

When the war started, there was much confusion in the air. Neither side had any definite types of machines ; both the British and German Flying Corps used French aeroplanes that had been acquired before the outbreak of hostilities.

The gunners on the ground therefore found great difficulty in recognising friend from foe and preferred to take no risks. They generally solved their problem by firing at every machine they saw.

But very soon the aeroplanes on both sides adopted distinctive devices ; the English and French machines had red, white and blue cockades painted on the wings and fuselages, while the Germans adopted a black Maltese cross as their emblem.

These badges were a great help to the gunners of the

anti-aircraft batteries and the men in the trenches, but for the pilots and observers they were unnecessary. Their trained eyes picked out the type of machine at a great distance, so that they never bothered to look for the distinguishing marks. But it is easy to see how such carelessness might lead to complications.

In a German aerodrome somewhere in the Meuse sector there lay a captured Spad. Its original pilot, a young, inexperienced and over-rash Frenchman, had one day encountered an old, wary foeman ; he put up a plucky fight, but the result was never in doubt, and ultimately he was fought down and forced to land behind the German lines, where his machine was taken in charge before he could set fire to it.

This Spad was under orders for transport to Germany, where the aircraft factories would examine it carefully to see if it contained any new devices worth copying. Afterwards it was destined to find its way to some flying school where an instructor would use it for mock combats with the pupils he had to familiarise with the types of machines they would encounter at the front. Meanwhile the aerodrome staff had painted out the red, white and blue cockades on its wings and fuselage, replacing them with black Maltese crosses to mark its change of nationality.

Several German pilots had flown this Spad behind the lines in their free hours, among them a certain Captain von Schleich, the pilot who had vanquished its original owner. Schleich, the leader of a Jagdstaffel that had scored many victories, decided that he liked the Spad quite as much as his own Albatros.

Moreover he was feeling in a merry mood. On the previous day his Staffel's bag had numbered six, while he himself had scored his nineteenth victory ; the binge that night had been worthy of the occasion.   To-day he felt pleasantly lazy, and as he had a certain amount of business to attend to, he let his second in command lead the Staffel.

But his work on the ground was finished earlier than he expected, and, as I have just remarked, his mood was of the best.   He was ready to see the bright side of everything.

Under these circumstances the idea occurred to him that it would be an excellent joke to fly the captured Spad over the front and see what the French airmen and Archies would do.

Thought was swiftly transmuted into action.   Schleich ordered his mechanics to bring the French machine out of its hangar and sent word to his own Archies kindly to refrain from firing on a Spad that bore the German emblem.   This was a very necessary precaution because the eyes of the gunners were now as skilled as those of the pilots, with the result that they shot at every machine of enemy type without troubling to look for its distinguishing device.

There was sufficient French ammunition for the Spad's machine gun to enable Schleich to protect himself if attacked in the air, so with a light heart he crossed his own lines and set off in the direction of Verdun. Warned of his approach, the German Archies held their fire.

Likewise the French Archies ; their gunners saw only a Spad, and it never occurred to them that it might bear a cross instead of a cockade. Then over the Argonne sector Schleich saw several French scouts in the air, but they paid as little attention to him as their brethren on the ground. Smiling to himself, he turned and made for Verdun again.

Above the famous city he saw a group of five Spads flying towards the German lines in close formation and, emboldened by the immunity accorded to him so far, he winged his way towards them. In less than a minute he had joined them and was endeavouring to follow the signals issued by their leader.

For the next five minutes he flew with the French Spads. Afterwards he admitted to a violent attack of cold feet, for if any one of the five had taken the trouble to look at his Maltese crosses, he would never have reached his aerodrome alive.

But when the Spads crossed the German lines, Schleich realised that something was bound to happen, for as long as he remained a member of their squadron the German Archies would be in a dilemma, as they could not open fire on the enemy without endangering him. He therefore put his machine into a right-hand turn and spiralled down.

It was not long before the Frenchmen noticed the sudden departure of the sixth Spad and began to observe its movements. As soon as their leader caught sight of the Maltese crosses on it and divined the trick that Schleich had played, he gave the signal for attack. All five started off in pursuit.

The German Spad evened out, turned and started to climb again while holding a parallel course to its pursuers. " I didn't do anything till they spotted me, so it's quite fair," thought Schleich when, having gained sufficient height for his purpose, he circled round and dived on the hindmost of the Frenchmen. A well-directed burst sent his late colleague down out of control.

Then Schleich half-rolled into a dive and dropped 6,000 feet with the other Spads after him. When he had gained sufficient speed, he caught his machine and made for his aerodrome with all the speed he could muster as his French ammunition was exhausted.

On the whole he decided that he had " got away with it nicely." He had secured his twentieth victory and pulled off a joke that would keep the mess amused for a week. Proceedings would not fall flat that evening, as they so often did the night after a binge.

He was welcomed home by comrades who had given him up, for someone had seen a Spad go down, and the inference drawn was that Schleich had asked for trouble and got it. But his safe return was made the occasion for a celebration that outdid the festivities of the previous evening.

It even took the sting out of the official reproof he received the following day when a curt communication admonished him that henceforth it was *verboten* under severe pains and penalties to take a captured machine into action, however clearly it might be marked with the German emblem.

When reading the accounts written by airmen of their exploits at the front, one is apt to gain an impression that the two-seaters used for reconnaissance, photography and artillery direction were easy fruit for the fast single-seater scout. But although the majority of victims sent down by any famous ace on either side are bound to be two-seaters, it does not always follow that the slower and heavier machine is inevitably doomed. Quite often the team-work of an observer who knew how to handle his gun and a pilot who gave him the right opportunities to use it caused the scout to sheer off hastily in search of easier prey.

Sometimes the two-seater proved more than a match for its nimbler opponent. In his *War in the Air*, H. A. Jones relates how an Albatros (then the latest type of German machine), was forced to land behind the British lines after a long duel with an old-fashioned B.E.2d, a most remarkable victory even though Captain G. A. Parker and Lieutenant H. E. Hervey, the British pilot and observer, were old hands, while their opponent was probably a novice fresh from the flying school.[1] But I doubt whether many observers can equal the feat of Lieutenant von Hengl who was attacked by ten Spads and escaped after shooting down four of them.

It was naturally due to good team-work. Von Hengl had flown for some time with his pilot, Lance-Sergeant Baur, so that each man knew by instinct what the other would do in a tight corner, and their work was highly valued by the batteries they served in the Rheims sector.

One morning they were instructed to locate a couple of French batteries that were making themselves particularly obnoxious. When they started out, the artillery on both sides was active, and the air literally hummed with shells.

Their objective lay some three miles behind the French lines, and as soon as they approached it, the Archies spotted them. That was, of course, all in the day's work; they took ordinary precautions, found their batteries, and von Hengl wirelessed the information back to his own artillery. Then Baur manœuvred their machine into a position where they could watch the effect of the German shells and correct any errors in the

[1] *The War in the Air*, Vol. II, p. 322.

range. But both men were so absorbed in their work that they failed to notice a squadron of ten Spads until escape was impossible.

Baur headed for a cloudbank in which he hoped to baffle the enemy, but it was too late. They were fairly trapped. Von Hengl was loath to leave his work undone. He knew that he could put his own artillery on to the correct mark if only he was allowed to watch a few more shots, and, after all, he could not hide in the clouds indefinitely. Sooner or later he would have to come out and take his chance with the Spads, so, mindful of Napoleon's maxim that attack is the best form of defence, he made up his mind to have a go at the enemy.

It is often said that Fortune favours the bold, and that day the fickle jade lived up to her reputation. Baur emerged from the clouds before the Frenchmen were expecting him ; the sun was behind him, and the Spads some 300 feet below him.

Tack—tack—tack ! A short burst from von Hengl's machine-gun stripped the wings off one Spad ; the mutilated machine fell like a stone, followed at a slower pace through the air by strips of fabric. Then the German observer swung his gun round on to the nearest of the remaining nine, and it promptly burst into flames.

There were Spads all round them, but Baur zigzagged away from their bursts as coolly as if he was showing off for the benefit of some pupil in a home aerodrome. His sudden dive and his observer's marksmanship had thrown the French squadron into such confusion that several Spads only missed head-on collisions by inches.

One Spad pilot headed straight for the German machine but saved himself from crashing into it by looping the loop. But as he came out of his loop, von Hengl sighted him and put in a burst that sent him spinning down out of control.

Meanwhile the other Frenchmen did not remain inactive. Hole after hole appeared in the German machine's wings, while every now and then the crack of wood proclaimed that a bullet had pierced the sides or floor of the cockpit. Finally a sharp sting in von Hengl's arm told him that one of the leaden messengers had reached him, but the next moment he forgot about it in the excitement of the fray.

He picked out a machine that bore the streamers of leadership and began a bout of tail-chasing with it. So furiously did the two machines whirl their circles that the other Spads had no chance to intervene. Their numbers were a hindrance rather than a help, and at last Baur manœuvred his machine on to the other's tail. Von Hengl put in a burst at short range, and the Frenchman went down in a spin, but contrived to catch his machine in time to land behind his own lines.

However his abrupt dismissal from the scene of action took the heart out of his companions, who with one accord turned and headed for their own aerodrome.

Von Hengl went on with his work. His wireless set was shot to pieces, but he dropped messages behind his own lines which were telephoned to the artillery. The German shells landed nearer and nearer to their mark, and when at length the French guns ceased fire, he dived down and peppered their crews with his Spandau.

Then home once more, and when he landed, the mechanics wondered how his machine had held together. Two interplane struts were so badly damaged that by every law of science they ought to have collapsed under the wind pressure.   Their resistance was nothing short of a miracle.

Von Hengl and Baur were always ready to take on any single-seater that tried to interfere with their work or join in any fight in their vicinity.   One day they hastened after a Jagdstaffel that had taken off to intercept a French bombing squadron heading for an important railway junction and arrived in time to take part in the fight, in the course of which they tackled one of the giant bombers and sent it crashing.   On another occasion they came to the rescue of a German single-seater, the pilot of which had been wounded after a long duel, and shot down the enemy who had him at his mercy.   Yet another victim was a Nieuport flown by an American pilot, whom they vanquished in single combat.

They had the luck they deserved.   When they were engaged on their usual work during the Aisne offensive, their engine was hit, and Baur had no alternative but to land behind the English lines, where they were made prisoners.   But before they could be marched off, a Wurtemberg battalion stormed the trench where they were held captives and set them free.

Later, one pitch-black night, they flew to Epernay— a long way behind the French lines—where they bombed a camp and shot up the Poilus with their machine guns. Neither of them ever knew how or why they got home safely, for, truth to tell, they were both gloriously drunk when they started out.   " We couldn't have got away with it if we'd been sober," both afterwards candidly admitted.

They finished the war with a score of nine acknowledged victories to their credit, a magnificent score for a couple of gunnery spotters who were not supposed to fight except in self-defence.

The contrasts of an airman's life in the war were extreme. When pilots returned from some grim encounter in the air, where perhaps several on each side had been sent down in flames, they landed at an aerodrome situated in some peaceful spot behind the lines. While their brethren in the trenches pigged it in rat-infested dug-outs, they ate and slept in comfort in dwellings provided with most of the amenities of civilisation.

These contrasts are well illustrated by an episode in the career of Captain Göring, who had the privilege of leading the famous Richthofen Squadron in the closing weeks of the war.

In the early months of 1917 he was in charge of a Staffel somewhere behind the Somme front. His responsibilities weighed heavily on him, for he was not yet an ace ; having only six victories to his credit, while the pilots under him were mainly inexperienced youngsters, fresh from the flying-school. But he liked his work and appreciated his quarters, which were situated at a bend of the Oise that emphasised the peculiar charm of the French landscape.

It was a beautiful day of early May, and Göring felt in a lazy mood. From a cloudless sky the sun poured down kindly rays, birds sang in the trees, and the artillery fire at the front was so restricted that it was almost possible for the pilots off duty to imagine that there was no war on. The midday patrol had gone out in charge of Göring's second in command, and with no work to do until the afternoon the leader reclined in his shirt-sleeves beneath the shade of an apple-tree in full blossom, dozing over the book he made pretence to read.

But his incipient nap was rudely disturbed by harsh sounds in the air, and he looked up to behold the blue sky dotted with fleecy shrapnel clouds, while high over head his trained ear caught the drone of distant engines.

"Enemy aircraft in sight, sir," called out a batman ; Göring sprang up, pulled on his coat and ran for his quarters.   Pilots fumbled at the buttons of their flying kit, while mechanics swore strange oaths as they pulled the machines out of their hangar.   It was a positive relief for Göring to climb out of the hustle and bustle of the aerodrome into the comparative calm of the sky.

Three other Halberstadts followed him as higher and higher he climbed towards the sun that would mask his attack upon the foeman who had so impertinently disturbed his peace and quiet.   At last he glanced at his altimeter, which showed 1,500 feet and swung northwards, followed by his youngsters in close formation, but though his eye searched the horizon he could espy no trace of the enemy.   He flew on, and at last, as he was nearing Cambrai, he saw the German Archies busily engaged with hostile aircraft.

Four F.E.s they were, accompanied by an escort of three Sopwiths.   Göring realised that he had to act quickly, also that it would be sheer suicide to attack the bombers 3,000 feet below him as long as the Sopwiths were free to dive on to his pilots' tails.   The F.E.s would have to go their way in peace until he had disposed of their escort.

This was easier work than he had imagined.   The four Halberstadts dived out of the midday sun on to the Sopwiths, who were completely taken by surprise and made off to their lines.   Göring made no attempt to pursue them.

He zoomed up to gain height for an attack on the F.E.s, then down again dived the Halberstadts in a long curve that brought each of them on to the tail of his intended victim. But for a few critical seconds the leader found himself isolated and exposed to a concentrated fire from all four F.E.s. Around him he could see the medley of smoke-trails left by their tracer bullets, as, disregarding the other three, he headed straight for the opponent he had singled out.

But his youngsters did not fail him ; from the corners of his eyes he saw them swing down to right and left of him, leaving him free for a single combat. The British observer in his opponent put in a burst at close range, but it only tore a few holes in his wings and he passed out underneath. When he had gained sufficient speed, he zoomed up, firing as he rose. The F.E.'s observer swung his gun over the side to get in a burst, but he was too late ; before the first bullet left his barrel, Göring's twin Spandaus shot out their leaden streams.

From the stricken F.E. a sheet of flame burst forth as the burning cockpit shot earthwards past the Halber-stadt. Fragments of wood and iron flew all about the German pilot, several narrowly missing his face, and he was truly thankful when he had climbed out of the danger zone.

From the peace of higher altitudes he looked down to see one of his youngsters hotly engaged with an F.E. which he forced down until it went into a nose-dive and hit the ground violently. His other two pilots were far away, chasing their F.E's, and his experience of previous combats told him that this time they stood little chance of getting them. In the airspace below him the broken wings of his late opponent fluttered gently earthwards, leaving a thin trail of smoke behind them.

The two pursuers rejoined their leader, who gave the

signal for all to return to the aerodrome.   The homeward
trip was uneventful ;   one by one the war birds dropped
down to land.   In the excitement of the fray Göring had
forgotten about the heat, but as soon as he was assisted
out of his cockpit, he felt himself near to suffocation in
his flying kit.

At last he was free of it ;   he questioned his pilots.
As he had anticipated the two youngsters pursuing the
F.E.s had no luck ;   the Englishmen were old hands who
fought them off until they reached the protection of their
own Archies.   But the third, who had succeeded in
bringing his opponent down, was exultant when his
leader complimented him.   " My second, sir," he
exclaimed.   " And my seventh," thought Göring, as he
went to make out his report, " but, Lord, how hot it is
to-day ! "

Back again in the orchard at last !   Göring pulled off
his coat, rolled up his shirt-sleeves, sank into his deck-
chair and picked up his book again.   It was open at the
page he had been trying to read when the alarm was
given.   He glanced at his wrist-watch ;   it was exactly
an hour since he left the orchard.

Overhead the sun blazed down as warmly as before ;
the birds still sang in the trees while the unwonted silence
of the artillery at the front seemed to signify that the
gunners there were also affected by the languor of this
warm spring.   He glanced around him ;   everything
was exactly as it had been an hour ago.

But within those brief sixty minutes he had climbed to
dizzy heights to fight a duel in the air with two brave
men, whom he had sent crashing to their death, besides
experiencing a narrow escape from sharing the same
fate when their machine burst to pieces in the air.   And

now he was taking his ease under the blossoms of the apple-tree, wondering whether he could summon up enough energy to read his book.

Truly this war was a strange business, thought Göring.

But it was not all sunshine on the western front, and after the hot summer of 1917 there came an exceptionally nasty winter.   It did not, however, interrupt the fighting, and in its November the famous battle of Cambrai took place, in which the British tanks played such a large part. Much has been written about this battle, mainly by persons concerned in the affairs on the ground, so that it is therefore interesting to have an account of it from the airman's point of view.

Captain Richard Flashar, who was at that time the leader of Jagdstaffel No. 5, has placed on record his impressions of the fight as viewed from the air, and his tale commences with the night of 19 November, when he was roused from his bed by a telephone message from G.H.Q.

" Enemy attacking in force," the man at the other end told him, " warn your Staffel to be ready to start at 7 a.m. on any mission that may be assigned to them by the General Staff."

Flashar relieved his feelings by a few round oaths. What, he wondered, did their High and Mightinesses of the General Staff think an airman's machine was made of ?   Or his eyes ?   Or his constitution ?

November had justified its reputation for fog and rain ; for the previous ten days no machine had left its hangar.   No, thought Captain Flasher, the English are not quite such fools as you gentlemen of the General Staff make them out to be ; besides, we have heard these tales of sudden offensive before, and they never come to anything.

But orders are orders, and so he told his batman that the pilots were to be wakened at 6 o'clock in case the weather cleared sufficiently for them to go up ; then he went back to bed to resume his interrupted sleep.

Brass hats are brass hats the world over, and the Cambrai sector was supposed to be a quiet one.   But when the din of a terrific bombardment awoke Flashar long before 6 o'clock, he had to admit that for once the brass hats knew their business.   Obviously something was going to happen ; he hurried into his flying kit and stumbled out into the darkness, uttering maledictions against the English gunners who had spoilt his beauty sleep.

At 7 a.m. all the pilots of his Staffel were shivering in the aerodrome.   From the thick mist heavy raindrops pelted them remorselessly.   " No one can possibly go up this morning," was the general verdict.

In Flashar's office the telephone bell rang incessantly. The English were attacking in force, it was said, and their airmen were out (break their necks, the damn fools, thought Flashar), and the tanks were supporting the infantry.   More tanks than had ever been seen at any battle, said his informant.

Then the general in command of his army corps came to the telephone and wanted to know why the —— his Staffel was not in the air.   Flashar tried to explain that it was absolutely impossible for the pilots to take off, and if they did, they would never find their way to the front in a fog that did not allow them to see a yard before their noses ; they would only have to come down again and land where they could, in which case they would probably write off all their machines. Flashar made much of this last point, tactfully reminding the general that his was the only Jagdstaffel in the sector while the number of aeroplanes at his disposal was limited.

" The English aviators are up," snorted the general, and began to talk of a court martial in the way generals of all nations do when anything upsets them.

Flashar went back to the aerodrome, cursing all generals and their staffs. The pilots of his Staffel were all redoubtable fighters and several of them had won the " Pour le Mérite " order. No one had a right to accuse them of showing the white feather.

Still, something had to be done, if only to show the general how unfounded were his insinuations. Flashar went up himself to see what it was like aloft, but a minute later he was down again, thankful enough to have found the aerodrome and landed safely. He reported that it was sheer suicide to try to carry out the general's instructions at present, but ordered the pilots to stand by their machines.

After a shivering interval of about half an hour the fog showed faint signs of clearing ; then, suddenly, the Archies in the vicinity of the aerodrome began to fire. " Enemy aircraft sighted," reported a sergeant.

" We'll have to go up after them," Flashar told his men. The invaders he guessed to be a bombing squadron that had been sent to drop their eggs on his aerodrome, though he wondered how they expected to find their target in the thick fog. But possibly they also had an irate general at the other end of a telephone who threatened courts martial when they showed reluctance to undertake the impossible.

Flashar picked out three of his best pilots. " Two

of us will go round in a left-hand circle," he instructed them, " the other two in a right-hand one."

Distorted through the fog, he heard the drone of an English motor. It was the right moment to intercept the raiders, he decided, though it would be sheer luck if any of them were caught.

Staring up, he fancied he saw black dots through the fog. He gave the signal to his mechanics ; his Albatros left the ground and as he banked, to turn he caught sight of the black dots again. He puts the machine's nose in their direction, but before he could reach them they were swallowed up in the fog.

After five minutes of blind man's buff, during which period he failed to sight a single English machine, he dropped cautiously down to the aerodrome, where he found that the other three had already landed.

" No luck," reported two of them, but Sergeant Mai claimed to have shot one down in flames. He blundered into him by pure chance and managed to get in his burst before the adversary. Lucky to avoid a collision.

An hour later came the confirmation of Mai's success. The wreckage was found.

Further news followed shortly. Two Englishmen were prisoners ; they had lost their way and were forced to come down where they could. Lucky to have got away with their lives—so ran the verdict of Flashar's Staffel.

They were certainly luckier than others of their squadron, for ten minutes afterwards came the report that two English machines had crashed into trees when they attempted to land. All their crews were killed. The Staffel decided unanimously that their decease was a striking proof of the folly of attempting to fly in such a fog, whatever the generals at the other end of the telephone might say.

But the weather took a turn for the better and Flashar thought that after all something would have to be done to satisfy the irate veteran. He gave the order for the Staffel to start, but as soon as he attempted to steer for the front the mist thickened. He gave it up as a bad job, and once again he considered himself lucky when he got down safely.

On the aerodrome anxious groups of mechanics awaited the return of their machines, and eventually five out of the eleven rejoined their leader. The other six rang up in the course of the morning.

Their reports were identical. "Impossible to find the front, had to land where I could. Machine more or less O.K. ; hope to get back some time in the afternoon." Flashar felt dubious on this point and swore that the general's unreasonable orders had halved the strength of his Staffel.

"But now is the time to rub it in," he decided, and rang up G.H.Q. to report that he had attempted to carry out his orders but only succeeded in losing six good pilots. He quoted the fate of the English bombers as an awful example of attempts to fly on such a day.

The same general answered the telephone, but luckily he was in a more reasonable frame of mind and replied that he would leave it to Flashar to decide when it was possible to fly. "Only, for heaven's sake try to get to the front as soon as you can," he implored.

Flashar learnt the news from the front. Things were looking bad ; the English had broken through the weakest part of the line after a short but intensive artillery fire. How far the offensive had penetrated it was impossible to say as yet, but the defenders were still holding on to Marcoing. Flashar made rapid calculations and deduced that the enemy could not be much more than five miles from his aerodrome. It looked odds on the Staffel having to move back to safer quarters if this push went on.

He enquired about the tanks, and received the reply that the English seemed to have brought out a bigger and more effective type that could jump the widest trench and knock a stone wall down—there was positive evidence on that point. Meanwhile they were giving hell to the poor blighters in the trenches ; no one knew what to do to stop them.

" Try what your aeroplanes can do against them," urged the general, and Flashar promised that he would, provided that the Staffel could reach the front.

After lunch he decided to let his six remaining machines start out in couples. Flying barely 100 feet above the ground he took as his guiding-line the long straight road between Le Cateau and Cambrai which ran past his aerodrome, as like so many French roads it was flanked by rows of poplars on either side. The tops of these trees were visible through the mist.

Flashar soon lost his companion but reached Cambrai, skirted the housetops and flew on towards the front. The din of the artillery was terrific ; below him the road was choked with batteries going full gallop through the fog, munition transports following them at a slower pace and infantry advancing at the double. " A hell of a mess on the ground," he thought, " fog or no fog, I'm better off up in the air." But the next moment he was inclined to revise his opinion when an aeroplane streaked past him.

It came so close that the wings of the two machines nearly touched, and yet he was unable to tell whether the other was German or British.   Several more followed at intervals, but he made no attempt to interfere with them and was only too thankful to escape a collision.

He saw the figures of advancing infantry, which he took to be English, and when he turned towards Flesquières and Ribécourt, he could espy dark smears moving through the mist which were obviously tanks.   Then a thick blanket of fog rolled up and blotted them from his eyes.

It was hopeless to go on, so he turned and, more by luck than judgment, made his way back to Cambrai, where he had the poplar-flanked road to guide him to his aerodrome.   When he landed he found that only two other pilots had succeeded in reaching the front, one of whom had attacked a tank with phosphorus ammunition that left it an easy mark for the artillery.   He served several others in similar fashion, which were then put out of action by the gunners.

The following day the fog showed no signs of lifting, but with the experience the pilots grew better at finding their way to the front.   It was, of course, out of the question for them to look for their usual opponents of the air, but, flying low, they undertook the work of contact patrols[1] and used their machine guns with good effect against the advancing English infantry besides

---

[1] The " Contact patrol flyer " (German : Infanterieflieger) had the task of watching the progress of an offensive and reporting to the staff by signals or wireless the changes in the front.   As it was impossible to distinguish friend from foe when flying high enough for safety, the infantry were supposed to signal their positions by lights or by laying down strips of cloth on the ground. When circumstances prevented them from undertaking their regular work, the Jagdstaffels were generally detailed to assist the " Infanterieflieger."   The fog must have rendered their tasks doubly hard in the Cambrai battle.

engaging the tanks with phosphorus ammunition whenever they sighted them.

But on 22 November, the rain ceased and the fog
blew off, so that Briton and German fought in the air
again.   The Staffel had four victories as a result of their
day's work.

They had fought against odds, but that evening they
were joined by eight machines from Staffel No. 15, and
Richthofen motored over to see what further reinforcements they needed.   But meanwhile the fighting on the
ground was turning out badly for the Germans, and the
English foremost troops were less than three miles from
the Staffel's aerodrome.   Flashar foresaw that their
hangars were bound to be destroyed as soon as they were
spotted for the enemy's heavy artillery—which the
English reconnaissance machines would be certain to do
if the weather remained clear.   To-morrow, it was
agreed, they would have to make a move.

But on the next day the fog came over again and
concealed the position of the aerodrome from prying
eyes.   Once more the German war birds joined the
infantry flyers for contact patrol work, and those who
survived the day were surprised to find themselves
still in their old quarters when they returned.   Every
moment they expected the order to pack up, for despite
the reinforcements that had reached them, the men in
the front line could barely hold their own.   It seemed
impossible to hinder the English from effecting a
complete break through.

But on 24 November, the offensive came to a standstill, much to the surprise of Flashar and his comrades,
who could only presume that the bad weather which
favoured its early stages subsequently prevented the

victors from fully exploiting the advantage they had gained. And so the defenders hung on for another six days until the German counterstroke was delivered.

Low clouds hung over the sky that day, but the war birds on both sides were active. From daybreak till dusk patrol after patrol went out from the hangars that had been crowded to their utmost capacity by the arrival of yet another Staffel of Richthofen's squadron. But no one minded the discomfort, for the great ace came over to take command of their operations.

Flashar's Staffel was placed under him, and remained subject to his orders until his death in the April of the following year. He was glad to have the responsibility taken out of his hands for the rest of the Cambrai battle, and he smiled when he reflected that not even the most peppery of generals would dare to order Richthofen to fly in impossible fogs.

But Flashar had a lucky escape on that busy day. In the afternoon he was flying over the English lines with five other machines when a Sopwith squadron suddenly attacked him. The usual dogfight took place, in the course of which he found himself separated from his companions and assailed by three English pilots who had singled him out on account of the streamers of leadership his machine carried.

As he went into a turn to shake off one of them that had succeeded in getting on to his tail, another put a stream of tracer bullets into his bus from above. He heard the wood splinter on all sides of him and felt the rush of air as one bullet whizzed past his face to bury itself in his seat. The next moment his tank was holed by another.

The Sopwiths had fought him down to 1,000 feet,

so that he saw no alternative but to land unless a miracle occurred, but just as he was resigning himself to his fate and wondering how and why he was still alive, Könnecke and Rumey,₀ two of his best pilots, dived unexpectedly from the clouds and sent one Sopwith down in flames. Another followed it soon afterwards, whereupon the third made off.

Flashar turned and headed for home, but just as he crossed the front line, his engine went dead. His last drop of benzin had run out, and when he tried to switch on to the emergency tank, he found that that also had been pierced.

He had to come down at once, and his machine was a total wash-out, from which only the engine could be salved. But the astounding feature of the whole business was that the tracer bullet which entered the main tank failed to set the bus on fire.

Miraculous as his escape was, the following incident, which resulted in an award of the Iron Cross, seems quite as incredible. The hero of it was a certain Corporal Gieler, who was the observer in a D.F.W. of a somewhat antiquated type. This machine, piloted by Corporal Kornder, seemed, however, to bear a charmed life.

But there is a proverb concerning the number of journeys that a cracked pitcher may make to a well, the day must come when it breaks. Neither Kornder nor Gieler believed that their luck would last for ever, and one day they were certain their last hour had come when they were surprised by three fast English single-seaters while engaged in shooting up a trench in the Ypres sector.

Before they had time to manœuvre into a defensive position one of their opponents put in a burst at close range. Kornder got off with two flesh wounds that did not trouble him greatly, but Gieler received a bullet through his shin. Worst of all, the elevator and the left lateral control were shot away.

As steering was impossible, the D.F.W. began to go round in circles, and the English pilots waited for a favourable opportunity to finish it off. But Gieler's presence of mind saved the situation.

He could hardly use his wounded leg, but with a desperate effort he hoisted himself out of his seat and crawled on to the left lower wing, where he contrived to hold on to an interplane strut. The resistance his body offered to the wind enable Kornder to steer a straight course, and with a desperate nose-dive he contrived to land behind his own lines.

Alpine flying is beset with trials and tribulations of its own, as the Swiss aviators discovered when they made the first attempts to steer their machines amid the summits of their mountains, where a forced landing must inevitably involve a fatal crash. The same fate awaited the war birds on the Austro-Italian front.

The traveller of to-day, journeying from a city of Northern Italy to Vienna, will probably use the Brenner route. His trip begins in the hot Lombardian plain, but after leaving Verona his train starts to climb. A cooling breeze is wafted to him from the high snows of the Alp-wall.

Several hours out from Verona the train will halt at Trento, which is the chief town of the district now known as the " Alto Adige." The old mediaeval town, with its battlements and turrets, fills the whole of the Adige valley ; to the right loom the pinnacles of the Dolomites to the left we see the foothills running up to the high mountains of the Adamello massif.

Trento is famous in history for several events, but the German and Austrian war birds of that front will remember it as the headquarters of the aircraft attached to the Austrian army that defended the valley of the Adige against the invading Italians. Their aerodromes were at the little neighboring villages of Gardolo and Pergine.

One day the order went forth that Milan must be bombed—Milan, the industrial capital and nerve-centre of Italy, with its network of railways, its vast factories and its dynamos that transformed the Alpine torrents into electrical energy. A blow struck home at Milan would inevitably be felt all along the front that stretched from the high snows of the Ortler to the blue waters of the Adriatic.

It would be a heavy blow, but the war birds who had to strike it knew that they must start off by crossing peaks 7,000 feet high, where descent meant death. The second part of the journey across the Lombardian plain might be easy, but if they survived the Archies of Milan the last stage would involve recrossing those peaks when benzin supplies were low and machines perhaps damaged. It was a cruel finish for a wounded war bird.

Dawn had not yet reddened the February snow that covered the foothills when the bombing squadron started, ten great Lohner-Pfeil double-deckers that required 270 litres of benzin to do the 120 miles each way of their journey. Weighted with 80 kgs. of bombs, they were bound to climb slowly and painfully, and all the pilots knew that it was touch and go whether they could attain the 9,000 feet which was the minimum, safety height at which they could cross the rocky wall that separated them from the Lombardian plain.

They were ready to start, but the leader waited for a few moments before entering his cockpit. He glanced round the group of pilots, all of whom understood the significant look in his eye. If any of them misdoubted their engines, now was the moment to say so and withdraw without shame rather than shatter themselves on the rocks in a forced landing. But as no one spoke, he took off, followed by the other nine.

Soon they were up in the snows—a white world that changed to red in the glow of the rising sun. Here and there dark patches showed rocks too steep to hold the snow.

But when they had flown some little distance, sharp thunder-peals rose up from below, to be tossed, re-echoing from peak to peak. Amid those snows there were men that confronted one another in opposing lines of trenches—to be smitten by the fierce summer sun of the rarefied air and chilled by the icy blasts of winter. From some lonely eyrie an Italian anti-aircraft battery had spied the raiders, and was roaring its defiance at them.

The still, crisp air was now alive with the fleecy shrapnel cloudlets, but the war birds had often passed that way and knew how to avoid the messengers of death. Yet in curving to dodge them, they exposed themselves to fresh perils, for amid the treacherous mountains it was bound to fare ill with the pilot who lost his course and so wasted too many drops of his precious benzin ; on the way home he would run short and be forced to descend, perhaps even on those same rocks.

The leader glanced at his compass and saw that the intense cold of the mountain air had frozen it ; that meant that he would have to pick his way by identifying on his map the labyrinth of ridges and valleys. If he erred, his followers, taking their direction from him, would suffer for his mistake, and none might reach Pergine aerodrome again.

But the man whose Lohner-Pfeil bore the streamers was an expert map-reader, and so he threaded his way out of the maze of peaks and at last brought his squadron to the Lombardian plain where no worse fate than captivity awaited the pilot whose engine failed him. With a sigh of relief he dropped to the comparative warmth of a lower altitude ; henceforth it was a straight course to Milan, where the giant cathedral stands high above the even stretch of the plain, a landmark far and wide to all who approach the city by land or air.

It was nearly nine clock when the squadron reached Milan, the factory town with suburbs that sprawl in disorderly fashion over the plain. From the cathedral spire the leader's eye roved over the buildings until he had picked out the railway station. As soon as he had found it, he knew where to search for the electrical works that were his main objective, but before he could approach them, the fleecy shrapnel clouds began to burst around his Lohner-Pfeil. The Archies of Milan were alert to repel the raiders that threatened Italy's nerve-centre ; in all probability they had been warned by telephone from the front.

From Milan's aerodrome a dozen Italian aeroplanes rose into the air, and the leader knew that they were a worse danger than the Archies because the gigantic Lohner-Pfeils were powerless to fight them off. To economise weight and ensure an adequate supply of bombs for the work of destruction and benzin for the journey, the Austrian machines had been stripped of all superfluous weight, including their machine guns. As a grudging concession, their observers were allowed to take revolvers or carbines to protect themselves against the full-armed foemen of the air !

If we have no adequate weapons, then we must fight with bluff, thought the leader, and noted with satisfaction that when he manœuvred into the correct position to fire on one of those Italian aviators that executed their turns with such dash, the latter sheered away quickly. How should he know that there were no Spandaus to fight him off !

So the pilot steered his way to the dynamos, and his observer gave them his largest eggs.   But as the Lohner-Pfeil was swinging over a huge adjacent factory that was such a tempting target, the leader observed with a sudden shock the presence of an Italian machine barely 200 feet above him.   He put his machine into a left-hand turn, his opponent did likewise.

Round went the Lohner-Pfeil in a series of left-hand curves, which were imitated by the light Italian scout that turned so elegantly.   The Italian pilot saw that he held an advantage over his heavier, clumsier opponent, whom he regarded as an easy prey, and waited for a favourable moment to put in the burst that would send him down in flames.

Aware that below him all Milan was watching his prowess, he resolved to treat them to a spectacle worthy of their eyes, and so—for a few vital seconds he concentrated his thoughts on the beauty of his dashing left-hand banked turns and ignored the opponents beneath him. His vanity was his undoing.

Watching his opportunity, the Lohner-Pfeil pilot manipulated stick and rudder with expert hands and feet and shot off into a right-hand turn. Before the outwitted Italian realised the trick that had been played on him, the two adversaries were more than a mile away.

The Austrian leader calmly swung round again and manœuvred his machine over a factory. Down went an egg, and the observer yelled his delight as a thick column of smoke belched up. The pilot then turned away to watch from a safe distance the destruction wrought by his followers.

The Italian gunners were now warming to their work, and the air was full of shrapnel. But they fired with more zeal than discretion, the Austrian leader thought, for most of their shells were bound to fall into the city and do damage ; moreoever they made such a hell of the upper air that the Italian war birds hesitated to close with the enemy they could have so easily finished off. One Italian machine went down in a vertical dive, but it was impossible to see whether the pilot had fallen a victim to his own Archies or taken a desperate way of getting out of a hot corner.

The leader saw a high factory chimney quiver and totter ; then followed explosion after explosion until the air was thick with smoke and dust. For a time he lost sight of his followers, but at last, one after another, they shot out of the haze. Their job was done ; all the eggs were dropped, so they set off homeward, the leader bringing up the rear. He glanced at his chrono-meter and noted that the whole business had taken half an hour.

The return journey seemed endless, for the excitement, that buoyed them up at the start had ebbed, and twenty tired men began to realise that it was brutally cold and speculated on the troubles that awaited them from

Archie and the mountains on the last stage. A strong east wind was reducing their speed, and, judging by the apparent permanence of certain landmarks, they seemed to be almost standing still.

The leader glanced at his benzin " clock " and saw that he had 90 litres left. The oil-pressure gauge stood at zero—probably frozen, he thought. Then his ear caught an ominous sound ; his engine was knocking. He noted the speed indicated on his tachometer and tried to calculate the distance still separating him from Pergine.

Fifty-five miles he reckoned it to be—the bus ought to do it. But the trouble was that they were not miles as the crow flew them, for he had to allow extra mileage for his climb to clear the mountain barrier. He tried to calculate what this addition would amount to, but the figures whirled in his head till he wanted to scream aloud. Yet all the time his hand manipulated the stick mechanically and efficiently, coaxing the utmost out of the knocking engine as he started to climb.

Suddenly his observer hammered joyously at his shoulder and shouted something ; after several efforts the pilot understood him to say that they had passed the Italian positions, and now, whatever happened, they could land behind their own lines and need not be taken prisoners. A loud vicious outburst from Archie confirmed the statement ; the Italian gunners had been caught napping but were now alive to their presence and exerting themselves to atone for the negligence by wasting as much ammunition as they could in the hope of escaping a wigging from their superiors.

But the pilot smiled wearily ; if the knocking engine failed him and he was forced to descend, the Italians would be welcome to what they could pick up after the inevitable crash. How many weary miles of jagged mountains were there still to cross, he wondered, glancing anxiously at his benzin " clock."

His engine was knocking worse than ever, but at last a well-known landmark came into sight. He relieved his feelings with a triumphant yell and told the engine that he did not care whether it went dead or not, for now he knew that he could reach Pergine aerodrome in a glide.

But strange to say, the engine went on working till he shut it off to land, though it continued to knock till the last moment ; it is a way that engines have sometimes. When, however, his mechanics made their examination, the pilot gave vent to a very long whistle, for the axle-shaft was found to be broken !

One by one the other nine Lohner-Pfeils dropped down to Pergine. None were missing ; not a pilot or observer had been wounded, and so they all trooped off to a late breakfast, proud of a job well done.

Though the average airman's life at the front was exciting enough, it would be wrong to suppose that he had a monopoly of the thrills. The instructor engaged on home service generally had his fair share of them, if only for the reason that in the air one is always up against the unexpected.

Such is, at least, the opinion of Captain Flashar, whose adventures at Cambrai have been recounted earlier in this chapter.

In September, 1916, he was the pilot of a two-seater that carried an observer to bomb or photograph, and when he was sent back from the front to Freiburg-in-Breisgau to instruct the youth of Germany in the science of flying L.V.G.'s, he looked forward to a rest after a period of strenuous activity. But one day, when he had finished his work, he received a telegram from the general commanding the district, who wanted him to send a pilot to fly over the town of Rottweil, some forty miles away, and make sure that the lights of the powder and munition factories there were sufficiently masked so as to be invisible to hostile aircraft.

" Nice little jaunt for someone," thought Flashar, and then it struck him that the someone was bound to be himself because he was the only certified officer pilot in the establishment. And the trouble was that he had never made a night-flight.

All the same the job had to be done, and he thanked his lucky stars that there was a full moon that night. He therefore rang up the officer in command of the Archies at Rottweil and said that he would come over the same night, starting from Freiburg about eleven. The gunner promised to listen out for his engine and send up a rocket as soon as he heard it.

Associated with Flashar in the instruction of youth was his friend and observer, Claassen, who had accompanied him on many bombing and photographic expeditions, on the western front, and though he too had never been up at night, he swore that he would see his pilot through with the job. When the time came the sergeant in charge of the aerodrome told them the regulations for starting and landing by night, and after their Mércèdes engine had been tested, they took off.

As the start was watched by a crowd of admiring pupils, Flashar was delighted when he found himself leaving the ground as neatly as though he had been doing nothing but night-flying all the war. But after he had circled twice round the aerodrome to show the youngsters what a fine pilot he was, horrid doubts began to assail him, for he knew that his way to Rottweil lay through the hilly, wooded country of the Black Forest, and though by day he could have picked out some spot to land in an emergency, he had no idea what he would do at night if anything went wrong.

Before he had been five minutes in the air his misgivings were increased by the capricious behaviour of the moon. For the last fortnight an Indian summer had prevailed, but to-night of all nights a thick bank of clouds had risen, and of course Madame Luna must needs go and hide herself behind them. In an incredibly short space of time these clouds covered the whole heaven, blotting out the stars, so that Flashar was enveloped in a pitch-black darkness.

Although he could see no landmarks, he steered by his compass, and in due course a rocket shot up into the air, showing that the Archie officer at Rottweil had kept his word. Claassen answered with a signal from his light-pistol.

Rottweil was as dark as regulations intended it to be, and when Flashar had finished his tour of inspection he felt he could conscientiously report that all the factories were properly masked from any French bomber. He breathed a sigh of relief ; his job was done, and in another half hour he would be back at Freiburg. Nothing so very difficult in this night-flying, he decided.

A moment later he swore profoundly and revised his opinion, for when he swung round to put the L.G.V.'s nose in the direction of Freiburg, he saw to his horror that the needle of his compass remained unaltered.

" Something gone wrong with the bally thing," he

made Claassen understand, whereupon the observer
studied his map by the light of his electric torch and
then leant over the side.

But what is the use of an observer who cannot observe ?
Flying over level country, even on the darkest night
and under war conditions, it would have been possible
to distinguish landmarks of a sort, but in the woods of
the Black Forest Claassen could see nothing that would
help him.

Every now and then Flashar cut off his engine to enquire
if Claassen had found the way, and his tones grew
snappier each time the observer was forced to admit
that he was still in the dark. But at last the badgered
Claassen could stand it no more, and pointing vaguely
ahead of him, said : " You're getting along splendidly,
old man."

But his tones were so unconvincing that Flashar resolved to ignore his observer for the rest of the trip.
" If I keep on long enough in some direction," he thought
" I'm bound to get out of this damned Black Forest
sooner or later and find somewhere to land."

Every now and then he cut off his engine and glided
down, but could espy nothing but wooded hills. But
after he had flown aimlessly for some forty minutes, he
fancied he made out the water of a large river. When
he dropped, he found his surmise to be correct.

" If it's the Rhine, we're O.K.," he told Claassen.

" It must be the Rhine," swore the observer. "There
isn't another river of that size anywhere within a hundred
miles."

" Then I'm coming down," said Flashar, " for we're
running out of juice, and there's bound to be a decent
spot to land on."

But as he pushed the stick over, the lights of a big town rose up before him.   He saw the outlines of its streets quite distinctly, and gasped with amazement ; what on earth, he wondered, had induced the municipal authorities to defy governmental regulations in that audacious fashion—serve the blighters right if some French machine came along and tickled them up with a few bombs !

But at any rate it was a town, and if he landed near it, he could get his tank replenished.   He dropped down to 200 feet and espied what he took to be a handy meadow.

But at the moment he put the bus's nose down he saw a tree—rows of trees. "Lord, what an escape," he gasped as he pulled the stick frantically, " that's a fruit farm ! " Then, resolving to elucidate the mystery of this town that blazed with light he flew over the housetops until he came to a sharp bend of the river running through its midst.   " Oh hell, it's Basel," he cried, " we've been violating Swiss neutrality ! "

Which was the truth.   When he left Rottweil, he must have flown nearly due south instead of west ; without being aware of it, he had then crossed the Rhine and flown over a considerable stretch of Swiss territory. If he had come down, as he had intended, he would have been interned for the rest of the war.

" Neutrality be damned," he swore, "I haven't landed, and I'm not going to—might run into another fruit-farm.   If I stay up, I've only got to follow the Rhine to get somewhere near home."

At Freiburg they had given him up for lost.   From Rottweil the Archie officer had rung up to say that after flying over the town the L.V.G. had made off in a southerly direction, while half an hour afterwards news came through from a frontier post to the effect that a German aeroplane had crossed the Swiss frontier in the neighbourhood of Schaffhausen.

Hoping against hope, they lit flares to guide him back to the aerodrome, and then, just as they were about to report him as definitely missing, the frontier guards near Basel rang up to announce that a mysterious aeroplane had entered Germany from Switzerland and was heading northwards.

Flashar just got home on the last drop from his emergency tank. He made a good landing in a thick mist that had sprung up during his absence, and by sheer luck he taxied to within five yards of his hangar. The pupils decided that Flashar was the most wonderful stunt-pilot they had ever seen, but their instructor began to wonder whether he would not do well to apply for a transfer back to the front if they expected him to live up to his reputation.

CHAPTER XI

"*IM Krieg geboren, im Krieg gestorben.*"
Born in the war, died in the war : such is the epitaph of the German Flying Corps. Death overtook it in its prime, for it was still doing lusty deeds when the conditions governing the armistice of 11 November, 1918, decreed that all German military and naval aircraft should be handed over to the Entente powers. The Treaty of Versailles confirmed the death sentence, so that to-day Germany possesses no Flying Corps.

But never did the doomed Flying Corps live such strenuous days as in those last months of the war. Let us look at a picture of a war birds' nest in the August of 1918 when the last of the German offensives has failed and the Kaiser's armies are beginning to reel under Foch's counterstroke.

The scene is "somewhere on the Somme," that battlefield where only two years ago the German armies were pushed slowly back, exacting a heavy price in blood for every inch of ground they ceded. Then, only a few months ago, they stormed forward, full of hope, and retook in days the positions which the English had needed months to wrest from them. But the offensive on which such high hopes were set has failed, and now the tide of war flows back once more. Bapaume, Peronne, St. Quentin, and all the other villages and small

towns with historic names are passing or have passed
into English hands again. Germany is making her last
stand.

Yet if we peep into the pilots' mess, we see no signs
of the bitterness of defeat. Snatches of song, lustily
chanted by vigorous young voices, deafen our ears,
while a sturdy pair of hands thump melody from the
battered piano that has been moved so often backwards
and forwards when the war birds' nest was shifted in
accordance with the advancing or receding tide of war.
Only yesterday it was bundled unceremoniously on a
lorry and dumped down in the new quarters, ten miles
to the rear, because the former aerodrome was en-
dangered by the advance of the English batteries to new
positions.

But the festive gathering disperses at an early hour,
because the war birds must be up and doing before
dawn. One by one they retire to seek what rest they
can.

It is a marvel that they can sleep at all. The whole
night long their ears are assailed by the thunder of the
heavy artillery, mingled with the sharp rattle of machine
guns. Then Archie joins in the infernal orchestra ;
an English bombing squadron is abroad, on mischief
bent.

Perhaps they are coming here, but what does it matter ?
Roused by the warning note of their Archies, the tired
pilots turn over and doze again.

Several times that night Archie barks his defiance,
the last occasion being the dark hour before dawn when
comparative peace and quiet generally prevails. And
this time the crash of a falling bomb drowns all other
noises. R*

The heaven is alive with hellish sound ; they are after us this time, realises Lieutenant von Greim, the leader of Jagdstaffel No. 34.   Hastily he leaps from his bed and goes to see whether all his pilots, mechanics and riggers are at their allotted stations.

Not a man is missing, but no sign of the enemy can be seen through the thick mist that has risen in the night. A good ally of Germany it proves, and a hasty inspection of the hangars shows that not a single machine has been touched.   The bombs that were intended to destroy them lie harmless in the mud some hundreds of yards away, and the pilots return to their quarters to snatch another brief rest before the dawn patrol.

Dawn.   The mist still holds ; no chance of taking off yet, although the din of the artillery proclaims that another heavy day has begun.

Ten minutes later the telephone tells von Greim that several English bombing squadrons are out ; can his pilots make an effort to intercept them ? He gives orders to the mechanics to bring out the machines.

Up through the clammy white curtain the Fokker triplanes rise into the clear blue heaven, but search as they may, they can discern no signs of hostile aircraft. The leader wings his way over the enemy's lines to see if there is anything doing in that direction, but there is not one speck in the sky, and the mist is growing thicker. Best get down while we can, he thinks, and gives the signal to return.

An hour later the Staffel starts again ; the weather is no better, but there may be a chance to take a hand in the battle going on down below and do some damage to the advancing enemy, who, judging by the noise of the various instruments in the infernal orchestra, seem to be advancing again. Von Greim flies low, and as soon as he reaches the front, he espies through the mist the uncouth forms of English tanks. Behind them little dots denote running infantrymen.

A rattle of bullets and half-a-dozen new holes in his wings tell him that he has no time to waste, so, throttling down his engine, he dives on a likely-looking crater and rakes it with his machine guns. Then he tugs at the stick and rises steeply to curve away from retaliation.

Down he comes again, and this time he is lucky enough to espy a light battery pushing forward on lorries. Before the crews can take cover, he has put in a destructive burst, and his Staffel, swooping down behind him, complete the work. That battery is now definitely out of action.

While von Greim is seated at his late breakfast or early lunch (meals grow more and more irregular every day), a telephone message from headquarters requests him to come to the assistance of the artillery flyers who are hampered in their work by several squadrons of fast British machines, Dolphins and Bristol Fighters. The meal comes to a hasty end ; once again the Staffel takes off, and von Greim notes with satisfaction that the mist is lifting. Now he will have a chance to put the fear of the Lord into those troublesome fellows.

He leads his Staffel some distance behind their own lines in order to gain the shelter of the clouds unobserved by the enemy. Over Villers-Bretonneux the war birds emerge into blue sky, where two enemy photographic machines are taken by surprise ; they put up a plucky resistance but are speedily despatched earthwards in flames.

Then down from the sky dives a squadron of Dolphins ;
a dogfight ensues in which a dozen Bristol Fighters
join.   One enemy machine is sent down to join the
unlucky photographers, but when a Sopwith squadron
makes its appearance, von Greim decides that the odds
are too great and gives the order to retire.   The Staffel
extricates itself neatly, but on the way home another
group of Bristol Fighters are encountered, two of which
are sent down in flames.   All von Greim's pilots reach
home safely, and the Staffel is well content with its
bag.

Over the telephone von Greim learns that several
Staffels of the famous Richthofen squadron are coming
to his aid, as the enemy appears to be concentrating
large numbers of aircraft in this particular centre.

Von Greim knows that he will get no rest that afternoon.   Quarters for men and machines, extra supplies
of benzin and munitions must be arranged for, and the
telephone is continually breaking down.   At 4 p.m. a
barrage patrol is due, but von Greim has no time to lead it.

He sends it up in charge of his second in command,
but the start is nearly a tragedy, for a Staffel which he
has been unable to warn over the telephone chooses that
very moment to land on his narrow aerodrome.   A
general cursing and swearing takes place, but luckily
no damage is done.

It is a relief for von Greim to get away from the
business on the ground and go up with the evening
patrol.   He takes part in a dogfight in which a Sopwith
is sent down in flames ; that makes the bag for the day
six, but the Staffel is too tired to indulge in any celebra-
tions that night.   Most of the pilots have put in ten
hours' flying.

But when they try to snatch some sleep, the night is again full of alarms. Once more the English bombers are abroad on their errands of destruction.

The enemy's forward movement is pulled up short on the following day, but the war birds have no rest ; the air is full of English machines, and encounters take place three or four times a day. The Richthofen squadron has distinguished itself ; although Weiss, Wolff, Scholz and other crack pilots have followed the great leader to the land of the shades, others remain to carry on the tradition. During those early days of August, Löwenhardt shoots down his forty-eighth, forty-ninth and fiftieth victims, and the mess begins to wonder whether he will beat Richthofen's own record of eighty. But Fate is against Löwenhardt ; three more victories she allows him, and then comes his hour of doom. No British war bird can claim the honour of vanquishing him ; like Boelcke, he crashes after a collision with a comrade.

Daily the drum fire increases in strength ; the English are planning a new attack. Orders reach the war birds to shift their nest, which is too near the front ; those of them who have time to think may indulge in gloomy speculations, for they must draw the inference that Germany's generals have little confidence in the resisting power of their forces against an enemy whose strength increases daily. But most of the war birds are too busy fighting to worry their heads over the Higher Command's strategy ; sufficient for the day is the work thereof.

Food is becoming scantier and of poorer quality ; it is hard to celebrate victories without good cheer So the German war birds fight and sleep, and sleep and

fight, and if they can get hold of some liquor, they try
to think that they are enjoying life.

They even fight on the day that they move house ;
needs must when the devil drives.   One morning they
take off from St. Christ and land at Hervilly where
everything has been made ready for them.   They wonder
how long they will stay there.

The drum fire ceases, but soon starts again.   One
morning, when the dawn patrol goes out, they find a
black mist obscuring the sun.   The enemy's smoke-
bombs have done their work, and behind the veil the
English artillery thunders.

They know that it means a combined infantry and
tank attack.   The enemy's war birds will be hard to
find to-day, but there is work enough for the flyers who
are ready to deal with the foeman on the ground.   With
a trusty companion von Greim goes out to hunt for such
ground-game.

He flies low over the German lines, where the comrades
of the trenches send up rockets and light magnesium
flares to tell him their positions.   Then onward, with
eyes searching the ground.

Through the mist loom up an ungainly shape ; further
on the airmen mark the outlines of a second monster.
English tanks !   Von Greim has never fought a tank
before and wonders how to set about the business ; from
above the brute looks invulnerable, and yet there must
be a weak spot somewhere.

" Well, here goes," he thinks, and curves to dive at
the tank's broadside.   His companion divines his
intention and makes for the other monster.

Greim holds his fire till he is quite close and then
puts in a burst from each Spandau.   A hit—a very

palpable hit, but the tank pursues its sluggish way untroubled. " Might as well have potted the brute with a peashooter," thinks von Greim.

The tank's crew manifest their derision with a burst of machine-gun fire that riddles von Greim's wings so thoroughly that he is glad to zoom out of range. Through the mist he watches the tank's progress.

" No good battering at his sides," he mutters, " I'll try if he has a weak spot in the lid." At a height of 1,500 feet he manoeuvres over his target ; then he pushes the stick hard and goes down in a nose dive that sets all his struts and spars creaking in protest. Then he puts in burst after burst from the two Spandaus. Neither gun jams, and though diving is supposed to be the Fokker's weak point, his machine holds together.

A few feet only seem to separate him from the tank when he catches his machine and evens out. And this time no fire follows him as he curves away. He looks round and can scarcely believe his eyes, but the tank stands motionless. Then he sees that the second tank has also come to a standstill ; his friend has finished it off in similar fashion. Thoroughly pleased with himself, he returns to tell his Staffel that he has found a new way of killing tanks.

They killed quite a number of tanks by means of the nose-dive attack, but they could not stem the enemy's advance. In September, scarcely a week passed without their being compelled to move their aerodrome back a few miles, and the lost ground was never regained. Who ever had a moment's leisure to think, knew that Germany was beaten.

It was a cruel irony of Fate. While the infantry beneath them gave ground daily, up aloft the German war birds won victory after victory. The new Fokker was more than equal to any machine on the Entente side, as their captured opponents were willing to testify.

All through October the Richthofen squadron distinguished itself. Udet, their star of greatest magnitude, celebrated his sixtieth, sixty-first and sixty-second victory in the last days of the month, while the last Chancellor of the tottering German Empire was exchanging notes with President Wilson about the terms on which an armistice might be granted.

In the first week of November twenty-five enemy machines were brought down by the Richthofen squadron, although bad weather restricted their flying hours considerably. Then, on 11 November came the death-sentence ; not only was the Richthofen squadron never to fly again, but all machines must be handed over to the enemy. The Richthofen war birds could hardly believe the order that stood written in black and white.

Outside their messroom all was confusion ; the strangest rumours flew from mouth to mouth. The Emperor had abdicated ; the Emperor had not abdicated, but would refuse to survive his country's defeat ; on the morrow he intended to lead a death-charge against the victorious foe. Germany was in the hands of the Bolshevists ; a Soviet Republic had been proclaimed in Berlin—all officers were degraded from their ranks by a committee of workmen and soldiers ; Hindenburg was a prisoner, Ludendorff had been lynched. Orders and counter-orders, all equally impossible to execute, arrived hourly.

But towards evening they learnt that, although beaten, the German army was not entirely demoralised. The

Emperor had certainly abdicated, but like a mighty oak-tree Hindenburg stood erect and would take charge of the German retreat from the soil of France, where their armies had fought for four years. They also learnt definitely that on the morrow they must fly to Darmstadt, the town which had been chosen as the squadron's peace headquarters. A brief respite was allowed before the parting with their beloved machines.

They flew to Darmstadt, and there the days of rest were used to compile the squadron's records. Seventy pilots, it was found, had made the supreme sacrifice ; one hundred more were crippled for life. Others were in hospital or prisoners in the enemy's hands. But the number of the squadron's victories was nearly a thousand, while eighteen pilots had earned the " Pour le Mérite " order.

The conditions of the final surrender were hard. It would have softened the blow if they had been permitted to hand over their machines to the commander of some famous British squadrons against whom they had fought so often, to the foeman they liked and respected, instead of having to fly to Strasbourg, the capital of the Alsace that their forefathers had wrested from France and had now become French again, to surrender them to someone whose name was unknown to them. But, remembering that the dead commander whose name their squadron bore had always insisted on smart take-offs and clean landings, they took a pride in carrying out the final scene as he would have wished it.

Im Krieg geboren, im Krieg gestorben. Germany has no Flying Corps and we all look forward to the day when no country will need one. But a few months before we celebrated the tenth anniversary of the armistice, two

Germans, setting forth from a Dominion of the British Empire, flew the Atlantic from east to west. The third member of their crew was a British subject. Germany has still a future in the air !

THE END